THE
WILD
GREEN
YONDER

Captions to inside covers

Front, clockwise from top left:

Bob L de Berry outside his 140-year-old sod cottage, Cambrian, Central Otago; The author milking Thelma the goat at Waihi Bush Organic Farm, Woodbury, near Geraldine; Shelves of preserved fruit at the Stone House, Clyde, Central Otago; House bus at Aradia Women's Community, Papaaroha, Coromandel Peninsula; Echinacea flowers at Totaranui Farm, Geraldine; Harvesting potatoes at Seacliff, near Dunedin; Mulching fruit trees at Treedimensions near Motueka; Colourful harvest at Little River, Banks Peninsula; Centre: The wwoofer caravan near Takaka in Golden Bay.

Back, clockwise from top left:

Corn plant and chicks at Hohepa Farm, Halswell, near Christchurch; Nathan, Steph and their dog Noel at Aroha Organics, St Andrews, South Canterbury; Grapevines at Sunset Valley Vineyards, Upper Moutere, near Nelson; Livestock at Hohepa Farm; Loading grapes into the de-stemming machine at Sunset Valley Vineyards. Centre: Tumbledown barn at Milmore Downs, Scargill, North Canterbury.

THE

Ten seasons volunteering

WILD

on New Zealand's

GREEN

organic farms

YONDER

PHILIPPA JAMIESON

NEW
HOLLAND

First published in 2007 by New Holland Publishers (NZ) Ltd
Auckland • Sydney • London • Cape Town

www.newhollandpublishers.co.nz

218 Lake Road, Northcote, Auckland 0627, New Zealand
Unit 1, 66 Gibbes Street, Chatswood, NSW 2067, Australia
86–88 Edgware Road, London W2 2EA, United Kingdom
80 McKenzie Street, Cape Town 8001, South Africa

ISBN: 978 1 86966 183 0

Publishing manager: Matt Turner
Design: IslandBridge
Cover design: Dexter Fry
Editor & cartographer: Sue Hall

A catalogue record for this book is available from
the National Library of New Zealand

1 3 5 7 9 10 8 6 4 2

Colour reproduction by Image Centre Ltd., Auckland
Printed in China at Everbest Printing Co

The paper used for the pages of this book
was sourced from sustainable forests.

CONTENTS

ACKNOWLEDGEMENTS

I wish to thank:

my parents Glennie and Don Jamieson for love and encouragement;

Helen for the laptop and constantly keeping in touch;

Quentin and Angela for living close to the land;

Margaret Holmes, my grandmother, for being such a role model;

Wendy Harrex for the idea of writing this book;

Stephen Stratford for constructive criticism and encouragement;

Antony and Jackie Wood, my fairy godparents;

Sally Crimp for your love and hard slog in the garden;

Andrea Bosshard, Meliors Simms, Liz Rawlings, Jacqui 'Sharkey'
   Bennetts, Gillian Newman, Richard King and Chris Forster for
   friendship and 'life coaching';

Chris Lynch and Andrew Sutherland for the witchy house in which
   to write;

Karen Dickson and Neil Mouat for the Punakaiki retreat;

and all the wonderful WWOOF hosts for their hospitality.

This book was written with the support of the Mentor Programme
run by the New Zealand Society of Authors (PEN NZ Inc) and
sponsored by Creative New Zealand.

Parts of Chapter 14, 'Heirlooms', have appeared in the article
'Treasures from the Garden of Eden', *Organic NZ*, vol 61 no 4,
July/August 2003.

INTRODUCTION

The first card in the tarot deck is the Fool, depicted as a carefree traveller, stepping jauntily off into the abyss, one foot on solid ground, one foot in the air, risking but totally trusting. He carries nothing but a swag and a cheerful air.

That was me, about to leave my comfort zone, my home, my job, my friends, my family and my cats, and leap off into the unknown, to go roaming around the New Zealand countryside working on organic farms – for no pay. Was I mad?

Most of my life had been spent burrowed in the den of Dunedin, my birthplace. It's a place that draws you in, where the houses huddle together on the hills around the heart of the city, around the harbour. Dunedin, where chilly winds gust up from the Antarctic, where stoic citizens brave the weather to stride down the main street with arms folded, chins tucked against chests.

The geography of Dunedin creates a nurturing nest, its isolation giving rise to its own unique creativity, but that nest can become a rut. Just to get up to the rim of the hills and gaze out to the world beyond is to draw in a fresh breath. I just had to get out of there and try something new and different.

Spring, 2001: seeds that had been gestating in my unconscious mind were now taking root, rising to the surface and beginning to sprout. Away from Dunedin, on a trip to Sydney, I got a new perspective, and with my friend Chris I thrashed around some ideas for my future. It was time to move on from the comfortable publishing job I'd had for six years, and as my girlfriend and I had split up earlier that year, I was a free agent and it seemed like a good time to hive off and do my own thing.

We sat and brainstormed lots of ideas. I wanted to do something environmental, to do with organics specifically, if possible. We tossed up the possibility of further study, but the thought of being back in another institution felt suffocating. I wanted to satisfy my wanderlust, and give back to the world by doing something hands-on. Chris suggested travelling or working overseas, and mentioned an environmental volunteer scheme she'd come across in Ladakh in northern India. But in the wake of September 11th, international travel didn't have quite the same appeal.

Back in New Zealand I went to a careers counsellor, and it soon became obvious to me that the WWOOF scheme was the thing for me. Willing Workers on Organic Farms was the original name of the scheme, but in 2003 it was renamed Worldwide Opportunities on Organic Farms. Either way, the initials spell WWOOF. The scheme was started in the UK in 1971 by Sue Coppard, a city dweller who wanted to spend her weekends in the countryside, gaining farming and gardening experience. The idea grew quickly and spread to other countries. It started up in New Zealand in 1974.

Organic gardening was a passion of mine that I wanted to develop to see where it might lead. I was already a member of the Soil and Health Association, New Zealand's oldest organic organisation and publisher of *Organic NZ* magazine. Volunteering on the WWOOF scheme would give me exactly the sort of adventure I was after, while also doing something meaningful and useful, learning lots and having fun.

By 2001 organics had become mainstream. It was no longer the preserve of oddball hippies living in communes, but was increasingly being taken up by farmers who wanted to increase their premiums and look after the environment at the same time. Organic food was becoming more readily available in city supermarkets and in smaller provincial centres.

Since its humble beginnings in the 1970s when all the host farmers could be listed on one sheet of paper, WWOOF New Zealand has mushroomed to include over 1000 hosts (at the time of writing) and about 4500 volunteers, or 'wwoofers', who join each year. Most of the wwoofers are young foreigners travelling through the country. Farmers pay a small annual fee to be listed in what is generally called 'the WWOOF book': a directory of host farms listed geographically, with contact details and a bit about each farm or property. The directory is also available online. The wwoofers also pay an annual fee and receive the book, then make contact with the hosts they want to stay with. They work about four to five hours a day in exchange for their food and board. There are hosts on a wide range of properties, including farms, orchards, market gardens, communities, gardens in cities and towns, and various ventures in self-sufficiency.

The idea of WWOOF is about learning. It's an excellent opportunity for wwoofers to gain practical experience in organic farming and gardening, and at the same time the hosts benefit from having an extra pair of hands, and enjoy the cultural exchange with their wwoofers.

The scheme gave me everything I wanted: practical experience in organics and travel in my own country. What with war and terrorism on the increase elsewhere in the world, New Zealand seemed by contrast a very safe, quiet place to be. And it would give me the opportunity to see lots of places in my own country that I'd never been to, and maybe find somewhere to live, that dreamed-of block of land. And, in the back of my mind, though rarely voiced, a new relationship.

There was nothing holding me back now! Things began to fall into place. Tenants appeared for my house, and I dispersed my possessions amongst friends and family. For Christmas my geek-girl sister Helen gave me her old laptop to take with me – she was upgrading – and unlimited free computer support and advice. Money, or the uncertainty about it, was my main worry, but I thought I could survive on a shoestring, getting a bit of rent, a little from freelance writing, and of course food and accommodation would be taken care of by my WWOOF hosts. What was the worst thing that could happen? If I fell down in a screaming heap, I could just stop and get a job again. At least I would have tried. So only three months after that talk with my friend, I was launching off into the wild green yonder.

SOUTH ISLAND

NORTH ISLAND

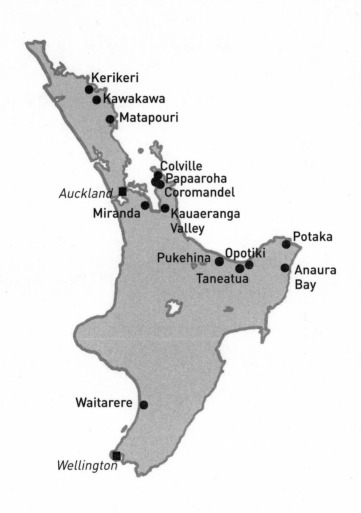

AUTHOR'S NOTE

I have used the past tense throughout the book, in order to describe what happened at the time I was wwoofing. While most of my hosts are still on their farms and doing the same sorts of things they were doing when I was there, some hosts have since changed what they are doing on the farms, or have sold and moved on.

1
STARTING OUT

The beginnings of my wwoofing adventure were characterised by the forces that pulled me in different directions. On the one hand, I launched into my new life with gusto, with an ambitious, if somewhat unfocused plan, to go to as many different kinds of farm as possible, covering the length of the country. I gave myself a year to do this, with no fixed plans after that, reasoning that something would emerge out of that year to show me a new direction.

On the other hand, my natural tendency towards caution ensured that I eased into things gradually, starting close to home, with plenty of visits back to Dunedin in between farming stints. My first rural sojourn was not in fact at an official WWOOF host's farm, but farm-sitting for a couple of weeks for my brother Quentin Jamieson near Little River on Banks Peninsula, following a few days of Christmas holidays with him.

Decades before, most of the native bush had been felled and the land sown in pasture for sheep farming. Steep ridges plunged down into valleys. The property was up a gravel road, in a valley with a sheep farm on one side, regenerating native bush on the other, and a stream tumbling down the gully through a boulder-strewn path. Poking above the canopy of manuka and broadleaf species was the occasional large podocarp that was probably saved from clearance by the awkward access of the sheer slopes.

It was a small property of about three-and-a-half hectares, and had been subdivided off the neighbouring farm along with several other small blocks about 10 or 15 years before. In more recent times there has been a rash of subdivision all over New Zealand, creating so-called 'lifestyle blocks' – a term that means different things to different people. For some people it's a peaceful place to build a huge house and still commute into town. For others, it's a chance to have a bit of land and practise at least some measure of self-sufficiency. Quentin was in the latter category.

On the cleared land were the house, a glasshouse and terraced vegetable gardens, fruit and olive trees, berry bushes, a henhouse and beehives, a handful of sheep and a goat, which had to go because of her Houdini-like ability to release herself from her tether.

Although I was reasonably familiar with the place, Quentin spent some time showing me around and pointing things out, like the intricacies of the water system (water for the house and garden was gravity-fed from the stream), and left me with plenty of instructions and phone numbers of people to contact if necessary.

'Now, the most important things are looking after the chooks, the sheep and the dog, and watering the tomatoes,' said Quentin. 'If that's all you do, that's fine with me, but here are a few other things to do if you want, and if the weather's OK.' He handed me a list scrawled in pencil on an envelope:

Check tomatoes, peppers etc. for whitefly and spray
   with neem if needed

Pluck out laterals on tomatoes

Plant leek seedlings

Harvest gherkins and any other veges

Harvest garlic

Pick and freeze blackcurrants

Weed herb and vege gardens

Cut back herbs that have flowered

Mulch fruit trees with old futon innards

Check water tank levels and troubleshoot if not filling

That should keep me busy, I thought. The list demonstrated the variety of activities going on at any one time. At the height of summer, planting was going on alongside harvesting and cutting back.

The gherkins were a new delight for me; they proliferated like rabbits, and swelled overnight from the size of a pea-pod into a fat saveloy shape. The gherkin patch was a sprawl of prostrate leaves and tendrils that hid their fat knobbly little babies from the ravages of the elements, nestled on a bed of straw. Almost every day there were more gherkins to collect, store in bags and refrigerate to be pickled later.

Unfortunately, harvesting was hampered by invaders in the gherkin patch: a number of deceptively thin and soft-looking Californian thistles. They had to go – from that spot, anyway. Californian thistles ('callies' for short) are one of the most common and invasive pasture weeds and spread both by seed and root. When digging them out, one has to be careful to get the whole root, or as much as possible, to give it the least chance of returning, as it will grow from even a tiny piece of root. Fortunately in the loose cultivated soil of the gardens there, this was relatively easy.

The idea of mulching the fruit trees with the stuffing of an old futon was a perfect illustration of the 'reduce, reuse, recycle' philosophy. I was struck by a pang of regret and guilt that, in the scramble to leave my house, I had rashly consigned my own mildewy old futon to the tip, when it could have been transformed into useful mulching material. Here there were a number of spindly young fruit trees that were competing valiantly with the long grass for nutrients. The addition of a circle of mulch at the base of a tree could mean the difference between life and death for the tree, or certainly between a vigorous heavy cropper and a struggling tree that was vulnerable to pest attacks and had a meagre yield. The futon stuffing was a multi-coloured mass of cotton scraps and threads, probably a textile industry by-product and therefore doubly recycled. What an ideal mulch: the dense wadding provided a barrier that would be, for some time at least, impenetrable to grass and weeds, and served as a kind of thick sponge that would hold moisture and ensure that the trees didn't suffer from the extremes of drought. And it was biodegradable in the long run.

Although I managed to tick off most things on the list, just looking after the chooks, sheep and tomatoes took up most of my time.

The first rude awakening of my new life was the rooster beginning to crow anywhere from 3.00 a.m. onwards, rending the still country air with an aggrieved, strangled cry. The hens began clucking before first light, their squawking rising in pitch and volume with their impatience to be let out of the henhouse. Before Quentin went away on holiday, these fowl cries roused me briefly from sleep, but I rolled over and fell asleep again. Now the bossy, skittish birds were my responsibility, and would not let up their screeching until they were released into the large hen run. Some time before, Quentin had been jolted from sleep by the frantic screams of chooks being killed by a marauding ferret that left several bodies in its wake, and ever since, the chooks had to be shut in at night.

Once they were released and fed, the chooks scratched and pecked and strutted around contentedly, occasionally letting out a jubilant, self-satisfied cackle that appeared to announce 'I just laid an e-egg!' The dozen or so hens were laying between five and seven eggs a day, so some of them weren't pulling their weight, but they certainly produced more than this household could keep up with, and the surplus usually went to the neighbours. Quentin had recently discovered that you can freeze eggs, and had begun freezing them in anticipation of the winter months when the hens would stop laying. Eggs must be cracked open and frozen in containers (otherwise they will burst out of their shells), and can be separated out if you wish. The yolks keep for about six months frozen, and whites for about a year.

In the unlikely event of one of the chooks getting sick, I was to isolate the invalid from the rest immediately and keep it under surveillance in the porch. The main cure-all was cloves of garlic in the chooks' drinking water in the event of sickness; both for the isolated patient and, as a precaution, for the rest of the chooks. Fortunately they were all perfectly perky during my stay.

Every morning I checked the glasshouse. It was midsummer and there were some hot days, and even on the cooler rainy days the glasshouse plants often needed water, as they weren't exposed to the rain. As well as 50 or so tomato plants, there were several capsicums, eggplants and chillies, all in large black plastic planter bags; some seed trays; and a few one-off experiments in tropical plants like lemon grass, ginger, carob and turmeric. Of these latter heat lovers, the lemon grass was so far proving the easiest to grow, although the others were sprouting, and the carob was already several centimetres high, and looked like a miniature tree with wavy-edged leaves.

Watering ostensibly meant just turning on one tap, as the main pipe ran around the glasshouse with little straw-like tubes or 'whiskers' going to each planter bag. In practice, though, one had to check the whiskers to make sure they weren't blocked and were, in fact, stuck into the soil and weren't squirting out onto the ground or drowning the plant next door. The plants in the central row of the glasshouse weren't on the irrigation system so I had to hand-water them. This incubator of steamy warmth was a peaceful world all of its own, where the plants were cosseted and sheltered from the cold and wind, from birds and rabbits and the occasional stray sheep.

Plants weren't the only ones to enjoy the protected environment of the glasshouse. Insects thrived in the still warmth away from some of their natural predators. Whitefly was the main problem for all the Solanaceae family, the capsicums especially, and to a lesser extent the chillies and eggplants. The tomatoes seemed to be more resistant. My brother's solution was to make up a mixture of neem soap and water and spray it on the leaves.

Neem is an age-old natural insecticide made from the neem plant native to the Indian subcontinent and, in recent times, popular with organic gardeners and commercial growers. There are neem sprays on the market, but Quentin preferred to use neem soap, as the soap adds to the effectiveness of the solution by sucking the moisture out of the insects. The solution was effective, but the plants needed daily spraying once the whitefly population had boomed.

Another insect proved to be my nemesis: the fly. My brother had warned me about flystrike and told me what to look for. He inspected the four sheep (Ricardo, Hannah, Frantoio and Kowhai) before they left, pronouncing them to be OK.

'Just look out for flies buzzing around their backsides,' said Quentin. 'If they're scouring, they're more likely to attract flies.'

'Scouring?' The only scouring I knew involved vigorous cleaning of burnt pots.

'It means diarrhoea,' he explained. 'Just break off a bit of koromiko for them to eat; that usually clears it up.' Koromiko is a native shrub (*Hebe salicifolia*) that grows into a leggy bush, its leaf growth being reminiscent of a buddleia: the new tips sticking up in the middle of graceful fountains of tapering leaves finger-length or longer. Its medicinal uses for human health are well documented, a decoction of the leaves being used to cure diarrhoea, dysentery, urinary and kidney problems, and used externally as a poultice on ulcers and sores.

Quentin explained what to look for when checking for flystrike: clusters of eggs about the size of a pea, in a pale lemon shade, usually around the sheep's rear end or on the back. Or worse, if the eggs had hatched, there would be maggots, in which case the sheep would likely be scratching itself against a tree or something. The only maggots I could recall were some that had hatched in a liquid compost brew I made once out of seaweed and left festering for rather a long time.

Because of the lack of internal fencing on the property, the four sheep were tethered, necessitating checks once or twice a day to make sure they had enough to eat, had enough water, were out of reach of the vegetables and fruit trees, and hadn't got loose or tangled themselves up. They occasionally wound their chains round and round their posts, or twisted them around trees, bleating plaintively for someone to come and rescue them from their predicament. Thus, there were plenty of opportunities to check for flystrike, but somehow the onset of this affliction escaped my notice until it was well underway in the youngest sheep, Kowhai. She was scouring, so I administered koromiko, which she ate rather half-heartedly, but it didn't seem to make much difference. One particularly hot day there were clouds of flies buzzing around her, and an inspection of her dirty derrière revealed not just eggs in her wool but also maggots.

Steeling myself for an unpleasant job, I donned plastic gloves and made up a bucket of Jeye's fluid diluted with water, which, although not organic, was my brother's anti-maggot remedy. I held Kowhai in a firm grip between my knees and gingerly snipped at the wool and dags around her rear end. Every cut revealed more maggots in varying stages of development, some like tiny writhing threads, some already plump from eating live lamb. They wriggled out of sight, burying themselves deeper into the wool and away from the light and from my hacking scissors, which seemed to work better than the hand shears.

Feeling sick, I realised with growing horror that she was flystruck on a large part of her body: her lower back, flanks and stomach. It would take me ages just to cut back the wool. It was time to ask for help. I doused her liberally with Jeye's fluid and went inside to phone the vet, who suggested that the farmer down the road might be willing to shear her. The farmer was on my list of People To Call In An Emergency, and he very kindly came and picked her up, and returned her later the same day, freshly shorn and suddenly skinny looking, with blackish patches here and there where the maggots had been feasting.

'Now, I've dipped her as well,' said the farmer, 'and she's still a bit wet, so keep her warm and under cover if you can. We're meant to be in for a bit of a cold spell.'

The dip wasn't organic, but when confronted with the possible death of another being, I quickly overcame my purist tendencies. As a thank-you to the farmer, I baked him a cake, using up some of the bountiful supply of eggs. The chooks, for their part, had earlier set upon the maggot-ridden wool with clucks of delight, devouring the tasty morsels with a feverish pecking. Might there be a bird that would eat the fly eggs and maggots on sheep, I wondered, in the kind of symbiosis that hippopotamuses have with the oxpecker birds that pick ticks and other parasites off their backs? But this kind of thinking has got New Zealand into trouble in the past: bring in stoats to reduce the rabbit numbers, and you end up with a whole new pest problem. Besides, hippos and oxpecker birds must have developed their own relationship over time, without the arrogant interference of humans.

I tethered Kowhai close to the house, where I could keep an eye on her and she could shelter under the house or in the old dog kennel. She seemed a little fragile at first, not moving or eating much, but she happily accepted an old blanket laid over her for warmth, not once shrugging it off, and after a day or so was munching grass contentedly.

I was relieved when my brother returned and Kowhai was still alive. I had done my duty, and could relax now. But the very next day the little sheep was sitting immobile for rather a long time and couldn't stand up, despite our efforts. Quentin felt her tongue.

'Her temperature's way down. Let's bring her into the porch and warm her up.' He administered warm water with a bit of milk via a syringe down her throat to try to raise her temperature, but it was too late. Kowhai died in his arms. The passing of my erstwhile charge brought tears to my eyes and questions to my mind. Could I have been more assiduous in my flystrike monitoring? What if I'd brought her into the porch when she came back? What else could I have done to save her?

'Don't worry, Philippa,' Quentin reassured me. 'She was always sickly right from the start. If it wasn't flystrike, it would have been something else. The only thing I might have done differently would have been to keep her in the porch, but who knows, she might have died anyway,' he said. He took the death with the equanimity of experience. I tried to put the incident out of my mind, or at least be philosophical about it. In retrospect, it was a good introduction for a townie to the harsh realities of rural life.

SAVING THE SEEDS

My first official wwoofing stay was at Kotare Vale, a hazelnut and chestnut farm near Little River, not far from my brother's. The sleepy side road meandered along the Puaha Valley, crossing a couple of single-lane bridges. There were a few lifestyle blocks along the road, an olive grove and sheep roaming on the hills above. A sign advertised 'Lemons for Sale', another gave the name of a property as 'Rivendell', and a house right by the road sported a number of aging, pre-loved road signs, the two most prominent of them helpfully indicating the directions of Christchurch and Akaroa for any traveller who had become disoriented.

Just before the road turned to gravel and twisted sharply up the hill, there was a large red toadstool with white spots that my would-be host, Martin Tickner, had said to keep an eye out for. This creation of Martin's was the most visible landmark indicating the entrance to the farm, although Kotare Vale had signs too: one announcing 'Proud to be GE Free' and the other stating 'Tree Crops Association Member', attached to the gate, which was tucked in off the road in a shady dell. Down a short drive lined with pines on the right, past a great pile of compost on the left, were a modest house, caravan and vegetable garden, all nestled in the crook of the valley.

This area was once sheep yards, and there was still a small round concrete structure that Martin referred to as the killing shed, which of course it was, only, being a naïve vegetarian townie, I had never come across one before. It had become a useful storage shed, the sinister butcher's hook above now innocently draped with pieces of twine.

There were shearing sheds too, somewhat dilapidated but still useful for storage, just across the stream and up the hill a little. The farm is named after the kotare, the native kingfisher, which can be seen from time to time darting up and down the stream there.

The hazel and chestnut trees were dotted on the slopes above, along with a swathe of native bush. Amid the bush was the only naturally occurring rimu tree on Banks Peninsula – all other rimu in the area appear to have been brought in as seedlings from other places. As rimu need separate male and female trees to reproduce, this old man rimu may not be able to pass on any distinctive characteristics that may have developed among rimu on Banks Peninsula.

Martin is an Englishman who first arrived in New Zealand in 1991 to visit his brother and was captivated by our environment. He wanted to become an organic grower and felt the opportunities were much better here than in his homeland: a favourable climate and much cheaper land prices. Sadly, Martin's brother died a few years later. He left money, which Martin and his sister-in-law Faye put into a family trust, and used to purchase the 18-hectare block and plant hazels. Like my brother's place, this property had been subdivided off the sheep farm that surrounded it.

A feature of Kotare Vale was the communal working bees organised for large projects like the hazel planting, and making tracks through the bush. One of the ideas for the land was to use it for educational purposes, so school groups and others could visit and learn about the natural world. The regular working bees established a community of mostly Christchurch people who had a connection with Kotare Vale and, judging by the photos and entries in the visitors' book, they had a great time working together and feasting afterwards.

Although the hazels would eventually be the main crop, they were only a couple of years old when I stayed, and hadn't yet started to bear nuts. They didn't need tending to then, so Martin planned to make use of my talents in the vegetable gardens – but the weather had other ideas.

It was a very rainy January on Banks Peninsula in 2002, and Akaroa suffered flash flooding when storm water drains became blocked with debris. For five days solid it poured. Fortunately Martin had some wet weather activities up his sleeve. He found the perfect job to satisfy my congenital aptitude for cataloguing (inherited from my librarian parents): I was to sort out his entire seed collection.

Martin was on the board of the Southern Seed Exchange, the Christchurch-based community seed bank, which has its own seed collection housed in a straw bale shed in the organic horticulture section of the Christchurch Polytech. Straw bales were used for construction of the shed because of their insulation properties, so the seeds were kept at a relatively constant cool temperature with no need for electricity. An enthusiast for rare and 'heirloom' varieties of vegetables in particular, Martin had his own large seed collection, from which he grew out and harvested seed, including unusual plants like jicama (a South American climber with edible tubers shaped like spinning tops), local varieties like the Takamatua black bean and an assortment of chillies (anaheim, jalapeño, habañero, serrano and aji).

'Heirloom' conjures up images of precious things: jewellery, perhaps, sets of china or antique furniture. But the term has also become applied to varieties of plants that our grandparents and earlier forebears grew, that have been passed down from generation to generation, nurtured and tended, selected and improved along the way. In recent times there has been an upsurge of interest in identifying and saving these heirloom varieties and establishing seed banks. There are now groups and individuals around the world who are dedicated guardians of our food heritage.

A century or so ago, seed catalogues boasted hundreds of varieties, many of which disappeared over the years with the advent of the industrialisation of farming, and its focus on a much smaller number of plants that fit commercial requirements: high yield, easy to transport and store, and with a long shelf life. Qualities valued by generations of farmers and home gardeners, such as flavour, nutrition, biodiversity, and the social and spiritual importance of regional – and family – varieties, began to fall by the wayside. And now humankind has opened up a Pandora's box of genetic engineering, threatening the purity of our plant heritage. Already much of the corn grown in Mexico, the home of corn, has been found to be genetically engineered (GE), whether by cross-pollination or through contaminated seed stocks, and we have had several instances of contaminated corn here in New Zealand. As existing seed stocks seem likely to continue to become contaminated by GE, it will be increasingly difficult to maintain heirloom seed lines, and there will be a reduction in biodiversity.

On with the job of looking after the seeds. Martin's seed storage receptacle was a large trunk, which he dragged into the living area where we tipped it up, letting the contents cascade onto the floor with a loud swishing sound of seeds in their packets that mimicked the rain outside. How on earth could I ever find anything in there? Although all the different seeds were carefully labelled and stored in envelopes, plastic bags or jars, they were all jumbled together in no particular order and Martin confessed that he frequently spent some time rummaging through everything to find exactly what he wanted. The collection was in dire need of a tidy up. Armed with Suzanne Ashworth's classic book *Seed to Seed* as a reference, I set to work, first sorting all the vegetable seeds into families: the Solanaceae family (including tomatoes, capsicums, chillies), the brassicas (cabbage, broccoli, rocket, etc.), legumes (peas and beans), cucurbits (pumpkin, zucchini, melon), Chenopodiaceae (silverbeet and beetroot), Apiaceae (formerly known as Umbelliferae [carrot, parsley, celery etc.]), Asteraceae or daisy family (lettuce, endive, globe artichoke) and the genus *Allium* (onions and garlic). There were also a number of flower and herb seeds.

Once the carpet had been covered with a collage of packets, the next tasks were to amalgamate any double-ups, throw out any that were too old, and confer with Martin about any unnamed or undated ones. Progress was slow, as every packet needed to be assessed. How old was too old? Parsnip seeds, for example, are notorious for not being viable for long: one, maybe two years at the most, whereas tomato seeds will keep for five to 10 years. The floor gradually became more visible as I threw out seeds that were past their use-by date. Seeds in used envelopes and plastic bags were repackaged into envelopes of a standard size to make storage easier.

The collection included seeds from a variety of sources: commercially available seeds, such as those from Koanga Gardens, Eco Seeds, King's Seeds, Mount Tiger Gardens and others, and seed that had been saved by gardeners themselves and swapped through the Southern Seed Exchange. Martin liked to have as much information about the seeds as possible: common name, Latin name, the date the seed was harvested, received or bought, and where it came from (in some cases from a person's garden or collection). If there was no harvest date or expiry date, Martin hazarded an educated guess.

The seeds themselves were fascinating. Each seed carried a signature of its parent plant, yet each one was also its own unique being, genetically different from the siblings that shared the same packet. Many of them were familiar to me from sowing and collecting seeds in my own garden: the knobbly cork-like seeds of beetroot and silverbeet; small, flat, cream-coloured discs of tomatoes, capsicums and chillies; the shrivelled pale green balls of peas. There were some that were new to me, like salsify; Martin had recently harvested some of these long, thin, somewhat ragged seeds and was drying them out on a tray. Also called the oyster plant because of the delicate flavour of its long slender roots, salsify requires similar growing conditions to carrots: fine light soil, not manured or composted in the few months before planting, and a sunny well-drained spot. The seeds are only viable for about two years.

As I worked away quietly the rain just kept falling, at times drumming heavily on the roof, then subsiding to a drizzle. Martin pottered about doing various tasks and popped in now and then to tell me the new height of the creek. The previous spring it had burst its banks and temporarily made a path across the yard, perilously close to where Martin's cosy caravan was parked, surrounded by raised vegetable beds and plants in pots.

In the end the whole trunkful of seeds was reduced to a couple of old card-file drawers, plus some others stored in jars that were just too bulky to fit in (large seeds like peas and beans). The seeds were now neatly assembled in alphabetical order within each reunited plant family. Only one packet of seeds remained a mystery, although, judging by their flat almond shape, they appeared to be some kind of cucurbit. At the time of writing, they have yet to be planted out to find out what they are.

As well as seed saving, gathering food in the wild was another of Martin's passions. He had an extensive knowledge of fungi, seaweeds, shellfish and edible wild plants in his homeland and, with his natural curiosity and sharp eyes, quickly became familiar with Aotearoa's wild harvest. One day we went on an expedition to collect seaweed for the garden and were driving down a steep, narrow Peninsula road when he stopped abruptly on a slope.

'What's wrong?' I asked, thinking there was something amiss with the car. But no, Martin was transfixed by something in a singularly unspectacular paddock beside the road.

'Look!' he said, pointing to a tree. 'See that narrow-leafed lacebark over there? Can you see the fungus halfway up its trunk?' There was indeed something jutting out.

'It's *Agrocybe parasitica*,' he rattled off. 'The Maori name is tawaka. A distinctive summer-fruiting, edible mushroom. You can find it on some of the trees in Hagley Park, too. We'll come back and collect it on our way home.'

We carried on down to Duvauchelle where the road flattens out and runs alongside the harbour, and parked right by the narrow strip of beach. The seaweed was as thick and springy as a mattress, and so plentiful it covered much of the sand. It was a type of seagrass with fine leaves, and was already partly decomposed – perfect for the compost heap. Once we'd loaded up the boot of the car with several heavy sacks, Martin decided it would be better to go home by the main road, so we missed out on picking that mushroom.

Another day he picked several shaggy parasol mushrooms in varying stages of development. He lined them all up for a photo, from the smallest one that looked as though it was wearing a beanie pulled right down over its face, to the tallest one with its parasol fully unfurled, shamelessly shaggy. Then we devoured these flavourful mushrooms in a delicious omelette, served with some bull kelp Martin had pickled, but he agreed with my somewhat lukewarm appraisal of this unusual condiment.

'Yes, it's rather bland, isn't it? It was a bit of an experiment really. Another partial success!' he joked, using his favourite phrase that he employed whenever something hadn't turned out quite right, or in fact had failed completely. His natural optimism combined with his unflagging sense of humour always saw the tiniest speck of silver lining on any cloud. In fact, that kelp pickle was the exception to the rule; Martin was a curry connoisseur, a spice aficionado, and every one of his meals was gourmet quality.

The kitchen hadn't been finished yet, so meals were cooked in the caravan. We usually ate breakfast in the caravan, which was decorated in Martin's idiosyncratic taste of toadstool and lizard figurines, and a plug with a frog on it. Lunch was taken outdoors on the Pink Terraces, weather permitting, at a pink picnic bench under a sun umbrella, from which dangled a pink flamingo. There was pale pink carpet underfoot, laid down to suppress the prolific blackberry, and a collection of kitsch pink ornaments on the table. Dinner was generally eaten in the main living area, the 'long room', which also housed a small but very interesting library, mainly consisting of gardening and natural history reference books.

A year later I returned to Kotare Vale for a couple of days. How things had progressed. There were new vegetable gardens just up the hill, with twisty-driftwood climbing frames (sorry, pergolas!) for the runner beans. The hazels had grown noticeably, and there was a massive pumpkin that Martin was growing for the Little River Pumpkin Festival – it was already about half a metre in diameter. In the long room was a new addition to Martin's non-living menagerie: a telephone with a receiver in the shape of a duck, which startled me by quacking instead of ringing. Even technology seemed to be organic at Kotare Vale!

3

THE RIVIERA
OF THE SOUTH

That first summer of wwoofing, I made a trip to Southland, through softly rolling lush green farms that were increasingly changing from sheep to dairy. My destination was Riverton, a pretty fishing village half-an-hour's drive west of Invercargill. The sleepy little town is enlivened in summer with an influx of holidaymakers, including townies who have cribs there, trampers and backpackers on their way to the then-new Hump Ridge track near Tuatapere, and an increasing number of tourists passing through between Te Anau and Invercargill or Stewart Island.

Approached from Invercargill, the town seemed plain enough at first; a ribbon of main street laid straight along the flat, edged with a few streets of houses. There's a bridge spanning the Aparima River, and a bluff forces the road to fork into two, the right-hand fork leading to points west: to Colac Bay, Tuatapere, and the delightfully named Cosy Nook. The left-hand fork snakes around the estuary, past boathouses, and further round to the Riverton Rocks, where the beach hugs the sea in a curve, rocks loom out of the white sand, and houses dot the hillside above. In one of the shops were some delightful postcards, somewhat curled and faded, that proclaimed Riverton to be the 'Riviera of the South'.

For a small town of 2000 people, Riverton was surprisingly well-supplied with WWOOF hosts, and boasted a total of four in the area. I'd chosen to stay with Robert and Robyn Guyton and their three children, because it sounded as though they were my kind of people. According to the WWOOF book, they used permaculture principles and biodynamic methods, and were involved in the local environment centre, organic food co-op and estuary care group. 'We welcome wwoofers who are genuinely interested in the environment and organics and are keen to help us with our many projects,' the entry stated.

A whirlwind of energy greeted me, first in the form of Sparky the dog, bounding out towards me barking and wagging his tail madly. Robert said a passing hello and then was off taking the kids somewhere. Robyn gave me a quick guided tour, talking nineteen to the dozen as she whisked me around the maze of paths through the large garden. She was a bright and friendly woman with a wealth of knowledge about plants and an incredible gift of the gab, like a long-playing record sped up to 45. Her words spilled out so fast it was hard to keep up, and all the plants and trees and chooks went by in a blur. Perhaps she always rattled off the same spiel for the guided tour? But I soon found that this tongue-twisting speed was her normal pace.

Then Robert returned and showed me my room.

'We thought we'd put you in the barn loft.' He pointed to a wooden ladder leaning against the barn, and my gaze travelled up the rungs to the hobbit-sized door at the top, fringed with a grapevine. Quaint. Picturesque. And perhaps a way to overcome my vertigo. Eight-year-old Holly was up in a trice.

'Come on, Philippa, I'll show you!'

Gulping down any trepidation, I placed my feet surely and squarely on each rung and climbed up, wondering halfway whether the ladder was attached, and would I overbalance with my backpack on? My mild fear of heights had been intensified a few years before by a car accident that left me with weak wobbly ankles and the need to be sure of my footing, but after a couple of times negotiating the ladder I was swinging up and down like a monkey, even in the dark.

The loft was a private haven away from the noises of the household, and had a view down over the garden and across the Aparima River. The whole family had lived in the barn while they were building the house, which was a two-storeyed place with plenty of recycled windows and doors, and a large, light, living/kitchen area. The most interesting item was the icebox, a small insulated cupboard with two shelves, top and bottom. I'd never seen an icebox before, or at least not one being used for its original purpose. It was their only fridge, and was kept cool by two slicker pads that were alternated daily between the freezer and the icebox. For a family of five, plus wwoofers, there wasn't much in the icebox, mostly dairy products and leftovers. Most things didn't last long enough to go off or wilt at room temperature, and whatever vegetables were in season were harvested as needed.

Ten years before, the Guytons had bought the property, which was then a one-hectare paddock infested with gorse, and gradually they had converted it into a productive garden using permaculture principles. The word 'permaculture' was coined by two Australians, Bill Mollison and David Holmgren, to denote permanent (i.e. sustainable) human culture and agriculture, a way of people living in harmony with each other and with nature. Drawing on the ideas of many cultures, and people like Masanobu Fukuoka (author of the classic book on natural farming, *The One-Straw Revolution*), permaculture involves close observation of the patterns of nature, and designing for maximum efficiency and minimum effort. It is not limited to gardening or agriculture, but is a way of looking at the totality of human culture, of devising fair, ethical and environmentally friendly ways of working, trading and living together in communities.

Permaculture is a design system in which people consciously implement ways of living that are in tune with nature. One of its trademark ideas is to organise things in different zones, as concentric rings rippling out from one's house (which is zone 0). Zone 1 is the area immediately around the house, for things that you need to access easily and often, like a recycling area, and kitchen herbs; zone 2 is for things that need to be reasonably accessible, like the vegetable garden, chook house and clothesline; zone 3 is an area you don't visit quite so often, for example an orchard; zone 4 is further out again, for perhaps cereal crops or grazing animals; and zone 5 is somewhere rarely visited and ideally not tampered with at all, like wilderness or native bush. These are not to be confused with the numbered climate zones you sometimes see on seed packets.

When I did a permaculture course in Dunedin, much of it seemed like plain common sense to me – encouraging biodiversity and recognising the multiple uses of plants and making maximum use of them – but it did encourage me to adopt a certain mindset; to observe, plan and design carefully and consciously. Permaculture overlaps with organics and biodynamics, in that all these systems aim to work with nature rather than subdue, tame or conquer.

As with many organic gardens, the Guytons' place had a slightly 'messy' look. Not for them the wide expanses of lawns mown to within an inch of their life, or plants surrounded by large patches of bare, meticulously weeded earth. Instead, it was a colourful riot of life, a profusion of flowers, herbs, vegetables and fruit. In keeping with the permaculture principles of efficiency and minimising the workload, there was very little lawn – apart from a couple of spaces around the house, the rest of the place was covered in food plants for humans and birds. Down one side of the property was an ample chook run, a pleasant habitat with trees and bushes. Sixteen-year-old Terry took responsibility for feeding the chooks and collecting the eggs. There were bees too, just one hive at that time, which produced honey and pollinated the fruit trees and other plants. Although both Robyn and Robert worked off the property, as teachers, they still managed – with the help of the children, and of course wwoofers – to keep the garden thriving.

There were two other wwoofers staying, a young American couple, Kit and Alex, who announced their engagement while they were there, and delighted in each other's company like puppies. Our work was varied: harvesting fruit, weeding the vegetable gardens, cooking and preserving, weeding around the fruit trees, scraping the wax off wooden frames from a beehive, and more weeding.

Southland's cool climate favours berry fruit; there were blackcurrants, redcurrants, gooseberries, worcesterberries and blueberries. Worcesterberry was a new one on me. Robyn described it as a cross between blackcurrant and gooseberry; it was a thorny bush like a gooseberry, but with a dark coloured berry. A native of the Pacific coast of North America, it has the Latin name *Ribes divericatum*.

33

Blackcurrants (*Ribes nigrum*) and gooseberries (*Ribes uva-crispa*) are in the same genus.

At that time, in late February, all the berry fruit had been harvested except the blueberries, which were planted in a line, forming a kind of hedge, and were draped with netting to keep the birds from eating the fruit. We flung back the netting and plunged in, parted the leafy branches to get at the succulent berries in the heart of the bushes, crawled underneath to reach dimly glimpsed clusters, and popped the juicy morsels into our mouths with a slightly guilty pleasure. Filling our ice-cream containers was a time-consuming activity, as the berries were small and not always easily accessible, and a certain percentage of the harvest made its way directly into our mouths, especially when young Holly was in our picking brigade.

There was other fruit to harvest, too: plums, apples and pears. Some of these we ate straight away, fresh or cooked in muffins and crumbles. When there was an excess we preserved it, like the apple jelly I made one drizzly morning, having left the cooked apples to hang overnight in a muslin cloth suspended from the ceiling. DO NOT SQUEEZE, warned the recipe book, OR THE JELLY WILL GO CLOUDY, but I couldn't resist, my frugal nature got the better of aesthetics and I squeezed a bit more liquid out of the muslin bag – and the result was a jelly that was somewhat dull in appearance but just as delicious.

For several days Robyn, Kit, Alex and I weeded around all the fruit trees, pulling up great tufts of grass and leaving them to wilt and decompose in situ as a mulch. Most of the fruit trees had thick clumps of comfrey growing around them, and we ripped off handfuls of their slightly prickly leaves and laid them around the dripline of the trees, where the rain paints an invisible circle and the feeder roots are concentrated, positioned to receive any nutrients washed off the leaves. With its deep taproots, comfrey draws up from the subsoil a wealth of minerals, including potassium, phosphorus, calcium and iron, and provides excellent nourishment for fruit trees. We could have simply left the comfrey to die down in the autumn, but Robyn wanted to distribute the nourishing leaves evenly around the trees to make sure they all got some while the fruit was developing, and comfrey is so vigorous it can handle being cut down several times in one season.

We spent some time weeding in the vegetable garden. This was the neatest garden in terms of lack of weeds – most vegetables struggle to compete with lots of weeds around them – but even so there were few areas of bare earth that might tempt more weeds to grow. Once we had weeded, we added compost to fertilise the soil and mulched with pea straw to suppress the weeds and keep moisture in.

After a week or so I was getting the hang of the garden layout, finding my way around all the twisty paths lined with fruit trees and native bushes, here and there opening out to areas of vegetable garden or compost heaps. Walking into that garden was to be transported into another world, one where people clearly had a part and an ongoing interest in creation, but a world where nature held sway. Entering it was to humbly acknowledge our human role as only one of a multitude of organisms and beings that share this earth. Certainly a meditative state made the sometimes tedious garden tasks pass more quickly – as did gardening with others, talking and working together.

The evenings were social; family and wwoofers chatted over cooking, dinner and dishes, and played games. The two teenagers, Terry (16) and Adam (14) both helped out with cooking, and on my first night Adam made the whole dinner. One night Robert pulled out the visitors' book for us to write in, and as I flipped idly through the pages, skimming the previous entries written in various languages, some illustrated with sketches or photos, one photo stood out – it was Robert, pictured outside the house with a bike. His entry, written tongue in cheek, had no doubt fooled a few wwoofers into thinking that he had arrived as a wwoofer and stayed to marry Robyn. I was almost convinced but for the inclusion of the cheeky email address: robert@hotmale.com

One morning Robyn took me down to the environment centre, a welcoming building down by the bridge, full of information, books, bright posters, organic food and seeds. It doubled as the town's information centre and in the summer received a steady stream of visitors. I weeded the carpark area while Robyn did the weekly ordering for the organic co-op. She and Robert were instrumental in setting up the environment centre, the co-op, a local seed saving group, and the estuary care group.

'How do you have the energy for all of these things?' I asked. 'I mean, you both work, you've got three kids and a big garden to look after.'

'Well it's not just us,' said Robyn. 'It's a matter of getting other people motivated too. And it has to be fun, not just a whole lot of meetings. That's boring! So we have social events, field days, pot luck dinners.'

'And you're just in time for the Riverton Estuary Festival this weekend,' Robert chimed in. 'Attendance is compulsory.' He shot me a mock stern look, then his face broke into a grin.

Saturday dawned clear but with a stiff, chilly wind. Who'd want to stay weeding the garden when there was a festival happening? I opted to help out at the festival. Headquarters of the day's festivities were at the environment centre, where there were kites, balloons and a sausage sizzle. At low tide there were races in which the participants started out running along the riverbank, then squelched, splashed and swam their way through the mudflats, across the river and back. Onlookers hung over the bridge to watch, or were ferried across to the 'island' in the middle of the river – an expanse of gravel exposed by the low tide – where we cheered the racers on and were entertained by musicians, including young Adam.

The festival was organised by the estuary care group, and was a way to celebrate the estuary by being in it, an opportunity most people had probably not had. The estuary care group had done several reafforestation projects along the estuary and river margins and had used 'seed balls' in some of them.

Seed balls were Robert's speciality; the previous year he had taken time out from teaching to study them, on the Teacher Fellowship Scheme run by the Royal Society of New Zealand. The idea of seed balls is to make reafforestation easy, and – in keeping with permaculture – get maximum gain from minimum effort. Instead of going to the trouble of raising seedlings and then planting them, one can just sow seed. But seed is vulnerable to being eaten by birds, blown away by the wind, washed away by rain, and, if the right soil micro-organisms are not present, the seeds may germinate but struggle to survive. Seed balls go some way to overcoming these problems.

Seeds generally do best in the kind of soil that is around the parent plant, so to give them a head start they need to be sown along with some of this soil. This is particularly important when reintroducing native trees and plants to areas from which they have long disappeared, because the soil micro-organisms that help those plants survive and flourish may no longer exist in that soil. Particularly important are various mycorrhizal fungi that have beneficial and symbiotic relationships with certain plants and help them to absorb nutrients.

During his fellowship, Robert had produced a video, which he played for us wwoofers to show us how to make seed balls. The balls can then be thrown around or into the area you want the seeds to germinate. Seed balls make reafforestation accessible to children, the elderly and people with disabilities, and also make it easier to sow seeds in inaccessible places. They can also be sown over large areas by helicopter. The only place where they don't do well is in thick grass – here it is better to plant seedlings and mulch them well. Robert continued to experiment with seedballs and had some sprouting down in the bottom of the garden.

Recipe for seed balls

(Robert's website explains in greater depth how to make and use seed balls: http://homepages.paradise.net.nz/sces/seedballnz)

Ingredients
- 1 part seeds (cleaned according to their needs)
- 3 parts compost from around the parent plant
- 5 parts powdered or fine red terracotta clay (not blue or white clay) – dry out and grind between two bricks
- water to mix

Method

1. Mix seeds with compost until the seeds are coated
2. Add clay and mix
3. Add water little by little until the mixture is sticky, like dough
4. Roll into marble-sized balls between the palms of the hands
5. Dry out in a shady place until the balls are ready to use (a few days)
6. Distribute seed balls in desired area

In the evening after the estuary festival, as the moon grew round, I sat up in the loft, looking out at the garden, the estuary, the bush and farmland all bathed in a silvery sheen. The chattering of ducks and a plover's plaintive cry reverberated across the water in the still night air. The swell of the sea was constant in the background. A horoeka was silhouetted black against midnight blue, caught, gawky but beautiful, in the transformation of puberty, a jaunty crown of short adult leaves sprouting above a skirt of long juvenile leaves. It was so peaceful to just sit, observe and slow my rhythm to match the natural world. I felt a million miles from my previous life, the routines and stress and deadlines of office work. My new life didn't feel like work at all – it was like a holiday – and I was only just beginning to unwind. Yet I was aware that the journey ahead would require emotional resilience and self-reliance. I had left the safe harbour of Dunedin, left the safety-net of friends and family and cast off into uncharted waters.

HARVEST TIME

It was March in Central Otago, when the days were blazing summer but the nights distinctly autumn. I rolled up to Bob L de Berry's place, down the end of the road at Cambrian, easily identifiable by the bright red Welsh dragon on a green background on his large letterbox, and a sign that said 'Beware of the Hug!'

As I got out of the car, a bearded man grinning from ear to ear came out of the little sod cottage, arms outspread.

'You must be Philippa!' He called out, enveloping me in a large bear hug. He was disarmingly friendly and instantly likeable.

Cambrian is a former gold mining village, near the better-known gold mining town of St Bathans in Central Otago, about half an hour's drive from either Ranfurly or Alexandra. The landscape is as enormous as the sky. Great long low ridges of mountains dominate, rugged but worn in barren but beautiful browns and golds. It's a harsh climate. The sun beats mercilessly down in the summer in this treeless, parched place and the winters are severe with temperatures of –17°C not unknown. Central Otago is probably the closest to a continental weather pattern as we have anywhere on these temperate isles.

Now, Cambrian is a dead-end road with a dozen or so houses strung out along it, few inhabited by full-time residents. Bob had been living there for 20-odd years in an old miner's cottage made of mud bricks – the material of this land, warm in winter, cool in summer. The house had stood the test of time well – 140 years on – and was still sturdy. There had been various add-ons, and a couple of sleepouts out the back for guests or wwoofers like me.

Bob led a semi-self-sufficient life, with chooks, fruit trees, a vege garden, Thomas the donkey, and Esther the retired house cow. Bob's vision for his land, and indeed for Cambrian, was of a large forest, which he had been steadily planting over the years. He had formed a trust, the Cambrian Common Forest, and welcomes donations of money and trees.

Already he had planted hundreds of mostly exotic trees, including maple, oak, sycamore, gingko, pine, fir, larch and birch. According to Bob the exotics do well in the climate, better than most natives.

'Surely, though, there must be sub-alpine natives that will survive?' I asked.

'Yes, but the exotics are much hardier,' he replied. 'There are a few natives over there.' He pointed to a patch of scrub which no doubt gave the trees some frost protection. I do remember seeing at least one matagouri bush: a lone specimen silhouetted against the skyline in stark and thorny glory.

I resolved to return with some suitable native trees. After all, this area must once have been covered in vegetation, scrub at the very least, if not taller trees, although many of the barren mountain ridges would just have had tussock and smaller plants. There's so much to learn about this land, about my own land, about how the landscape has been altered, whether by natural changes or by human beings. I wonder what sort of changes Cambrian Common Forest will be making to the landscape. Like tree-planting projects on the fringes of the Sahara Desert, it may help to increase the precipitation in this arid land.

Water didn't seem to be a problem at Bob's, though. There was an old water race, built by miners during the gold rush, and water ran through it across Bob's land at a reasonably constant rate. So there was plenty of water for household needs and for the young trees. It was just a matter of getting the water to the trees, and for this Bob had a series of pipes and hoses rigged up. That was one of my jobs: watering the trees on the flat paddock and also on the hillside. The ground soaked up the water, and in the dry heat of that March it was hard to imagine how the place would look in a few short months, covered in snow.

But for the time being it was harvest season. There were plums, apples and pears to be picked from the trees around the house, and there was plenty of pipfruit to share with Thomas and Esther who would amble over to the fence to eat from my hand. The numerous elder trees scattered around the property yielded nine kilograms of berries – enough to make wine, which I did under Bob's supervision, in two large lidded buckets. Elderberry wine was the house wine at this establishment, and a very nice drop it was too: rich and smooth like an aged port. Bob also made rosehip wine and home brew.

There were blackberries growing wild in thickets. I made some jam from the blackberries, but not having had much experience of cooking on a coal range, I found it hard to get an even temperature. After a slow start and much hovering over the range and feeding it more and more wood, the fire eventually roared and the jam overcooked and set into a rather stiff paste. Still tasted alright!

The little copse near the house was perfect for exploring. Many of the trees were overgrown ones that had been planted over a century before, or were the offspring of said trees. They grew thickly, covering up the sky, and in their midst were the ruins of an old house. Further up the slope just out of the shade was a large ring of blackcurrant bushes, and elders growing wild here and there.

Bob used to be known as Bob Berry, but then discovered his ancestors on the Berry side possibly came from France and were originally called by the more elegant name of de Berry. So Bob took this on, and in his characteristic humorous fashion, added his middle initial L for fun: Bob L de Berry – say it out loud.

While I was there, another Kiwi arrived – only one of three other New Zealand wwoofers I've met. From a farm in Southland originally, now resident in the Coromandel, John was a gentle soul and a gun fencer. He fixed a couple of damaged fences up the top of the property, after we had all gone up to chase the sheep back through to the neighbour's land, running and stumbling across a small plateau dotted with pines and spruces stunted by exposure to the weather. He was always a participant in some great philosophical conversations around the kitchen table at the end of each day.

One day we extracted honey from Bob's hives. John and I worked in the honey house while Bob collected the supers (bee boxes), a couple at a time, carefully balanced on a wheelbarrow. John and I took turns with the hot knife, slicing the wax off the tops of the cells, while the other loaded the frames into the extractor and turned it on. The extractor was simply a large drum that spun around, blasting the honey out by centrifugal force onto the sides of the drum, from where it slid down and collected in the bottom. Once in a while we turned on the tap at the bottom of the drum and the honey flowed out, a sieve catching any dead bees or bits of wax before the golden lava was stored in large tins.

Once the honey extraction was over, Bob took us down to the swimming hole, a small and very deep lake surrounded by reeds and pine trees, which had been a gold mine once.

There was a little circle of grass, ringed by stones, in a sunny spot overlooking the pond, and after a swim the three of us gathered there on our towels to read and relax. Bob had created this little fairy ring: had planted the grass, watered it from time to time, and even mowed it once or twice. Beauty was just as important as mere utility and survival. One morning the three of us dug up some patches of snowdrop and bluebell bulbs to replant, spreading them around to help them multiply and provide a spring display in the paddock across the lane from the house.

Bob must be one of the longest-standing hosts, having become one in 1981. His long-term vision for the trees extends into other areas of his life – in fact beyond his life – he has already made his own coffin, with a little verse beside it:

'This coffin was made with much levity
Its owner desires longevity
But regardless of health
Irrespective of wealth
Don't stuff around with negativity.'

When I left, Bob furnished me with my first wwoofing reference, written on groovy paper in a flourishing hand:

Cambrian Common Forest

11th March 2002

To Whom it May Concern

It is with much pleasure that I give Philippa Jamieson a reference as an excellent 'bona fide' wwoofer. Her skills at making jam are well set in my mind and she did a creditable job at extracting all that honey from the poor little bees.

No job needs to be described twice, and her culinary expertise puts quite a spell on you. Don't turn down this wwoofer or you might end up a frog!

Bob L de Berry, caretaker, CCF

It was March, still autumn, still harvest time, and it seemed like a good time to continue wwoofing in Central Otago. I had heard of a lesbian couple living nearby whom I wanted to interview for the national gay newspaper, *express*. They owned the White Horse Hotel at Becks, a small settlement on the road between Ranfurly and Alexandra, at the turnoff to Cambrian. While staying at Bob's place I went and checked it out. The women were no longer there, but had bought the Stone House, an orchard near Clyde, so I followed them up and went to visit them.

Kaye Chamberlain and Clair Higginson, with Clair's sister Stephanie as a business partner, had an orchard where they grew a variety of fruit: the stonefruit that Central Otago is famed for (luscious apricots, plums, peaches, nectarines and – a new one to me – peacherines); pipfruit (quinces, apples and pears); and blackberries. Kaye and Clair were happy to be interviewed, and it just so happened that they needed an extra worker for a week or two to help out with the harvest, so they put me up in a little flat behind the coolstore and packing shed.

The farm wasn't certified organic, but they grew everything organically, as had the previous owner. They weren't listed in the WWOOF book, but there are a number of organic farms that will take volunteers on the same basis as wwoofers even though they're not part of the WWOOF scheme. Most of them know other WWOOF hosts, and sometimes take the 'overflow' from their friends or neighbours, or take on people whom they know or meet up with.

The Stone House was, in fact, a stone house, though not as I had romantically envisaged, an old stone miner's cottage. It was a much more modern, two-storeyed house perhaps 20 or 30 years old. And it was the name of the business, which included an orchard and a pickle-making enterprise.

In the commercial kitchen Kaye, Clair and Stephanie made all sorts of delicious concoctions, such as blackberries soaked in port, fruit liqueur toppings for desserts and quince 'cheese' (really a super-thick paste that you can cut in slices and serve with crackers and cheese).

As well, they sold the fresh fruit in season from their roadside stall and direct to customers around New Zealand. Every morning we would open up the stall, put out boxes of fruit, and replenish any of the lines of pickles and sauces that were selling well. The sound of a car driving up to the stall, or the ring of the bell, would alert us to the fact that customers had arrived.

A mixed business like this ensured a variety of jobs. Picking was the main one at that time of year. The blackberries needed to be picked almost every morning as new berries were continually ripening, and all hands were on deck for this task, including two or three local women who were employed on a casual, seasonal basis.

The blackberries were a thornless, cultivated variety, so picking them was a breeze compared with the rather more ferocious bushes that grew wild at Bob's. Here the canes were grown in orderly rows and trained up against wires and posts, although they grew so vigorously that here and there the canes arched overhead. Even so, a certain detached concentration was required so that the eyes kept a couple of steps ahead of the hand, finding berries that hid in behind the foliage, assessing their ripeness. Zen and the art of berry-picking.

When the day's berries were picked, we took them inside for grading on the long stainless steel benches. As we were picking we were also grading and throwing out any that were too far gone or were somehow stunted, hard little things that would never develop and ripen properly. The plump, juicy, ripe berries were either sold fresh and/or packed in plastic bags and frozen. Fruit sales were in full swing at that time of year, but it was the pickles that made the money, as with any 'value-added' product, and they could be sold all year round, ensuring a steady cashflow.

'How would you like to make quince cheese?' Clair asked me one day.

'Sure,' I said, following her into the commercial kitchen beside the house. At one end was a small storeroom, where all the pickles were stored and packed in cartons. There were tall bottles of fruity ice-cream toppings, hexagonal jars of assorted pickles in wooden gift boxes, and a whole wall of large, old-fashioned bottling jars in an autumnal rainbow of greengages, peaches, apricots.

The storeroom led into the main kitchen area, where the fruit was washed, graded, cooked and bottled. Hygiene was important, so we wore caps and gloves, washing our hands thoroughly beforehand. Clair showed me the large steel gas-heated cylinder used to cook the preserves. Although there were ripening quinces in the orchard, we used frozen quince pulp, so it was simply a matter of adding sugar and cooking it for a while on a low heat, stirring fairly constantly so it didn't stick, until it was stiffer than jam, and finally ladling it into trays to set. A sort of kitchen alchemy occurs when cooking quinces, only instead of creating gold, the colour of the fruit turns from gold to pink.

After I'd finished my work for the day I would lie in the grass in the shade of the quince trees, reading a book. The quinces hung in the trees like pendulous, greenish-yellow Christmas baubles, with a faint white fuzz on them that was easily wiped off. They exuded their own distinct heavenly fragrance, and I put a couple in my room just so they could release their perfume there.

I had a sense of freedom and lack of cares that I hadn't had for so long. There was physical work to do, not usually too onerous, and then there was all this free time, stretching ahead of me like holidays. I was really beginning to unwind from the years of 9–5 routine, from the stress of deadlines and city living. I was just three months into my new lifestyle and on a recent trip back to Dunedin several people had commented how relaxed I was looking.

Planning ahead is a good idea for wwoofers, especially in the summer months, and if you want to ensure a place at some of the more popular farms. But sometimes I just played it by ear, and in May 2002 I met up with Annie Wilson at the Soil and Health conference and instinctively knew she'd be a good host. Her Otago origins were not immediately obvious because of the overlay of a soft American accent picked up from a decade of living in the US, but we soon established common ground and mutual acquaintances.

Annie lived with her partner Sean (also a Wilson, by happenstance) at Miranda on the Firth of Thames, near the bird sanctuary. Down on the tidal mudflats thousands of migrating birds from Eastern Siberia and Alaska begin arriving in late September and stay till March, thus escaping the cruel Arctic winter. Like me, they sought out benign weather, although they get two summers, and I was merely swapping a South Island winter for a North Island one.

The property, Miranda Orchards, was about an hour south of Auckland, off the main drag and down a picturesque country road through rolling farmland. A colourful sign advertising organic produce greeted me as I neared a sharp elbow bend in the road, and there was the roadside stall (a good-sized shop-cum-shed) and the driveway. Up by the house, two Jack Russell terriers excitedly heralded my arrival, followed by an elderly golden Labrador, and then Annie appeared to show me around.

The 5.6-hectare Bio-Gro certified property had mandarins, tangelos, lemons, limes, tamarillos, feijoas, apples, nashis and plums, and, on a smaller scale, vegetables and herbs. Annie had worked as a gardener for years and really knew her stuff.

On the first day, she and I weeded the vege gardens and asparagus patch, chatting companionably as we got to know each other. Sean commuted into South Auckland for work most days, but helped out on the farm as well, and during my stay he spent some time in the shed tinkering with the tractor, until the engine's triumphant roar announced his success.

Near the house was a small orchard of nashis, which to me were indistinguishable from ordinary pear trees. Each tree had a veritable thicket of the past season's growth that shot straight up in the air. Over a couple of days, Annie and I pruned them all, taking care to separate out a few branches that were afflicted with fire blight, and move them to a pile to be burnt so the disease would not spread.

After 10 years of pruning my own fruit trees, I was reasonably confident, and Annie's trust in me helped my confidence. Even my fear of heights diminished when Annie brought out her pruning ladder, a sturdy A-frame design with spikes on the bottom to grip the earth, and once up the ladder and in some cases up the tree, I forgot to be afraid, so absorbed was I in the task at hand.

Pruning is a rewarding job, transforming what we call 'overgrown' trees into shapely forms to encourage more fruiting, to let more light in to help ripen the fruit, and to let the air circulate freely. Traditional wisdom dictates that you prune when the trees are dormant (which is what we were doing), so they do not bleed sap and therefore energy, but there is a school of thought that promotes pruning in summer, or immediately after the fruit has been harvested.

We kept the existing fruiting spurs and pruned so that more would develop, training the branches outwards, as the spurs generally develop on the more horizontal branches. We cut off the water shoots (the new season's growth around the base of the trunk), and pruned a good deal of the vigorous leggy growth at the top, leaving just a few main 'leaders'.

While the pipfruit and stonefruit was entering the dormant phase of winter, other fruit was ready to pick. Annie seconded me into harvesting fruit at another nearby property, also organic.

'Here we are,' she said, pulling the ute over onto the grass verge. Over the fence was a paddock with some big spreading trees, perhaps six or seven metres high, looking to my untrained eye not unlike avocados.

47

'These are the casimiroas,' said Annie. I had to get her to repeat the name, which was new to me. Originally from Mexico, they are also called white sapote, although they are no relation to the black sapote.

'Some people call them ice-cream fruit,' she continued. 'Try one. They've got a creamy texture.' She picked a couple and we sampled them. Mmm. It was rather like a custard apple (also known as cherimoya), which I'd tried in India, only more delicate.

'Be careful when you pick them and handle them,' Annie advised, handing me a picking bag. 'They bruise and get soft easily.' Hence, they are not a great commercial success. The height of the trees made it hard to harvest all but the lower branches, and there were only a few that were ripe anyway.

Next we went after the bright orange mandarins, which peeked out from between glossy leaves. Annie showed me how to snip close to the fruit so the base of the stalk was still left on but it didn't stick out and pierce the skin of the other fruit in the picking bag.

A few persimmon trees huddled under some bird netting, which was draped over them like a shroud. We lifted up the edges of the netting and an orange glow shone out – from the ripe globes of fruit, and from the leaves on the ground and some still in the trees. A few birds had snuck in through holes in the netting and now were flying around in a panic, trying to get out. Some of the fruit looked perfectly whole from underneath but when picked revealed varying degrees of bird damage, from a few pecks to the whole of the flesh eaten out, leaving the skin like a shell.

Across the road were some long rows of tamarillos, looking for all the world like lanky teenagers laden with numerous pendulous earrings of fruit in hues of blood red, ruby and dark wine. The fresh green of feijoas added to the colourful array of fruit stacked up in yellow bins in the back of the ute. The feijoa is one of my favourite fruits, from its distinctive scent, which perfumes a whole room, to the tangy acid taste and slightly grainy texture. Native to South America, the feijoa thrives in our climate, and while it isn't in quite the same category as the adopted kiwifruit (known as Chinese gooseberry in my childhood), New Zealand is the biggest exporter of feijoas, and lots of people have them in their gardens. I always wondered why they were conspicuously absent in Australia, given that the conditions must be favourable for them, but recently discovered that growing them is discouraged in several states because they are a prime host of fruit fly.

Back at Miranda Orchards, Annie set me to work in the tangelo orchard. The fruit wasn't ready yet, but there was weeding to be done. There was a bit of ragwort, which was easy enough to pull out, but the thorny weeds (barberry and blackberry) were trickier: as was the tap-rooted privet. It was satisfying, though, to pull out the small barberry plants whole, by the roots. There were a few gaps in the tangelo orchard, into which we planted a handful of avocados.

The variety of tasks made it an interesting and enjoyable stay. Up the top of the property there was a strip of native trees, which Annie and Sean were extending, and one day we planted flax, hebe, kohuhu, karaka and whau up there. We also planted elderberry, which I'd never heard of anyone doing, because it grows wild in Otago, to the extent that it's almost a weed.

On a rainy day, there were plenty of indoor activities. Down in the fruit stall by the roadside, I weighed and bagged fruit ready for sale, tidied up and swept the floor, and cleaned garlic – which meant taking off any dusty outer layers of skin, and cutting off excess roots.

It wasn't all work and no play: Annie took me off to the local thermal pools for a well-earned soak, and in the evenings we would all relax with some good food and a glass of wine in front of the fire.

Direct sampling of the food is one of the joys of harvesting on organic farms. Being a gatherer at heart, I already had a well-developed sense for browsing on wild food, roadside fruit trees and weeds like chickweed, although I was always mindful of possible toxins from sprays and car exhaust. Being let loose on organic farms gave me such a heart-bursting feeling of freedom. Here I had no compunction about taking a fig every time I wandered past the tree, or picking wild blackberries, knowing with certainty that they were toxin-free.

Sampling of the harvest itself is not simply for immediate gratification, of course, but also for Quality Control, to ensure that what you're picking is ripe enough and not too ripe. One soon learns to rely on the senses: vision for the size and colour; smell in some cases; touch for the texture, firmness and ease of picking – but what more thorough way to familiarise oneself with ripeness than by tasting?

Tasting is also an essential part of Product Knowledge: one has to learn about what one is picking and selling, in order to knowledgeably answer the customers' questions. And sometimes it was simply a case of the fruit being perfectly ripe but unable to survive storage or packing, so the wwoofers might as well eat it.

At the height of a South Canterbury summer, Aroha Organics was bursting at the seams with raspberries at varying stages of ripeness. This small market garden near St Andrews, south of Timaru, also grew strawberries, potatoes, garlic, lettuce and other vegetables, and had a number of newly planted fruit trees. The raspberry season lasted for several weeks, and as the summer raspberries gave out, the autumn varieties would be waiting in the wings to take over the next act. For a couple of weeks my main task was picking, alongside a couple from Uruguay, Nathan Davis the farm manager, and Steph from England, who had arrived as a wwoofer, but became Nathan's partner and stayed – a not altogether uncommon phenomenon in the world of wwoofing. The following year they were married.

I had originally met Nathan when he introduced himself to me after eavesdropping on a conversation in Golden Bay the previous winter. I was sitting with a newly acquired friend at the Wholemeal Café in Takaka, deep in conversation about our shared interests: organics, Green politics and genetic engineering (GE). Aided by a glass of organic wine, the conversation jumped and somersaulted around activist tactics to promote organics and to oppose the imminent lifting of the moratorium on GE in the environment.

The only other patron in that part of the café was a young man eating dinner on his own, and after some time, as engrossing as our plans for the ideal world were, we both began to realise that he was sitting as still as an alert dog, with his ears pricked absorbing everything we were saying. Finally he turned around.

'Um, excuse me, I couldn't help but overhear ... you've been talking about GE,' said the young man, politeness personified. 'It's a topic dear to my heart, and well ... do you mind if I join you?'

'Of course not,' we chorused, delighted to find someone of like mind. By the end of the evening Nathan had booked me in for a wwoofing stint at Aroha Organics, at a time to be organised. As we left the café we saw the full force of Nathan's ebullient, sunny personality and the strength of his beliefs embodied in his lime-green and purple VW combi van, and a red octagonal sign emblazoned on the rear window, screaming STOP GE!

So there we were, six months later, in the dry heat of the South Canterbury sun, with the surf close enough to hear but down at the foot of this shelf of coast and out of sight. Carrying punnets on flat wooden trays, we talked and ate and graded as we picked. The first grade raspberries were just on ripe but still firm enough to survive for a couple of days in a punnet in the chiller and in transit to one of the organic shops. Second grade were ripe but overblown, soft as a maiden's blush, so had to be sold that day, made into jam, or become an integral part of the wwoofer's diet. They had the sweetest and fullest taste, although if left just a little too long became watery and insipid. The speed of ripening was astonishing. We could pick from every row every day and there would always be more coming on. Occasionally we could even go over a row twice a day and find more ripe berries. There were always berries hiding in the middle of the bushes that could only be found by parting the slightly prickly canes at regular intervals.

We picked strawberries there too: huge, bright, juicy ones with such intense flavour that one could never go back to eating the synthetically grown kind again – the kind that might look a treat, but their flavour is merely bland and sweet, without tang or depth or joy. Nathan grew the strawberries under netting in mounded-up rows, each plant emerging from regularly-spaced holes in long strips of black weedmat. The weedmat was very effective, but even so, we had to weed along the edges of the mat and immediately around the strawberry plants as the grass and wire weed threatened to engulf the strawberries if we gave them half a chance.

When I left, Nathan and Steph loaded me up with a box of strawberries and raspberries for me to deliver to Fleur's Place, a café in Moeraki, and some for me to take away.

Since Aroha Organics is on the main highway, I try to stop by, if passing, to say hello or check out the produce and leave payment in the good old-fashioned honesty box if no-one's around.

5

COSMIC COW HORNS

In the early 1990s when my interest in organics was growing, and I read anything and everything on the topic, I came across a book titled *Biodynamics, A New Zealand Perspective*. Until then, biodynamics seemed rather far-out to me. Planting by the moon made sense, but filling cow horns up with cow manure, burying them for six months, diluting the transformed manure in water down to homeopathic proportions, and then spraying it on the land seemed pretty strange. But this book sparked my interest and increased my understanding, and on my wwoofing journey I jumped at the chance to visit some biodynamic farms. The farmers seemed totally down to earth, with a respect for the land and an acknowledgment of a spiritual dimension that I found very welcome.

In 1924 an Austrian called Rudolf Steiner gave a series of lectures about agriculture to a group of farmers who were concerned that their soil was slowly becoming degraded. These talks formed the basis for a new way of farming that became known as biodynamics, and which was part of a wider movement started by Steiner, called anthroposophy. Steiner was highly spiritual and an extraordinary thinker whose ideas have come to be adopted around the world, particularly in the areas of education, care of people with disabilities, and in farming.

Farmers in Europe who followed Steiner's ideas started selling their produce under the name Demeter (the Greek goddess of the harvest), which in time became formalised as a trademark name and certification label, with international standards and associations around the world, including the Bio Dynamic Farming and Gardening Association in

New Zealand (commonly referred to as the BD Association). A few farmers began using biodynamic principles in New Zealand as early as the late 1920s. Biodynamic farmers have been seen by some as being crackpots, or at the very least a little odd, but in recent years, with a shift towards organics and natural farming practices, biodynamic ideas have gained much wider acceptance.

Biodynamics acknowledges a spiritual dimension, a life force present in everything, and takes into account the influence of cosmic forces on all living things. Farmers and fisherfolk the world over have always considered the seasons and the phases of the moon in their activities, but biodynamic farmers go further and observe major planetary configurations, and not just the waxing and waning moon but also the ascending and descending phases of the moon (the moon's changing path across the heavens – sometimes it's higher in the sky, sometimes it's lower). They also use eight special preparations, two of which are sprayed on the land, and the other six used in compost heaps or liquid manure. The two most well-known, and most likely to be used by dabblers in biodynamics, are preparations 500 and 501. There is no special significance to these numbers; they are just numbers that were assigned in a catalogue.

The first winter of my journey I got some first-hand experience of using preparation 500, at Pakaraka Farm near Thames, the home of Harry Parke and Green Party co-leader Jeanette Fitzsimons, who was, as far as I know, the only Member of Parliament to be a WWOOF host.

The road twisted up the scenic Kauaeranga Valley, following the river's curves, along a flat valley floor that gradually narrowed as steep bush-clad hillsides took over. Harry and Jeanette farmed about 16 of their 87 hectares; most of it was fairly inaccessible slopes covered in regenerating native bush (and a number of weeds: gorse, woolly nightshade and pampas grass). On the river flats there were nut trees: pecans, chestnuts and a few macadamias. On the flats and slopes were several paddocks where they had about 150 sheep and a handful of cattle including the house cow. They also had chooks, bees, a vegetable garden and a number of fruit trees.

The house was one of the most eco-friendly I'd come across so far. It was made mostly of macrocarpa, which needs no treating, had a composting toilet, and was built according to passive solar design principles, facing the sun, and with dark heat-absorbing tiles in the dining area. The farm was not on the grid; electricity was generated by solar panels and a wind turbine. Most of the cooking was done on the woodstove, which looked like a coal range but burned only wood. They had a couple of gas rings, too, for quick stuff like boiling water for tea. The house had cost around $140,000 to build, not counting Harry's labour, and including about $20,000 for the solar and wind power systems.

Most weekdays Jeanette was away in Parliament or doing constituency work in the Coromandel electorate, so Harry was my main boss, if you could call him that. He was a considerate, soft-spoken man, wiry and weatherbeaten, with a silver beard, checked shirt and battered hat. He was always up at first light listening to National Radio while he had a cup of tea. Every morning he stood over the house cow to make sure she fed the foster calf, and twice a week he milked her. Most days he zoomed around on the farm bike to check on the stock and do various jobs around the farm. Harry was brought up on a dairy farm in the King Country, and had done a lot of shearing in his life, including competing in the Golden Shears.

At lunchtime he would spread out the newspaper like a tablecloth to pore over while we munched in companionable silence, broken occasionally by comments on the news, and discussion about the forthcoming general election. The paper would remain there for further perusal in the evening over an organic beer or a tot of whiskey, before being added to the stack for recycling. The phone was in frequent use, and Harry would often take it outside and have a cigarette as he chatted, pacing the sun-warmed flagstones or sitting on the little stone wall.

The farm, with its fresh air and activity, seemed to be a welcome antidote to the life of an MP, with its meetings, speeches and plane trips. Jeanette would come home from Parliament for the weekend, and before you knew it, she'd have changed her clothes and got stuck into some farm chore like collecting the eggs, checking on the bees or pulling up leeks.

Also staying at the farm at that time were Sophie, the daughter of some friends, and her two horses. She was a petite but strong, capable young woman, always active. If she wasn't off riding, she would be feeding out to the animals, or doing any number of chores with me: grubbing gorse, rounding up sheep, filling potholes in the farm road.

One weekend we mixed up a batch of preparation 500. It was my first experience of the biodynamic preparations, and I was curious, if somewhat disappointed, to see Harry emptying the contents of a small plastic bag into the mixing vessel, a 44-gallon drum (200-litre) full of warm water. There were no buried cow horns here, just an innocuous handful of what looked like rich, dark, loamy earth, which Harry had bought from the BD Association. In times gone by, Harry and Jeanette had made preparation 500 themselves, but after a while they found it easier to buy it.

Because we were mixing up enough to spray all over the farm, or at least everywhere accessible to the farm bike, all hands were on deck. Jeanette, Sophie and I took turns mixing the preparation, and Harry dispersed it all over the paddocks with spray equipment on the farm bike trailer. We mixed the brew with a large stick that was attached by a rope to a wooden strut sticking out from the barn (this took some of the weight of the stick and made it easier to stir). One of us stirred clockwise until the momentum got going and the water swirled into a deep vortex. Then another one of us would take over and change the direction to counterclockwise, throwing the whirlpool into chaos for a time before the constant stirring recreated the vortex again. Although an hour of stirring off and on seemed like a long time to begin with, we got into the rhythm of it, and there was even something primeval, something magical about it. We were like the three witches in *Macbeth*, concocting a magic brew in the cauldron. Each batch was thoroughly stirred for an hour, then Harry mixed in some liquid fish manure at the end before straining it into the spray tanks.

The idea of the stirring is that it will oxygenate and enliven the mixture, which in turn enlivens and revitalises the soil and the micro-organisms in it. The clockwise and counterclockwise stirring imbues the water with a rhythm. According to biodynamics, everything is influenced by the moon and other cosmic forces. We mixed and spread the preparation according to the recommendations: 500 is best sprayed in the afternoon, in autumn (or early spring), and while the moon is in its descending period. Biodynamic farmers and gardeners use the ascending and descending periods of the moon rather than the waxing and waning phases. The ascending period, when the moon's arc rises higher in the sky, is the time when the sap rises, the earth 'breathes out', growth above the earth is more evident and seeds germinate more successfully, while the descending period, when the moon's arc becomes lower, is when the earth 'breathes in' and draws the growth forces beneath the soil, to the roots and soil organisms.

One day I helped Harry drench the sheep. First we had to round them all up from the hill paddock into the yards. Harry, Sophie and I grabbed some noise makers (plastic milk bottles filled with small stones) and set off up the sloping paddock. The sheep put on a great show, demonstrating their agility and speed on the uneven slopes before we finally got them all in the yards, and then in the race, where they squashed up in single file and were easy to handle. Harry had a drench gun and backpack spray pack filled with cider vinegar and garlic, and proceeded to squirt the mixture down their throats with a practised hand, while I opened and closed the gates.

In a paddock of their own were three sheep that had been separated from the rest of the flock. They had suffered from internal parasites and had not responded to the organic drench like the other sheep, so had to be given a conventional drench. Organic certification rules state that animal health must be paramount, and if organic remedies are not working for sick animals, then conventional remedies must be used, and the animals kept in a quarantine paddock. While Pakaraka Farm was not certified organic, Harry and Jeanette used common sense and compassion when it came to animal welfare, just as the certification rules require. Harry said he would keep these sheep separate until he sold them, and he could not sell them as organic. The paddock was close to the farm road and next to the house cow's paddock, so it was easy to keep an eye on the sheep and make sure they were OK.

As well as all the usual chores on the farm, there was a flurry of activity associated with the lead-up to and aftermath of the 2002 election. The phone was in constant use: there were calls from various media, Green Party MPs and members. Sometimes we went to the neighbours' house to watch the news, as Jeanette and Harry didn't have a TV, and on election day I picked flowers and helped to decorate the Thames racecourse, where the Coromandel Greens – and the media – gathered for the election night party. Although Jeanette lost the Coromandel seat (which she had won in 1999, but which had previously been held by the National Party for decades), the Greens romped back into Parliament with nine MPs, an increase of two since the previous election.

After the anxiety and elation of election night, Sunday morning was a quiet one spent reading the paper and listening to the radio, absorbing the election results and political ramifications, followed by a clean-up of the racecourse hall.

John Warmenhoven from the Mahana community in the Coromandel recommended Ewen and Jan Willis' biodynamic orchard near Opotiki as a great spot to wwoof. Called Fruit Forest, it consisted mainly of avocados, with some mandarins, persimmons and feijoas. Ewen and Jan had been there for 20-odd years and the avocado trees were huge and spreading, like fully-grown walnut trees in size, with large canopies you could hide under.

The driveway was flanked by strips of herb garden, with the avocado trees towering on either side, and led to a large barn, part of which was a small packhouse and tool shed, and the other side of which was a very pleasant house, facing the afternoon sun and, over the bush, a view of the sea. Jan had planted a number of yuccas in the garden out the back, giving the place an exotic feel. At that time of the year,

Jan worked most days at a nearby kiwifruit packhouse, while Ewen worked full-time at Fruit Forest.

Hass and Reed were the main varieties of avocado there, with a few Fuerte and Zutano, and the main rootstock was Zutano. There were a number of grafted avocado seedlings in a shade house, and my tasks included repotting some of these into taller planter bags with a mix I made up of compost with a bit of coarse sand. I gave all the seedlings a top dressing with vermicast (the elegant way of saying worm poo).

There were seeds to plant: tamarillos, passionfruit and a few vegetables for the home garden, and I also pricked out some tiny passionfruit seedlings from a tray into another, giving them all more space to keep growing. Subtropicals flourished in the warm damp climate. A few bananas were grown for home consumption.

The place was Demeter certified, and one day Ewen and I mixed up a batch of preparation 500. Ewen had made the preparation himself, and dug up the cow horns, removed the rich, dark, crumbly contents and put them into the biodynamic farmer's cauldron (a 44-gallon drum filled with water), which we took turns at stirring.

Although there were avenues in amongst the trees that the tractor could traverse, spreading the preparation by hand meant we could get into more places in between and under the avocado trees. The two of us walked around the farm in the gathering dusk under the rising moon, each carrying a bucketful of the preparation. We spread it by dipping a hearth-brush into the water, then flinging it out around us in great arcs of droplets as we walked all around the orchard.

It was a peaceful, mystical, meditative activity, and I could almost feel the earth and the trees breathing in the preparation, absorbing it. Below me were millions of microscopic creatures, many more species than live above the earth's surface, all going about their various activities. How would this magic rain pattering down help them?

As I flung the preparation out wide, in that dreamy twilight, it seemed totally right and understandable. As at least a couple of bio-dynamic farmers have said to me: 'It's like electricity – you don't need to understand *how* it works. You just need to try it and see that it *does* work.'

One of the main problems for avocados is the fungus *Phytophthora cinnamomi*, which is present in many avocado producing regions.

'So what does it do?' I asked, ever-curious.

'The fungus causes the rotting of actively-growing feeder roots and generally weakens the tree,' Ewen explained. 'See that tree over there?' He pointed to a fully-grown avocado that was looking a bit leafless at the top. 'It's just starting to suffer. And that one over there,' he indicated a large stump with a forest of new shoots emerging from it. 'I cut that one down because it was pretty bad, but now it's growing back again vigorously.'

To combat this phytophthora, conventional avocado growers drill holes at intervals around the trunk and insert syringes of a solution of neutralised phosphorous acid into these holes. The tree sucks it up, and it helps control the fungus. But this isn't allowed under organic standards, so organic growers have to deal with it in other ways. Ewen's philosophy is that if you encourage a fungal atmosphere in the soil around the trees, the phytophthora has to compete with lots of other fungi and won't dominate. In order to get a lot of fungal activity, he puts literally heaps of mulch under his trees: lots of old branches and other woody material, which attract fungi as they decompose.

Certainly, most of his trees looked bloomingly healthy, although he pointed out the odd one or two that weren't doing so well and which he was thinking about taking out altogether. Even if you think they have succumbed to phytophthora, they sometimes have a new growth spurt if you cut them right back, as the flourishing stump illustrated.

Mulching the trees was a major activity, and Ewen enlisted me to haul branches and bamboo debris, semi-rotted pine needles, seaweed and compost onto the tractor trailer to distribute around the trees. A large windrow compost heap (a loose pile in a long row, not confined by a bin) benefited from an addition of organic chicken manure and sawdust, offloaded from the trailer and onto the heap by me and a wheelbarrow.

It was at Fruit Forest that I undertook with solemn diligence one of the most difficult wwoofing tasks yet encountered. It was my first morning there, and over breakfast Ewen was outlining the tasks for the day.

'Now there is one thing I'd like you to do every day without fail,' Ewen said. I nodded, ever conscientious, wanting to do the right thing. 'And that is to eat at least three avocados a day,' he continued, keeping a straight face. 'Well, you might get away with two a day,' he conceded. I laughed.

'Sure, that shouldn't be a problem!' I promised. 'I love avocados.' One for breakfast, lunch and dinner. In a salad or sushi, made into guacamole, or simply chopped in half, drizzled with lemon juice and sprinkled with pepper. How hard could it be? But in fact, I fell woefully short of the daily quota, sometimes only managing one. They're delicious, but so rich.

In my first year of wwoofing I wrote an article about heirloom apples in New Zealand for *Organic NZ*, and during my research was pointed in the direction of Dieter Proebst as someone who was highly knowledgeable in that field. Twenty years before (in 1982) Dieter established an orchard near Motueka called Treedimensions, and until 2000 also ran a nursery selling a wide range of his own grafted fruit trees. At the time of my visit he also ran Treedimensions Landuse Consulting Service, was an auditor for the Demeter certification agency, and was one of the tutors for the biodynamic course in Havelock North. It was clear he had a wealth of knowledge about fruit, was a truly dedicated biodynamic orchardist, and someone who could teach me a lot. After a couple of phone interviews for the article, I said I'd love to arrange a wwoofing stint at his orchard later in the year.

That spring I crossed Cook Strait and returned to the South Island, drove through the sun-drenched landscape of the Nelson area, past orchards and vineyards flushed with the bright green of fresh leaves, and up the Motueka Valley a little way. Up a gravel side road there was a fringe of native trees and beyond that the orchard: neatly planted rows of trees fanning out and down a slope and across the flat, edged by a stream that coursed along the bottom of a steep hillside. Then the house came into view, a unique hexagonal wooden place that spoke of someone innovative and unconventional living there.

I knew I'd come to the right place because the red on white Demeter logo was emblazoned on a building directly ahead of me on the driveway.

Dieter appeared in green overalls. He had a thick head of hair, a piercing gaze, and a certain German intensity. The stereotypical German orderliness was in evidence too; the stack of firewood by the front door was the neatest I'd ever seen. He gave me a quick tour of the gardens and orchard immediately around the house, and the newly built self-contained farm stay accommodation, then showed me to my quarters: a caravan with native trees behind, and a vista out over the orchard on the slopes below.

After settling in there I joined him and my fellow wwoofer, a 20-year-old American called Ashley, in the house for dinner.

'I hope you like pizza,' said Dieter.

'You bet,' I replied, eyeing the homemade pizza with all the trimmings. Ashley was just putting some grated cheese on as the finishing touch.

'It's all organic,' said Dieter, 'and so is the wine. It's a lovely drop from Sunset Valley over in Upper Moutere.' He poured us all a glass and we savoured the sauvignon in the late afternoon sun. Dieter was one of the staunchest people I'd met for eating only organic food. His pantry and cellar were well stocked, and wwoofers were encouraged to take part in cooking. It was certainly a pleasure with a wide range of whole grains, various organic luxuries, and fresh vegetables from the garden.

The only downside was that it was just about the worst time of year to sample fresh apples from the orchard. There were still some left in the coolstore – late varieties that had been harvested in May or even later – but come November many of them, even the good keepers like Sturmers, were past their best. There was, however, fruit leather of various kinds, including apple and blackberry, apple and apricot, apple and persimmon. Fruit leather was a good way of using fruit that was slightly damaged but had pieces that were still perfectly edible, and it had a longer shelf life than fresh fruit so could be sold throughout the year. First the fruit was steamed into a purée, then dried out in a dehydrator, cut, and rolled up. Each fruit leather roll was individually wrapped in cellophane with a simple label (bearing the Demeter trademark) and sold, as was the fresh fruit, to organic shops and directly to individual customers.

Dieter's citrus fruit was still in season, and there was a large basket of hazelnuts from the trees we could see from the kitchen window. These were not commercial crops but grown for home use. It became my habit to crack and eat a few nuts every day. One rainy afternoon Dieter suggested we make hazelnut praline, and he instructed us to shell a whole lot of hazels, chop them up and toast them in the oven, then mix them with melted chocolate (organic, of course), pour the mixture into a flat dish, chill in the fridge for a few hours before cutting into bite-size pieces. Divine!

Every morning, Dieter cooked up buckwheat pancakes, which were surprisingly filling and, because of the stickiness of the flour, could be made without eggs if need be – not that there was any shortage of eggs at Treedimensions; there were both hens and ducks in large runs with plenty of bushes and trees.

At that time in late spring, the main job in the orchard was grubbing weeds around the trees, and applying compost and mulch. Ashley and I were supplied with a grubber each, and Dieter showed us how to swing it so we cut the weeds off at ground level, making a weed-free circle around each tree about a couple of feet in diameter. We pulled out by hand the weeds that grew immediately around the trunk, so we didn't risk swiping the trunk with the sharp blade of the grubber. The work was somewhat monotonous, as is a lot of horticultural work, but at least there were two of us wwoofers, and we worked our way down adjacent rows, chatting from time to time, and singing all the songs we could remember to make the work pass more pleasantly.

The first block we worked on was a neat grid of young trees laid out on one of the few flat areas of the farm. The trees were apples and pears, relatively newly planted, spindly things about the same height as us that cast little shade. The sun was hot in the middle of the day;

we wore sunhats and carried water bottles with us, carefully secreting them in small patches of shade so they would remain cool. After grubbing the weeds, we used pitchforks to gather up the 'herbage', as Dieter called it, that lay in clumps here and there where the mower had left it. The herbage consisted of cut grasses and mixed herbal ley, including clover, plantain, lucerne, sorrel and yarrow. (A herbal ley is a carefully chosen mixture of living ground cover which allows for and promotes biodiversity.) We gave each tree a generous helping to cover up the weeded area, keep the moisture in and prevent weeds from growing and competing with the tree's feeder roots. We had to make sure that an area immediately around the trunk was kept clear so air could circulate and keep the trunk dry.

After we finished the newest block, we moved up onto the gentle slope above where there were more established trees. These larger trees afforded more shade, and there were other trees dotted in amongst the apples and pears, including some cork oaks, which had curly leaves and a much denser growth habit than other oaks. We did the same job, only this time after grubbing we applied a layer of rich compost before mulching. The younger trees had been given a good dose of compost when they were planted, but these older trees needed a top-up to keep them healthy and productive. Dieter drove the tractor over, pulling a large trailer full of compost, which we then shovelled into wheelbarrows and distributed around the trees in a layer about five to ten centimetres thick. Then the herbage mulch went on top of this.

Dieter made the best compost I'd ever seen. He had five cows, which he penned in every night, making it easy to collect the manure that built up on the floor of the barn. With the manure mixed with bedding straw and fallen hay from the cows' feed holders so that it wasn't too wet and slimy, the composting process was already underway right there in the barn. At regular intervals Dieter – or a wwoofer – dug out this rich mix and incorporated it into his large windrow heap, which was more or less triangular if seen from one end, several metres long, two or three metres high, and weighed about 50 tonnes. To help the decomposition process and to enliven the compost, Dieter used the biodynamic compost preparations in the heap. The finished product, which we shovelled around the trees, looked good enough to eat, like a crumbly dark chocolate brownie, and with an almost sweet earthy smell. Dieter recommended using compost, because of its microbial activity, in preference to rock phosphate or blood and bone.

Late one afternoon, after we had finished work, showered, and were thinking about dinner, it began violently pelting down with hail. Dieter stood in the kitchen, gazing out over the orchard, transfixed by the hailstorm. Thousands of white lines, like the afterimage of a barcode, indicated the plummeting trajectory of the hail. It was as if the sky were stabbing the earth with white javelins. Hailstones, some as big as cherry plums, pounded down and bounced as they hit the trees and the ground. We both knew the hail would damage many of the developing fruits, and that there was absolutely nothing we could do about it. Later Dieter discovered that the hailstorm had been quite localised, and that orchardists across the river had missed out on it.

'Ah well, we'll have more fruit leather and juice this year,' he said philosophically.

6

A WEED BY
ANY OTHER NAME

No-one told me when I first began gardening that 90 per cent of the work is weeding. Well, some huge amount, anyway. When I moved into my first flat at 19, I wanted to plant some vegetables, and enlisted the help and advice of my mother. The house had very little garden, only a poky concrete yard out the back, and masses of ivy and other weeds tumbling down the retaining wall that held up an inaccessible terrace, also covered in scrubby weeds.

It must have taken the two of us a whole day, or maybe even a weekend, to cut back the vines and other weeds to reveal a narrow strip of earth that bordered the concrete. Mum advised that the best things to plant would be silverbeet and parsley – hardy and likely to survive for a while at least, as February wasn't an ideal time to be planting many things in Dunedin. The calendar year of student tenancy has no regard for would-be gardeners. I have no recollection now if the plants thrived, or even if we ate them. The act of hacking back the weeds and planting something that could be eaten was more a symbolic gesture: both a taming of the wilderness, and a flag planting to claim territory.

It was not until I had my own house and garden that I began gardening – and therefore weeding – in earnest. The section was a typical size for Dunedin, an eighth of an acre (508 square metres), a long narrow ribbon that climbed up the sunny north-west-facing slope of the suburb of Opoho in several terraced strides. At least one of the previous owners had been a keen gardener, as evidenced by the number of fruit trees, carefully spaced and with matching male and female pairs when necessary for pollination. There were apples, plums, pears, a cherry, blackcurrants, redcurrants and gooseberries, all of which flourished in the Dunedin climate.

There were also kiwifruit and a grapevine, which grew perfectly well but were somewhat borderline in terms of fruit production; if looked after, they did produce enough to justify their existence even if it was more as a novelty than anything. The handsome fig tree and two struggling feijoas were the only failures: the former produced fruit that remained hard and green, and the latter only ever fruited when I hand-pollinated them, but the quantity and size were miserable. The little garden also had a glasshouse and patches where vegetables had clearly been grown.

Over the next 10 years I cleared and weeded, planted, weeded, harvested, weeded again, aided first by my flatmate, then by my partner, and sometimes by my mother, particularly during the summer when she came to help harvest the currants and we made jam together. Gradually I came to realise that most of the plants we rely on for food have to be carefully tended, mollycoddled even, compared with weeds. Gardening was a never-ending battle with weeds, and especially for an organic gardener like me, there were no 'simple' solutions like spraying synthetic chemicals to magic the weeds away. Over the years I gathered as much information as possible, by reading, by observing the patterns of nature and the rhythms of the seasons, by talking to other gardeners, and from the courses and workshops run by a local group called OGGO (Organic Gardeners and Growers of Otago, now defunct), and a permaculture course.

Along with all the information about garden plants, I started to accumulate knowledge about weeds, and came to develop a kind of grudging, or in some cases unabashed, respect and admiration for these survivors. After all, what is a weed? The best, and simplest, definition I've come across is 'a plant in the wrong place'. Wrong as defined by the gardener; what is a weed in one place might not be in another. What defines a weed usually has some component of human control, or lack of it; if a plant grows profusely in an area where we don't want it, and is difficult or time-consuming to remove, and smothers out other plants, it's a weed. But all plants have their place in this world, and if they're out of balance in some way it's very likely due to the activities of human beings. Weeds are nature's bandaids, immediately moving onto cultivated, disturbed or neglected land to begin the process of regeneration that begins with the smallest plants and, if left unchecked, would in most places slowly evolve into some sort of forest.

The organic outlook on weeds is somewhat different from the conventional attitude that weeds are enemies to be controlled and conquered. There is still the need to control weeds in an organic system, but there are many ways of doing this without using toxic chemicals. Indeed, mechanical and manual weed control are common in both organic and conventional systems. There are also organic chemical weedkillers, and gas-flame weeders. But rather than a quick-fix blast, organic philosophy takes a more holistic approach, encouraging the farmer to take a step back and closely observe what is going on, and ask why those weeds are growing there in the first place. Are they really causing harm, or are there positive things about them?

If they are harmful, either to crop health or yield, can the conditions be changed to make them less favourable for those weeds? One way is simply to change the soil pH. Different weeds grow in different areas, and in fact can be used as soil indicators. The dock and dandelion in my garden indicated that the soil was slightly acid, so to make the area less attractive to those weeds (and improve the chances for my vegetables), I added some lime along with compost to sweeten the soil. Certain weeds indicate the presence or lack of particular elements. For example, thistles indicate the presence of copper; chickweed, cleavers, nettles and fathen grow in fertile soils; buttercup indicates poor drainage and acidity; plantain indicates acid soil; and spurge (euphorbia) indicates alkaline soil.

Over time certain weeds became less common, or less invasive, in my garden. Some of them were reduced in big bursts like the concerted effort three of us put into getting rid of the ivy that spread its tendrils – and seeds – ever further over from the neighbour's garden every year. We found it had two trunks as thick as my arms, which we sawed right through. Other weeds gradually became less common as, over the years, I persisted in pulling them out whenever they appeared (like convolvulus), or at the very least cutting off any flowers or seed heads (like dock).

So I set off on my wwoofing adventure with 10 years of practical experience of home gardening, and no illusions about that major component of gardening: weeding. Since most organic weed control is manual, and therefore more labour-intensive than using herbicides, it was inevitable that my adventure would involve lots of weeding. And it did. At every place I visited, without a single exception, weeding was one of my tasks. Even at a place like the lavender farm on Banks Peninsula, where it was harvest time, the host asked me to whip out any weeds that were easy to remove by hand as I worked my way along the rows cutting the lavender.

Weeding can be problematic for wwoofers, as most of them are foreigners and not usually familiar with what our plants and weeds are, and there may also be a language barrier to overcome. More than one host had a story about explaining carefully which plants to weed, only to come back later and find that the vegetables had all been carefully weeded out, leaving the weeds. One host wrote in the WWOOF newsletter about a system he had devised whereby he put pink pegs on the plants he wanted kept.

Over time the line between weed and plant became blurred as I discovered the beneficial qualities of many weeds, and discarded my prejudices. Now they seem to me like rambunctious children, needing to be disciplined and brought back into line, but as deserving of love as the next plant, and for all their frustrations they have something to teach us. Here are a few notes about my favourite weeds.

Gorse

One of the most widespread weeds in New Zealand, and a bane of pastoral farmers, is gorse. Even its name is unpleasant, spoken as it often is with a scornful tongue, spat out like a curse – as it must be for many farmers. In Scotland and England, gorse makes a very useful hedging plant, providing a dense thicket impenetrable to stock, but when introduced here by the Scottish settlers the hedges began to spread out, taking advantage of the more favourable climate, of the bigger farms and much sparser populations of people and animals to control it. Whether you see gorse as unflaggingly cheerful or brazenly bilious, its bright egg-yellow flowers are a common sight in many parts of the country right through winter and into spring, sometimes again in summer, and occasionally covering whole hillsides.

Gorse seeds are notorious for the length of time they remain viable – up to 30 years, and some say many more – and during the summer one can often hear the pop-pop-pop sound as the pods burst open and scatter their seeds around. Gorse has an excellent protection mechanism in its all-over sharp prickles, and is only vulnerable to being eaten by stock when it's very young and the prickles are still soft.

One summer I spent a week on my friend Pav West's 42-hectare farm in a remote area of the Grey Valley on the West Coast. It was surrounded on three sides by Department of Conservation (DOC) land that was covered in native bush, and had its fair share of bush too. The remainder was pasture, under constant threat of being engulfed by gorse and blackberry, which grew rampantly in the steamy heat.

In order to give the flock of 80 or so sheep enough grass to eat, gorse duty was an ongoing task. Pav had a great steel-jawed pair of forestry loppers that seemed to be permanently fixed to his arm as he rarely went anywhere without them. In the hot sun we toiled, chopping gorse plants off at the base, or in some of the thicker patches we simply cut off any branches that interfered with human or animal movement, to maintain tracks through the gorse so the sheep could reach other areas of pasture. By the following summer Pav had signed up as a WWOOF host, glad to get help with the ongoing gorse control, among other things.

Over the years I have come to admire gorse and appreciate it for its good qualities. For a start, it's one of those plants that takes nitrogen from the air and 'fixes' it in the soil, making it available for other plants to use. Pav, a beekeeper, pointed out that gorse is one of the few plants that flowers in late winter and early spring and provides much-needed food for bees at this lean time of year. He also makes good use of the hot-burning firewood provided by larger gorse bushes. En masse it makes an excellent nursery for native bush; it gives good protection for small native trees and plants from browsing stock and possums, and then dies off eventually as the bush grows and blocks out the light. This has been ably demonstrated by, among others, Hugh Wilson at the Hinewai Nature Reserve on Banks Peninsula.

It wasn't until my second year of wwoofing that I discovered an unexpected delight: the sweet coconut perfume of gorse flowers, a scent that hadn't come through in the fairly hideous gorse flower wine I sampled once. Did the Scots, when they first encountered coconut, think 'doesn't this smell just like gorse flowers?'

Now it seems curious that I could have gone through so many years of life without noticing the smell, especially living in Dunedin where several of the surrounding hillsides are smothered in thick capes of bright yellow during spring, where the gorse flower fragrance wafts on the breeze.

Wild oats

It was midsummer at Waihi Bush Organic Farm in South Canterbury, a diverse farm with the foothills of the Southern Alps as a picture postcard backdrop. Waihi Bush is known for its flaxseed oil, and that business has grown so big that most of the flaxseed is now grown by contract growers. On the farm there were sheep, cows, a woodlot and several kinds of grain: barley, oats, rye, triticale (a hybrid of wheat and rye that has less gluten than wheat) and spelt (an old variety of wheat that some people who are allergic to wheat and/or gluten can still tolerate).

Even on this commercial grain farm there was hand-weeding to be done. There was no need to sow wild oats here; they just grew cheekily in the spelt field, distinguishable by their ranginess, their height. Our task was in fact called 'roguing' the wild oats, which sounds, if anything, more nefarious than the common saying.

As with many of the activities at Waihi Bush, it was all hands on deck. David Musgrave, the farmer, his 17-year-old son Oliver, myself and the other wwoofers, Julia (Canada) and Daniel (USA), were kitted out with blue overalls bearing the farm's logo on the back and headed for the field with a ute and plenty of sacks to put the wild oats in. We spread out over the field, aiming to go through it in an organised fashion, but once we had waded in a few metres it was easy to lose one's bearings in the chest-high grain.

'I'll just go over there and get that patch,' I thought, more than once, only to find myself wandering off course. There was a tree at the far end of the field that I had lined up in my sights to head towards, but no matter where I was, there was always a straight line to it. Following patches of wild oats, I eventually zigzagged over to the far corner of the paddock where a whole community of oats had invaded the field, displacing the spelt. Head down, pulling oats with both hands, stuffing them into bags, it took me quite a while to hear the strains of the others calling me at the top of their lungs. Their voices skimmed over the waving grain and dissolved in the wind. Finally a concert of yells brought my head up above the sea of gold. A couple of the others were standing on the cab of the ute.

'We're knocking off now!' they called. We dragged the heavy bags through the tracks we'd made in the grain, loaded up the ute and then dropped them off in a massive compost pile of flaxseed from which the oil had been pressed.

Wild ginger

The weeds in New Zealand vary greatly depending on the climate, and as I ventured into the North Island there were some I had never come across, but started to recognise, like the pretty flame tree, its striking red blooms standing out against the greens of paddocks or native bush, and the tall stalks of wild ginger that flourished in dense stands on riverbanks and roadsides. Also called kahili ginger, the plant is native to the Himalayan foothills, and has become an invasive weed in several countries, notably in the Pacific (kahili is a Hawai'ian word) and northern New Zealand, where it has been declared a noxious weed.

Seed dispersal is done by birds and, unwittingly, by people carrying seeds on their shoes or feet, and the plant will also grow from small pieces of root.

At Harry Parke and Jeanette Fitzsimons' farm in the Kauaeranga Valley near Thames, one of my tasks was digging out a patch of wild ginger down by the river. The council said they would come and spray unless it was removed. Harry and Jeanette certainly didn't want whatever herbicide spray the council chose to use on their property, so the alternative was removing it manually.

In the pale winter sunshine Harry and I gathered a spade and grubber and walked down through the leafless, dormant nut trees, to the riverbank where the offending patch of wild ginger had taken hold. The stalks towered above me, tall as bamboo, until I struck them down and laid them together. Then I attacked the roots, which exuded a faint, pleasant gingery fragrance. They were much larger than edible ginger roots – about as thick as my wrist – but a similar slightly stringy consistency.

The work wasn't onerous, although sometimes the roots were tricky to get out as they had wrapped themselves around tree roots, and around each other. I gathered up all the bits and placed them on sheets of corrugated iron, where they would stay until they no longer had any life in them; either because they had dried out or, if they were at the bottom of the pile, rotted.

Pampas grass

In the tiny patch of garden at the front of my house there was a large toetoe. It was like a huge unruly mop of hair, its long leaves sprawling out into the pathway by the front door, and bushy plumes sprouting up towards the sky. Over the years it spread out at the base, growing like an insidious tumour and requiring frequent haircuts so we could enter the house without having to brush past wet leaves in the rain. One day I was discussing it with my mother.

'I'm really getting sick of that toetoe at the front,' I complained.

'That's not a toetoe, that's an Argentinian pampas grass,' she said.

Immediately I saw the plant in a whole new light. No longer did it bear the sacred halo of the native plant – it became an alien invader.

'Oh yes, you want to get rid of that,' Mum continued. 'It'll just keep spreading, and it might seed too. Could be a tough job though.'

'Right, that's it. It's going!' I needed no further encouragement. My partner and I set upon it with an axe and a grubber, chopping it out bit by bit and flinging it into a skip. We excavated a little bit underneath it in order to get all the roots out, and eventually there was no evidence of it but for the depression where it had been, and the busted handle of the grubber.

Now I can tell the difference between toetoe and pampas grass. The former is generally much more slight in its form, with seed heads that arc over in a graceful curve, whereas the pampas grass is a thick clump, with dense bushy seed heads that stick straight up. Pampas grass has a slightly sticky feel on the undersides of the leaves, and the bushes are often surrounded by dead pampas leaves that break up into small spirals like wood shavings.

While wwoofing in the North Island I drove around the East Coast for the first time. There was a stretch of road near Potaka, about an hour east from Opotiki and a couple of hours north of Gisborne, where neither power nor telephone lines had reached yet, and there I wwoofed for a woman called Dixie Brightwell. The house was powered by solar panels and a woodstove, and a satellite beamed down phone signals for the party line she shared with a handful of neighbours. Dixie lived a quiet, semi-self-sufficient lifestyle, growing vegetables and some fruit amid an area of native bush and forestry.

Most of my work was weeding the vegetable garden in preparation for spring planting. A thick pampas grass was encroaching on the edge of the garden, and looked as though it would keep expanding. I offered to take it out. It took three mornings of concerted effort, digging and hacking away. Then there was the problem of how to dispose of it. There was no skip to whisk it away to the tip, and if we dumped it in some far corner the roots might just start growing again. So we decided on bundling it up in some large pieces of plastic until it rotted.

Couch

Couch (rhymes with pooch) or twitch, as some people call it, is one of those invasive grasses that send great long runners out in all directions. At first glance, the slender, white roots look fragile, but this look belies the tenacity of the plant. It's like a burrowing animal, blindly feeling its way through the earth, creating a maze of tunnels, and reproducing in an indiscriminate manner. Every tiny piece of root that breaks off can grow into a whole new plant.

At one farm I was harvesting potatoes and discovered a mass of couch roots in the soil. Some of the roots had pierced the potatoes, wormed their way determinedly through the firm flesh and come right out the other side. With a tug, the roots slithered out, leaving a clean hole, giving a new meaning to the phrase 'couch potato'.

At Kotare Vale, my host Martin asked me to weed the vegetable garden; a task that sounded simple enough, except that the main weed turned out to be couch. The whole plot had to be dug over thoroughly with a fork and then painstakingly hand-weeded to get rid of the couch, following the fine white roots under the soil to get them out whole, if possible. The plant had no regard for human borders; roots that started out in one bed plunged under the barrier of a partially buried wooden slat fence, and ran riot in the neighbouring vegetable plot, requiring a minor excavation all along the fence line. In some places the couch had even tried to penetrate the wood.

What to do with such a prolifically fertile weed that would take root anywhere it could? Like gorse, couch has its good points. Its long roots gather up minerals and trace elements from the soil. Martin got me to collect it in the wheelbarrow and then put it into a 44-gallon drum of water to rot and make liquid compost, to return to the garden the goodies extracted by the couch. If left in the drum, the couch would have risen to the top and simply kept growing, so we had to hold it under water with a board and stone. Into the mix we also lowered a hessian sack of sheep manure, left to steep like a forgotten teabag.

7

EAST COAST

The East Coast was hitherto unknown to me, so it was a must on my travels in the North Island. The road from Opotiki snaked around a rocky coastline with beautiful little beaches, small settlements, and a few signs declaring that this was Maori land, or more precisely, belonging to Te Whanau-a-Apanui. 'No beach access' some of them declared, erected on strips of paddock that separated the road from the coast.

I had no problem finding other access routes to the beaches. The rocky point at Te Kaha was a good lunch spot, and on a wander round the rocks I spotted a small seal basking in the sun.

There were plenty of places to explore along the way. Lottin Point was a worthwhile detour off the main road, and the rocky beach was all mine that fine September day.

The East Coast was a world away from city life, and was like an island in terms of its physical isolation.

A week's stay at Dixie's place in Potaka, with its party-line satellite phone, solar power and no electricity grid to connect to even if you wanted to, was a good reminder of how simple life can be, and how little technology we really need. The limited light meant that we went to bed earlier, and although my house truck accommodation was only a few paces from the house, I would always spend a few minutes gazing up at the countless stars, trying to imprint on my memory whole new constellations that couldn't be seen from our light-polluted cities and towns. I was inspired to write a poem:

Full Moon in Potaka

The moon through Dixie's telescope is like a crystal ball
like white marble, lines tracing its surface
Venus, surprisingly, is a bright crescent
partially eclipsed by planet Earth
moonlight casts shadows as I walk to the house truck
All light and power here is from the sun and moon
We're in a gap here untouched by electricity and phone lines
Another celestial body beams down the phone signals
– a satellite

Potaka marks the boundary between the iwi of Te Whanau-a-Apanui and Ngati Porou. As a Pakeha I was definitely in the minority in this area. The countryside was dotted with marae; every small bunch of houses seemed to be gathered around one. The only place Maori were not in the majority was at East Cape itself, where foreign and Pakeha tourists climbed up all those steps to the lighthouse at the top. Dawn would be spectacular from here. I had to make do with imagining a flaming sun rising up out of the sea. It was nice to linger up there and breathe in the expanse of view, get enough of the slightly curved horizon in my vision, watch the other Kiwis arrive, read the plaques, have their photo taken with the lighthouse, and go back down again.

I met three Germans and struck up a conversation with them, trying out my rusty German and reverting to English when the going got too hard. They took my photo with the view and Whangaokeno, the island just off the coast there. On the way back down I showed them the kawakawa bushes that grew on the hillside, and told them how you could make tea from the leaves.

The next stop on my tiki-tour was Ruatoria, half asleep in the soft afternoon sun, where I dropped off some preserves that John from Mahana Community in the Coromandel had given me to deliver to his daughter. I was looking forward to a soak at the hot pools at Te Puia but unfortunately a sign announced that they were 'out of order', so I carried on driving through the hills and dales of sheep-farming country to my next host at Anaura Bay. A former flatmate had rated Anaura Bay as one of her favourite places, so with this mystique attached to it, I had to at least visit, or better, wwoof there. Fortunately there were three WWOOF hosts in the bay, and the ones I chose were Louia and Scrubbs Blakeney, who lived in Waipare Homestead, a seven-bedroom historic house at the northern end of the bay. Their listing said 'No television or newspapers', which intrigued me. Were they hermits? Old-fashioned religious people? Hippies opting out of society?

Night had fallen by the time I arrived, and after negotiating various driveways and gates, I finally pulled up outside a white picket fence with the large two-storeyed house beyond. Scrubbs, tall and straight-backed, with a trim beard and an easy smile, strode out to meet me from the garage-cum-office where he had been working, and showed me into the house. My bedroom was upstairs and was narrow, plain, but charmingly old-fashioned, and had probably been a maid's or child's room at one time. Later I moved to a more spacious room in one of the outbuildings, and was lulled to sleep every night by the sound of the sea. The house had been built in 1887 and much of it was still original – including some of the plumbing. The modern shower downstairs was more reliable than the old bath upstairs.

Louia was warm and welcoming and served up pasta, her homemade pesto, and various vegetables for dinner on the big wooden table that dominated the room. The couple had two girls, seven-year-old Honey Lee and five-year-old Juliet. Louia reigned supreme in the farmhouse-style kitchen, turning out all sorts of gourmet dishes, including the aptly named (and decadently delicious) chocolate sludge cake, Lebanese and Mediterranean dishes and various pestos, pickles and sauces. There were always treats from the sea: fish, paua, eels and koura, and one day a neighbour brought around some freshly chopped off lambs' tails, which they barbecued.

Far from being recluses, opt-out hippies or belonging to some exclusive sect, Louia and Scrubbs were simply less interested in following the news of the day and more interested in being actively involved in their community. Louia, of Rongomaiwahine and Nga Puhi descent, ran workshops for local Maori women on various aspects of healthy living, including healthy low-calorie cooking, reflexology and permaculture (taught by Joe Polaischer from Rainbow Valley Farm in Northland). She also did some catering work.

Scrubbs, a Pakeha accountant, had worked as a film producer for several years, notably for the film *Utu*. While I was there he was on the Tairawhiti District Health Board, and the light in his office burned long into the night as he did his board work and accountancy work for community groups.

The setting was idyllic. In front of the house was a large lawn on two levels, surrounded by huge trees, including Moreton Bay fig and pohutukawa, with a treehouse perched in one. It was a great setting for a wedding, as indeed it had been for Scrubbs and Louia. A little gate opened straight onto the beach, and Scrubbs could often be seen returning from his early morning dip with a towel slung over his shoulder, padding barefoot up the lawn to the house. Then he would pick fresh kawakawa leaves and make tea – not just steeping them but boiling them on the stove, which made for a stronger taste, and no doubt more medicinal value.

My chores were fairly undemanding, mostly weeding around the house, in the large vegetable patch, and in the woodland garden where bulbs were blooming in the dappled shade. There was lavender to harvest, sheep manure to shovel, and watering to do. A Malaysian wwoofer called Chaichin came for a few days, providing some company for me in the garden when the others were busy.

Beyond the picket fence and the large vegetable patch and compost heaps was a tiny summer house that the family used over the holiday period while they rented out Waipare Homestead as holiday accommodation. We all pitched in to weed and plant the garden by the summer house so there would be salad vegetables and herbs to pick by the time summer came. In between the volunteer lettuces, calendula and nasturtium that were popping up between the stones of the raised garden bed, we planted tomato seedlings.

'Dad,' Louia would say to her husband, 'we need a bit of compost around here.'

'Righto, Mum,' he would reply. 'I'll get a wheelbarrow load.' They had a charmingly old-fashioned habit of calling each other Mum and Dad, no matter whether the children were around, or for that matter anyone else.

One day I pulled a muscle in my back while digging up weeds, and was put on to light domestic duties for a couple of days, including cooking and laundry. Doing the dishes was a common wwoofer job anyway, and Chaichin and I learnt how to do it Louia's way. She was particular about washing the glasses first before the dishwater was sullied by anything else, rinsing them, then standing them upright with a small amount of rinsing water in them. They were then emptied and, while still hot, were dried to a crystal clear shine with a fresh teatowel, elevating the art of doing dishes to a new and surprisingly satisfying level. I was pleased to see that the children had their own chores to do and Honey Lee was already doing dishes at age seven.

One of the things about wwoofing was having to fit in with different domestic arrangements. I had to be flexible and suspend my own ideas about how things should be done, increase my tolerance for mess and dirt in some cases, or pull up my standards in others – as with the glasses. Wwoofing involves a bit of give and take on both sides. Most of the hosts seemed fairly laid back and weren't too worried if they found tools in the wrong place, for example, though some found it necessary to lay down rules, like certain places that were off-limits. Although I almost always had my own room, sleepout, caravan or house bus, privacy was something I really missed, and didn't realise how much until I returned to my own home.

Waipare Homestead was always busy with wwoofers, friends and family members staying or dropping by to visit and sit around the big kitchen table talking. One night a cousin of Louia's came to stay after the Maori Women's Welfare League conference in Gisborne, and it turned out I knew her from Dunedin. The hub of the household was most definitely the kitchen, and a glance at my diary reveals how much food figured in this house: 'Lunch: pauas in cream, salads, couscous, avocados from the Willises.' 'Chaichin cooks marinated chicken, veges and noodles.' 'Lunch: pita, labneh, olives, mint, hummus etc.' 'Prepare curry for tea.' 'Help make bread.' A workshop was held in the house one day, and we served up a three-course lunch for the participants.

Light duties also encompassed helping Honey Lee and Juliet with their Correspondence School lessons. Chaichin helped out with teaching too. On top of their usual maths, science and English lessons, the girls obviously learnt a lot from having wwoofers from all over the world, including cultural differences, international cuisine, and smatterings of different languages. My special offering was yoga lessons, which is what my early morning yoga sessions turned into once the girls discovered me doing a headstand in the living room before breakfast. They were eager learners and being children, were ridiculously, unfairly flexible, achieving in minutes some poses that had taken me months.

Further down the East Coast I stopped at Morere for a soak in the hot springs, indulging in a night's paid accommodation to make the most of it. The springs were in a beautiful bush setting, with little tracks between the pools. There's something social about hot springs – you're there to relax, not to do lengths – and these were no exception. Within minutes of inching into the hottest pool I could manage, all of us in the pool had introduced ourselves and took turns at singing songs at the top of our lungs in our respective languages: Maori, German and English.

While my physical journey continued apace, my spirit was beginning to long for a slower rhythm of life. I was still on a fairly fast-paced trajectory around the countryside, but felt nourished by the trip to the East Coast. It was like going to another country, or going back to a time when the pace of life was slower, and Louia and Scrubbs with their news-free zone were illustrative of this. While writing this book I rang the Blakeneys to check some facts, and was delighted to discover that they were resisting the tide of technology and information overload, and still had a perfectly good life with no TV (well, only one to watch movies on), no computer, and no cellphone coverage at Anaura Bay.

8
COMMUNITIES

There's no getting around it: working the land is hard slog, even with all our modern machines. No wonder farming has been a communal, or at the very least a family, activity in most cultures. Times are changing, but there is still a strong sense of community in rural New Zealand, of sharing resources and helping out your neighbours.

And there are some people who work the land together, in what were often called communes a generation or more ago, but are now more likely to be called eco-villages, intentional communities, or simply communities. A number of them are well-known on the wwoofer circuit, including Tui Community in Golden Bay, Wilderland in the Coromandel, and Riverside Community near Motueka, which was founded in the 1940s and is the oldest intentional community in New Zealand.

Tui, founded in 1984, hasn't been an official WWOOF host for a few years but, like a number of places they host people on the same basis as the WWOOF scheme, and are very popular amongst wwoofers; you usually have to book ahead to get a place there. I've been there three times, but to visit friends rather than to wwoof. Wilderland was full with a school party when I rang to enquire about wwoofing there, so instead I just stopped by at their roadside shop south of Whitianga and bought some of their produce. And the closest I got to Riverside was to drop off some organic wine to the café, from Sunset Valley Vineyards up the road.

The first community I wwoofed at was Mamaki Eco-village, out on the coast near Whangarei. The road traverses vivid green farmland, hugs the coast, winds through lush bush, and takes you to picturesque Matapouri Bay, one of those almost perfect beaches, a crescent of golden sand stretching out enough for a good walk, and framed by rocky points at either end.

Just a little inland up the valley was Mamaki Eco-village, home to five families, with room for a couple more. Each family had their own patch of land (half a hectare or so) for their own use, and the rest, about 80 hectares, was held in common, in a trust, for all to use and enjoy and look after. Most of the common land was native bush, home to a few kiwi. The community worked with DOC (Department of Conservation) on predator control. The wwoofer hut was right next to the bush, and I would lie in bed listening to the sounds of the night: the rain drumming on the roof, the unmistakable hooting of moreporks, a high-pitched eerie cry I hoped was a kiwi (but my hosts told me was probably a weka), and the biggest, emptiest sound of all – silence.

The set-up at Mamaki seemed to be a good blend of individual and group needs. People could do their own thing in their separate households and gardens, and join together with like-minded neighbours for certain activities. The communal land had an orchard planted by everyone, an area for picnics and birthdays and bonfires, and some land leased for grazing. My hosts were Chris Bone, a skipper who ran boat trips out to the Poor Knights Islands, and Julia Alabaster, a homeopath. Their wooden house was built on a slope, with a big deck positioned to catch the sun, and at the perfect height to reach out and pluck fat little bananas from the trees that grew up beside the deck. I soon met several of the others living at Mamaki, particularly the children, who enjoyed the freedom of roaming around socialising in the different households. At the driveway entrance to the community were signs exhorting drivers to slow down and warning of 'free-range children'.

I arrived in the middle of a wet Northland winter, well-equipped with a brand new pair of gumboots (best wwoofer buy!) and an old but serviceable oilskin parka. It rained for much of the two weeks I was there, but that was fine because, by prior arrangement, my main job was not the usual wwoofing work at all, but helping with the

GE-Free Register, a list of properties all around New Zealand whose owners wanted to declare – and retain – as GE-free. It was June 2002; the Prime Minister had just called an early election to be held at the end of July, and the Green Party and other groups were campaigning to keep the moratorium on genetically engineered organisms in the environment and to keep GE out of food.

The purpose of the register was to create awareness about the issue and to gather information to strengthen the GE-free movement. The idea had taken off, and hundreds of people from all around New Zealand had sent in forms, or registered on the internet, and Chris, who was volunteering his time on this project, needed help to catch up with the backlog. My job was mainly data input, entering all the details in a confidential database: names, contact details, size and location of the property; and also sending out GE-Free gate signs for those who ordered them.

Some clear trends emerged: Northland and the Coromandel Peninsula in particular had large numbers of people wanting their area to be GE-free, but there were people from all over, and properties from the smallest city garden, to large farms, to multi-owned Maori land. Many people also voiced their concern about GE in comments along with their registration, and I felt caught up in a wave of fervour, an upswelling of feeling, a real movement.

It was not just organic farmers and growers who were concerned; there were conventional farmers who were worried about the damaging effect GE might have on their exports, on their own crops through cross-pollination, or on New Zealand's 'clean green' image. The story of Canadian canola farmer Percy Schmeiser was becoming well known. This third-generation farmer who saved his own seed every year sued biotech giant Monsanto for contaminating his crop via pollen drift from neighbouring farms, only to be sued back by the corporation for illegally using its intellectual property.

After intensive bursts at the computer, it was good to get some fresh air when the sun shone. I went to the beach, or did some outside jobs for variety: weeding, composting and planting in the vege garden, digging up gorse seedlings, and rounding up cows. I was wary of cows and had not the slightest idea about how to herd them. When confronted with a group trotting towards me along the drive, my instinct was to get out of the way, rather than try to stop them and turn them around. Chris showed me how to make myself look bigger by spreading my arms wide, or holding out a stick. He coached me in making the cows go in one direction or another: raising and waving my left arm would make the cows head off to the right, and vice versa. It seemed obvious once I'd learnt it and put it into practice, but it took several more encounters with cows for me to become more confident and at ease.

In the first year of my new life I had an itinerary roughly mapped out in my head, but where I went within those vague notions of direction evolved organically, as it were, taking shape as I travelled. One host might recommend another down the line, or some chance meeting would indicate my next destination.

While I wwoofed briefly at Gaia's Garden, a herb nursery near Kerikeri, my hosts held a workshop for Maori about growing herbs. It was part of a series of workshops for Maori interested in horticulture that were organised by TOPIS (Te Tai Tokerau Organic Producers Incorporated Society). At the end of the workshop I stood up and offered my services as a volunteer, and three people came and chatted with me afterwards.

One was Turei Hura, more commonly known as Shan, the chair of Te Roopu Whakatupuranga o Waiomio, which roughly translates as the group from Waiomio that makes things grow. Rather than a community where everyone is living together on the same land, this was a hapu trust whose members were joined by common ancestry and the tribal area of Waiomio where they had two marae. The primary, or at least initial, aim of the trust was to find jobs for Maori, and they had placed about 25 people in employment: fruitpicking, packing and pruning at orchards around Kerikeri. About six months before, the trust had also set up a market garden on tribally owned land, with the intention of developing it into a commercial concern, providing jobs and food for the workers. Long-term they also planned to have orchards.

Shan invited me to come and work on the market garden, and stay at his house, and gave me instructions for how to get to the village of Waiomio, just south of Kawakawa (famous for its funky public toilets designed by the artist Hundertwasser). I turned off the main road and drove past the Waiomio Caves, past the old school that had become the office of the trust, past soggy paddocks steaming in the sun. No-one was home at Shan's house, and the old school was similarly deserted. Back on the main road there were several cars parked outside the marae, and I cautiously entered the wharenui to find Shan and several others engaged in a hui. TVNZ was there to film an item on the appalling state of housing for Maori in Northland. I was immediately invited in and plied with kai after the meeting.

Shan was amazed that someone would volunteer to do gardening and farmwork, and was vocally appreciative of my efforts, although I didn't accomplish much in 10 days there. The trust wasn't in the WWOOF book, and indeed Shan hadn't even heard of the scheme, although the trust is connected with Te Waka Kai Ora, the national Maori organic growers' network. I met some of the others involved in the trust: Waimarie, the office administrator, and Piki, who ran some workshops at the old school, and members of Shan's family.

I stayed with Shan in his modest weatherboard house. A man in his sixties of simple needs, he grew up in another era, when he and his brothers and sisters had to get up before dawn and milk the cows, wash in the cold creek, then walk to school, often in bare feet. He still bathed in cold water, and used the electric jug to heat water needed for cooking or washing dishes, and he turned the hot water cylinder on specially in my honour. His home was simple and uncluttered, but he did have a few mod cons: car, TV and cellphone.

The work was varied, and at three different places strung out along the road. At the old school I planted herbs, potted up rosemary and grapevine cuttings, and weeded a koru shape that had been cut out of the lawn and filled in with pebbles. At the market garden Shan and I planted calendula at intervals in the rows of vegetables (as companion plants) and harvested vegetables. There were also vegetables to be picked at Shan's own garden. The produce of July was mainly green and leafy: silverbeet, broccoli, lettuce and bok choy, which I wrapped in damp newspaper bundles to be distributed amongst the hapu's orchard workers at the end of their working day.

Shan was the consummate host, and took me out on trips to see the local sights, and sites (like an old pa site), giving historical comment along the way. The limestone caves at Waiomio, complete with glow worms, were the local tourist attraction, and worth a visit. Limestone cliffs loomed eerily up out of the paddocks, mysterious and atmospheric, apparently riddled with numerous little nooks and caves. For $10 you could get a guided tour of the main caves with a bit of myth and history thrown in.

As Shan talked and showed me around, his vision for the place grew before my eyes: of thriving food-producing gardens, of lush growth in the damp Northland heat, of the hapu sharing in farming and gardening tasks, sharing knowledge and equipment.

'I remember when our people would all work together harvesting kumara,' he said, 'and I want to bring that back, bring back that sense of us all working together, bring back that knowledge, ask the old people how things were done.' Many of the hapu's young people have moved to the cities for education and jobs, and Shan said the educated ones often don't want to come back to the backblocks as they see no future. What the trust needed was skilled people who were committed to the project and prepared to stay and see it through.

A couple of months later, I found myself at Mahana Community, in a remote spot near the northern tip of the Coromandel Peninsula. Half an hour from Colville on a gravel road winding through bush and then up onto a ridge, there was a colourful big rural mailbox – a dead giveaway that some alternative sorts dwelt here. Teetering on the edge, I looked down a sheer hillside, and could see only a few small dwellings peeking up from the thick bush. Then began the descent down a steep gravel road with hairpin bends and the evidence of a recent washout.

Mahana was founded in the late 1970s, and covered about 200 hectares of hilly bush-clad country. Originally there had been a strong community spirit, with a schoolhouse for the kids, three shared meals a day in the communal building, and communal gardens and chooks. Gradually, though, people stopped contributing to the communal meals, and more and more people ended up doing their own thing in their individual houses. Lots of the former residents moved out once their children were high school age. When I visited there were about 50 people living there, and a communal meal was a special occasion. In more recent years, Mahana has attracted people on the benefit; there's not much work in the area, and it's a cheap place to live, with only a small amount needed from each person to pay rates and maintenance of the road into the community.

My hosts, John and Gisella Warmenhoven, had been there for 15 or so years. Gisella was a small, calm and capable German woman with dark curly hair and a ready smile. She always seemed to be on the go with one project or another around the house and garden, and began her day at 5.00 a.m. with two hours of meditation, followed by a session of yoga. She seemed undaunted by a slight back problem, and had perfected various techniques of digging and so on that required virtually no bending over.

John was a Dutchman who had lived in New Zealand for his adult life. His tousled hair and boyish grin made him seem younger than his 50 or so years, but his feet could have belonged to another creature, a hobbit maybe. He never wore shoes, and his feet were tough and leathery, the toenails hard and thickened. Apparently he had squeezed into some shoes a few years back for a wedding or some such, but that was an exception. He was a staunch advocate of going barefoot and, even in the damp chill of a Coromandel August, didn't seem to feel the cold from his shoelessness.

Gisella and John lived a simple life unencumbered by power-hungry modern gadgets in a modest wooden dwelling of their own design and making. They had a minimal electricity supply from solar panels, enough to power some lights, a radio and a tape deck, which was essential for their daughter's Correspondence School education. There was no fridge; instead they kept things cool in a heavy earthenware crock on the floor. A large wood burner heated their house, water and food (supplemented by gas rings for quick cooking). One day Gisella baked a cake, using a contraption that looked like an oversize lid for a roasting pan, complete with a thermometer, which she placed on top of the wood burner until the desired temperature was reached, then put her cake underneath it to bake, raised up off the hot surface by a wire rack. So simple, yet perfectly effective.

Communication with the outside world was via post, particularly lots of parcels going to and from the Correspondence School, and also via cellphone, but to get coverage you had to go up the winding drive to the top of the hill near the road. The house was TV-free, and the radio station of choice was National Radio, which John liked to tune into for news of the nation and the world.

My bed was a small loft above the living room, with a rope to help swing oneself up and down. Next to the loft, on the outside of the house, was a small dovecote, and I quickly became used to the doves cooing me awake in the mornings.

The garden was highly productive, and creatively constructed: there were vegetables in raised beds edged with corrugated iron, and old car windshields ingeniously reincarnated as cloches over freshly sown seed. Gisella and I hoed some beds, sowed carrot and beetroot seed, and reclaimed a patch for vegetables that had been planted in comfrey. Comfrey is famous – or notorious – for its deep roots; it pays to think carefully about where to plant it because of the difficulty in getting rid of it. Gisella had already been over this bed some time before and got out the largest roots. Now we were digging and sifting through the soil for any smaller pieces of root that had broken off or been missed before.

John had an extensive collection of bromeliads: dozens, if not hundreds, of different types. A couple of large ones stood alone in large pots as feature plants, and others were sprinkled around and about amongst the fruit trees and even into the surrounding bush. The cycad, an ancient plant that looks like some sort of palm, was another favourite plant of John's, and he grew a number of different varieties in a plastic tunnel house.

Fruit trees grew on terraces radiating up the slope, like members of an amphitheatre audience looking down on the dramas of the house. Many of the fruit trees had their own little individual terraces – box seats, perhaps. My hosts had used a few manuka or other branches stuck upright in a semi-circle into the side of the hill, then cut soft brush, often also manuka, and laid it inside the semi-circle of branches to create a pocket. Into this went earth and compost, and the fruit tree. The effect was like a series of wall-vases around the hilly section.

There were apples, plums, peaches and so on, plus semi-tropical fruits that I was less familiar with: citrus, bananas, loquats, figs, guavas, naranjillas, cherimoyas, macadamia nuts, even mangoes and pineapples (though these last two were marginal in the Coromandel). I was deputed to 'release' some lemon trees from a tangle of invasive weeds and from the encroaching jungle that constantly reasserted itself in the garden. There weren't many fruits in season at that time of year, but Gisella emerged from the garden one day with a handful of naranjillas. These exotic-sounding South American fruits are in the Solanaceae family along with tomatoes and a fruit that they are similar to in taste, the cape gooseberry. The naranjillas were small and round, covered in small brown hairs like a kiwifruit, only with an orange skin glowing through. The tangy, acidic flavour resembled lemon crossed with pineapple.

Gisella was an accomplished pruner, and told me that the traditional vase shape for pruning pipfruit and stonefruit is out – it makes more sense to keep a central leader, otherwise if you cut it out to create a vase shape, other branches simply keep on trying to grow in the centre to compensate.

Gisella and John wanted to reintroduce some of the former community spirit to Mahana, and initiated the idea of a communal orchard. There were already fruit trees planted on communal land; I recall apples and olives (John boiled up some olive leaf tea every day for his health), but this new orchard was to be mainly citrus. There was a working bee the day after my arrival, and I worked alongside half a dozen community members. Some of us dug holes for fruit trees to be planted in later on, and some removed a few small manuka trees that were invading the paddock that had been designated for the orchard.

One of the projects I helped with was making mud bricks for the bush bath. In a secluded clearing not far from the house, Gisella was making a mud brick structure for a bath to rest on, so that it would be raised up off the ground to make room underneath for a fire, and a bit of a chimney at one end to take the smoke up and out of the bather's way. To make the bricks, we mixed up mud, sand, cement, water and – the secret ingredient – fresh cowshit. Apparently this acts like an emulsifier and makes the bricks less likely to crack. It also gives them a distinctive smell – or at least it does while you're making them. We used a similar but sloppier mix for the mortar. While I was there the bath was delivered, shouldered by a bevy of brawny blokes, but unfortunately I left before it was fired up and christened.

It was so peaceful there surrounded by the bush, away from the stresses and hype of city living, yet not isolated. There was a criss-cross of paths between the various houses, and plenty of socialising and sharing.

'Why don't you stay here for a while?' Gisella asked one day. 'It would be good to have some fresh energy at Mahana. And there's a place that's empty at the moment.'

'Well …' I stalled. 'It's really neat, but right now I just want to keep on wwoofing.' This kind of invitation to join a community or stay in a certain area was repeated several times during my wwoofing journey and, although there were lots of special places, none of them beckoned to me with the certainty I needed to make me move there. So I just enjoyed the tranquillity of Mahana while I was there, the ruru calling at night, the clear light of the waxing moon, and the soft chimes of korimako (bellbirds) waking me in the early morning.

I did manage to have a wonderful bush bath in another community, Aradia, down the road at Papaaroha, midway between Coromandel township and Colville. Deb was one of just two residents there at the time. She and I fired up the bath and just on twilight we took it in turns in the deep hot water, gazing up at the stars as they blazed brighter, with a glass of bubbly in one hand. Indulgent.

Aradia is the name of the Queen of the Witches, highly appropriate for 'women's land'. I had visited about 10 years before, when there were several residents and different abodes, including house buses, caravans, houses and huts.

This time there were only two women living there. Tahi had lived there since the community was set up in 1989, and was a trustee of the land. She had her own house bus, and was now spending a lot of time working at the environment centre in Coromandel township. Deb, the other resident, was taking six months or so out to destress and reassess what she was doing with her life. She was staying in a little house not far up a track in the bush from the communal kitchen area.

The kitchen was open to the elements on one side, had an outdoor dishwashing area, and provisions in rodent-proof tins. An aura of faded feminism hung over the place, embodied in the women's posters, books and art and a visitors' book with entries expounding enthusiastically about women's land and the wonderful time women had resting and retreating from city life. It was like a university women's room from the 1980s only more idealistic and cosmic.

My abode was a house bus, equipped with a pot belly for heating and cooking and a gas ring for quick cooking and cups of tea. Water had to be collected from the nearby stream every day, as the gravity-fed pipe wasn't working. Here where there were no lights at night, my solar-powered radio and torch came in very handy. It could also be powered by batteries, but as long as it sat on the windowsill, it usually soaked up enough sun to see me to the long drop at night or down the little track from Deb's. If it ran out of solar power, you could wind it up as a last resort, cranking the little dynamo handle.

No power meant early nights, and few distractions, so I was alone with my thoughts. It was sad to see many of the dwellings and caravans around the place in sorry states of repair, and Aradia so empty, compared with what it had been like before. Where are all the women who used to live here? Has the back-to-the-land idea gone out of fashion? Is the idea of a women's community not so attractive any more? Is it too hard being self-sufficient? Are we too trained as individuals now to work effectively in small communities? Is there a lack of money to upgrade or build? Or are these sorts of communities too remote and apart from the rest of society to function well?

Whatever the answers may be, there is still the basis for a good community here – 160 hectares or so of land, most of it hilly and bush-covered, but a good amount of usable land too. There are lots of fruit trees planted, particularly citrus, feijoas, apples and pears. During my short stay I pruned some fruit trees, released some native trees from weeds, and weeded the vege garden and asparagus bed. I left feeling sad not to have spent more time there, but to stay there longer would have meant spending a lot of time on my own when I wanted to be around people. It would be good to revisit in the summer when there are no doubt more women there to share work and meals, and more of a community feeling.

9

HERBS

Most of the farms I visited had a few herbs growing, even if just a patch of mint and parsley by the back door. The use of calendula as a companion plant was widespread, and herbs have become de rigueur in organic pastoral farms and orchards, where mixed herbal leys are planted. These often include such species as chicory, clover, phacelia and plantain. Biodiversity is the key, and each species is chosen for different properties: clover to fix nitrogen, deep-rooted chicory to bring up minerals from below, phacelia to attract beneficial predator insects like lacewings, and a mixture of herbs to increase stock nutrition because of the different minerals made available by the plants.

There is increasing demand in New Zealand and elsewhere for organically grown herbs, for teas, medicines and cosmetics. Several places I visited were growing herbs as cash crops, such as the lavender farm at Takamatua Valley near Akaroa on Banks Peninsula.

The farm was compact, a narrow strip reaching up the hill from the valley road, planted in lavender running like neat rows of rounded vertebrae down the slope, about 3000 plants altogether. There were also several olives, some walnut trees and a home orchard. The owners, Pete and Polly Smith, had left jobs in Wellington to try something different, and set up the farm from scratch, planted the lavender, and invested in a new barn and equipment for distilling lavender oil. They sold the oil and other products like lavender handcream and soap directly from the farm during the summer, and all year round from the gift shop-cum-gallery they ran in Akaroa.

'I'll show you up to the barn,' said Pete, welcoming me when I arrived. 'There's a bed for you upstairs in the loft.' Up a short drive was a modern-looking wooden barn, with a little shop in the front part of it. Pete swung open a large side door and a heady aroma enveloped me. Freshly cut lavender lay in huge piles all over the floor of the barn, emitting such an overpowering fragrance I felt faint as I picked my way over the heaps to the stairs.

'Wow! The scent is so strong. I hope I can sleep OK up there,' I said.

'You'll get used to it pretty soon,' Pete assured me. No worries about sleeping; the herb is a time-honoured remedy for insomnia, and within a day or so I was completely accustomed to the scent, and slept soundly in the little attic.

Harvesting lavender sounds romantic, but any such notions must be swiftly cast aside. The reality is that you sweat in the heat of the midday sun, get a stiff back bending over the bushes, and risk bee-stings and cuts. We harvested with charmingly old-fashioned hand-held sickles, straddling a row of lavender bushes in order to cut from both sides evenly, and making our way up or down the rows like bow-legged cowboys. There were heaps of bees and despite the heat we wore long pants, long sleeves and leather gloves for protection against getting stung – or cut by our super-sharp tools, which Pete sharpened from time to time. Fortunately the bees were kind to us.

The oil rises in the plant as the day heats up, so to get the maximum amount of oil, and to be sure the dew has evaporated, it's better not to start before about 10.00 a.m. To harvest, you grasp a bunch of lavender in one hand, and with the other hand cut the stems about 10 centimetres below the flower head, as most of the oil is concentrated in the flower and upper stem.

Then the weather turned and we couldn't harvest in the rain. So we turned to those enormous piles waiting in the barn; harvested lavender should be distilled within a few days to keep its quality. The distilling process involved packing the lavender into tall metal cylinders that have a kind of mesh bottom (called 'baskets'), then compressing it by jumping up and down on top. Crushing grapes with the feet, now, I've heard of that, but stomping on lavender was a new one on me. Once we'd packed as much lavender in a basket as possible, up to around 25 kilograms, Pete would hook up the basket to a hoist and lift it up and into the steamer. A generator boiled water to create steam, which was then forced through the lavender-filled baskets at pressure, evaporating the oil. The steam and evaporated oil then ran through a cooling tube into another container, by which time the steam became water again and the oil floated on top. One of my jobs was to siphon the oil off the top via an overflow pipe, and at the same time release the water via an 'underflow' pipe so the water level didn't rise and go up out the overflow and contaminate the oil.

The main varieties of lavender planted there were Grosso, Impress Purple, Super, Pacific Blue, Twickle Purple and Tarras. Pete and Polly had the oil put into various products like soap and handcream. They also got lavender-flavoured honey from their bees. Even the lavender water (the steam that had been squirted through the lavender and then condensed back to water) was sold, as a refreshing addition to the bath, or to splash on as an aftershave.

Neat areas of brown, bare earth surrounded the lavender, and I wondered what sort of weed control they used. Pete said they used Round-Up once a year, after trying an organic weedkiller but finding it too expensive. Apart from that they were organic. Lavender is fairly hardy, and I haven't heard of any pests that attack it. At other lavender farms I've seen weed mat, black plastic, or mulches such as newspaper and straw used against weeds, apparently to good effect. At Takamatua we did a bit of spot-weeding by hand as we were harvesting, if we noticed a hawkbit or sow thistle or something easy to pull out.

After only four days we had distilled all the harvested lavender and there was nothing more to do until the unseasonable rain let up and we could harvest again, which according to the weather forecast wasn't going to be any time soon, so there was nothing for it but to leave. Even a week later the scent still lingered on my clothes like a memory.

A couple of places I visited were growing golden seal (*Hydrastis canadensis*), a North American herb that is becoming rare in its native range due to its popularity as a herbal medicine. Originating in Canada and the eastern USA, golden seal is found growing in rich soil in shady woodlands, and is a traditional Native American medicine. It has gained a reputation as a cure-all, and is used to treat a huge range of disorders, including colds and flu, eczema, inflammations of the ear and eye, and disorders of the liver, digestive tract and bladder. It is anti-bacterial and soothing on the mucous membranes. Golden seal is a potent herb, to use with caution, and never during pregnancy.

At Waihi Bush Organic Farm near Geraldine, one of my jobs was to put iceblock sticks by the golden seal plants so that in winter, when the leaves died down, their location would be marked and the roots could be harvested. Julia the Canadian wwoofer and I daubed the little sticks with splashes of bright yellow paint to make them stand out.

'Where *is* the golden seal patch, by the way?' I enquired. This was my second stay at the farm, but I hadn't seen these herbs before.

'In the bush down by the river – Lorina will show you,' said my host David, dashing off out the door to a board meeting. So Lorina (David's wife), Julia and I set out down towards the Waihi River, through an area heavily wooded with sycamores and an understorey of native scrub. Our host strode confidently along something that looked like a path, with us single file in her wake. A damp chill closed around us and then we came out onto the rocky bank of the river.

'I was sure it was around here, but we've come too far down now.' Lorina set off again along another path. How easy it would be to lose your golden seal crop, if you couldn't find it in the first place. And even harder in the winter, when the plants have died right down, only the valuable yellow roots remaining, hiding away their antibiotic qualities in the cold earth.

Soon we came out into a couple of adjoining clearings that had the solemn hush of a cathedral, tall columns of trees all around and sunlight filtering through the stained glass of their leaves. Lorina showed us the golden seal plants, small and innocuous, but most of them easily distinguishable on the forest floor by the bright red berries, reminiscent of small raspberries, that adorned them at that time of year (mid-February). It was a sparse plant, barely a foot high, with only two leaves the size of small hands and one berry per plant, resulting from the previous spring's single flower. Lorina left us to mark the plants by planting an iceblock stick beside each one – and to find our way out afterwards.

I liked Naomi Pond from the outset. When I rang to ask about wwoofing at her place, she was enthusiastic, and immediately invited me along with a group that was going to the theatre that night. The theatre, in Coromandel township! It turned out to be a local production of Terry Pratchett's *The Wyrd Sisters*, a highly amusing spoof on *Macbeth*. My witchy self felt right at home.

I also felt an affinity with Naomi's herb garden, her knowledge of herbal medicine, and the dispensary, a cool room lined with shelves of brown bottles containing herbal medicine. The property was just over a couple of hectares, but there was plenty of room for several sheep, occasional grazing for a horse, vegetable gardens and fruit trees, and the herb garden. The whole place was nestled in native bush, with one stream cutting through the property and another running down the back of it. A curving driveway led to the adobe brick house that was topped with solar panels to heat the water.

The herbs hugged the contours of a sunny north-facing bank and were planted in different areas according to what part of the body they heal: all the herbs for the liver were together in one area, the kidney herbs were grouped in a kidney-shaped section, herbs for the heart, the skin and so on all congregated in different areas. What a wonderful teaching resource it was, and indeed various groups came to visit the garden and learn about herbs.

Weeding the herb gardens was the ideal time to ask Naomi about the different plants, what they were, and what they were used for medicinally. I had only recently begun to distinguish some of the common weeds, and found two fine examples of a dandelion and a hawkbit. These plants are often mistaken for each other, although when comparing them the differences are obvious, particularly when they are flowering. Dandelions have a rosette of smooth, deeply serrated leaves close to the ground, out of which rises a relatively short, fat, hollow stem that oozes a white milky substance if snapped. The yellow flower turns into the familiar 'dandelion clock': a seed head of thistle-like down that children love to blow. Hawkbit also has a rosette of serrated leaves, but the flower stalk is much taller and spindlier and the flower is smaller. Naomi took photos of me and the plants for her reference collection. The two bright yellow flowers and their green leaves stood out well against my black singlet.

Naomi was also interested in the healing properties of native plants including kumarahou, which is used externally for skin problems and wounds, and internally as a decoction for coughs, colds and chest complaints. The native plant I saw most of there was kawakawa, as the tea was an everyday drink in this household, and the beams were hung with the drying plant to be ground up when dry and sold as a herb tea. I found it hard to believe that people would pay for this when the plant is common throughout the North Island and grows in the South Island as far south as Banks Peninsula, but they do. It's convenient, I suppose.

A forest understorey bush, kawakawa (*Macropiper excelsum*) is related to the kava plant of the Pacific Islands, and is well-known for its medicinal properties. It is reputed to be a blood purifier, and is used for numerous ailments, including kidney and urinary complaints, arthritis and digestive disorders. The leaves and bark made into a decoction are applied externally for skin problems, boils, burns and eye inflammations. The shiny heart-shaped leaves are often studded with holes eaten by an insect – some people say these leaves have a higher medicinal value. It's a Maori gardening tradition to burn fresh kawakawa leaves in between rows of kumara to make an acrid smoke that kills insects.

Naomi had a great sense of design, order and beauty in her garden. In addition to the medicinal herb garden, there were five circular gardens around the house. Each contained flowers and plants of different colours: green, red, white, yellow in the four directions around her house, and a ring of blue flowers immediately surrounding the house. These colours are important in Tibetan Buddhism, of which Naomi was a devotee. She regularly attended meditation sessions at the Buddhist centre near Colville, and took me there once. They were establishing gardens at the centre, and after our meditation session Naomi roped me into planting some flowers along the side of the meditation hall, and putting stakes in the ground in two large concentric circles as part of the design of a new garden. Her enthusiasm and unflagging good cheer made gardening fun, and not at all like work.

In Halswell near Christchurch I met Jenny and Larry Burrows. Larry was a plant ecologist at Landcare Research, and Jenny had a small herb nursery, Whincops Herbs, and was also studying herbal medicine. She inherited her love of herbs from her mother, Gillian Polson, who is well-known in herb circles, and is author of such books as *The Living Kitchen* and *Kitchen Herbs for Health*. Gillian came and stayed one weekend, and generously gave me a copy of *The Living Kitchen* when she discovered that I was also a writer. Jenny and her sister grow herbs to sell as plants at Whincops Herbs and also supply some organic outlets in Christchurch.

One of my tasks while at Jenny and Larry's was to harvest the lemon verbena. I cut long stems off the small bushes and piled them up on a bedspread in the sunny spare room to dry, turning over the pile a couple of times a day to speed the process. Then all the leaves had to be stripped off the stems and placed in baskets to continue drying. The aroma was heady and pleasant to work with; it filled the room and wafted out into the hallway. It was April, and the basil also had to be harvested before the frosts came, the plants pulled out completely, leaves stripped, bagged whole and frozen immediately.

The herb nursery needed a bit of a tidy up. Most of the plants were in a shade house, a wooden structure with shadecloth for the walls and ceiling that provided a sheltered spot from the prevailing nor'west winds, but allowed rain to water the plants. There was also an overhead sprinkler system for watering during dry spells. One of my tasks was to unclog the sprinklers and pipes, something that had to be done from time to time as earwigs often crawled inside and blocked the water flow.

In the nursery there were several plants to pot up, including hedging plants *Buxus sempervirens* and *Lonicera nitida*. Although not herbaceous, they are good sellers at Whincops Herbs because people would generally buy several of these plants at one time. Jenny also sold a number of native plants and trees, some of which I potted up into larger pots, and there were trays of little arnica plants (*Arnica montana*) to pot up for sale. Jenny was growing an experimental patch of arnica, but a number of the previous season's plants had not thrived, apparently due to some sort of fungus around the roots. They are alpine plants, as the second part of the Latin name implies, so growing them at a low altitude is a bit of a gamble. Tinctures of arnica are used to heal sprains, bruises and muscle aches, and homeopathic remedies are made from arnica for treating shock, injury and pain.

I had come across arnica plants once before, at Aroha Organics market garden south of Timaru, where there was also an experimental row of arnica plants that seemed to be doing well.

'Hey, Philippa, how d'ya feel like weeding the arnica plants today?' Nathan, the farm manager at Aroha Organics, asked one morning in his customary laconic, easy-going approach to wwoofers – and people in general.

'Sure,' I said, always willing to do something new. 'How do I recognise the arnicas?' They were a complete unknown to me at that stage.

'They're the ones that look like weeds,' Nathan said, laughing. Sure enough, these unimpressive looking plants were at that time of year (January) nothing more than a flat rosette of leaves growing close to the ground and could, to the untrained eye, pass for something like a broad-leafed plantain. They were much bigger than the little arnicas I later potted up at Whincops Herbs. Here, the row had a healthy crop of weeds, and the only way I could tell the arnicas apart from the rest of them was that they were obviously planted at intervals.

Another herb nursery I stopped at briefly was Gaia's Garden near Kerikeri, run by Julia Geljon and Chris McIvor. It was winter, and the tasks were similar to many other horticultural enterprises at that time of year – weeding and tidying up generally. At Gaia's Garden we plucked out rogue weeds in the gravel of the nursery, and weeded and mulched the garlic patch. Chris and Julia were growing garlic and florence fennel as small cash crops, as well as selling the herb plants at the nursery, and Julia wrote a regular column on herbs in *Growing Today*.

There were two other wwoofers there. Beate, from Germany, worked for a TV company doing travel bookings for the staff. Due to the downturn in travel following September 11, the company, rather than lay off staff, had given them the option of taking a few months off on a reduced wage. Beate had jumped at the chance to take some time off and travel. The other wwoofer was a tall Japanese guy called Keiishi. Perhaps I should call him a wolfer; he ate more than I have ever seen one person eat. There were never leftovers when he was around.

One night one of Chris' teenagers was out for the evening. It was towards the end of dinner and Keiishi was just about to polish off all the remaining food.

'Hey, we need to save a helping!' said Chris, catching him just in time. Later, Keiishi and I were doing the dishes – he washed and I dried. There were two sinks, one for washing and one for rinsing, but instead of filling up the rinsing sink, Keiishi kept the tap on continuous drizzle into the sink, so he could rinse the dishes in running water. Chris explained to him that they were on tank water and had a limited supply.

'But you have so much water in New Zealand!' he exclaimed. 'And this is the cleanest way.'

'Maybe,' said Chris, 'but if you want to have a shower tomorrow, you'd better turn off that tap.' That got through to him, and he filled the rinsing sink.

In the garden the next day we mulched the garlic, the three wwoofers working as a team. We loaded up wheelbarrows with pitchforks full of straw from a big pile, transported it to the garden, and forked it on. Once Chris had explained the job to us and was out of sight doing something else, Keiishi simply stopped working. Beate and I carried on for a while, but finally I had to ask:

'Keiishi, are you OK?'

'Ah, yes, OK,' he replied.

'Why have you stopped working?'

'My back is sore.'

'Well, why don't you tell Chris? Maybe she can find another job that doesn't hurt your back.'

The sore back didn't seem to be in evidence any time Chris passed by; Keiishi jumped up and immediately started pitchforking or wheeling a barrow.

One day Chris and Julia hosted a workshop that was part of a series organised by Te Puni Kokiri on Maori business development, focusing on horticultural opportunities. Percy Tipene, the organiser of the workshops, was the chairman of Te Waka Kai Ora, the national Maori organic growers' organisation.

About 40 people attended, and Julia and Chris talked about the possibilities for Maori in growing herbs. They talked about various herbs that might be lucrative, recommending that Maori do the research first to find out what herbs are needed, in what quantities, and what price they could be sold for. Cosmetics company Living Nature, nearby on the highway at Kerikeri, uses New Zealand flax, calendula and other herbs, and there are several herbal medicine companies that occasionally advertise for growers to supply herbs.

One herb that Julia and Chris thought had potential, particularly in Maori communities because of the incidence of diabetes, was stevia (*Stevia rebaudiana*). They passed around a bowl with some leaves for participants to try, with the recommendation to take only a tiny piece. The taste is immensely sweet, many times sweeter than sugar, although the strength of the sweetness varies from plant to plant, depending on the concentration of stevioside (the ingredient that makes it sweet). Stevia is native to Paraguay and is used in several countries as a natural sweetener that has virtually no calories. It appears to be safe for diabetics and hypoglycemics, is anti-bacterial, and does not cause tooth decay. It is reported to reduce cholesterol and strengthen the immune system. There is a debate over its safety for human consumption because of possible adverse effects on male fertility, and a mutagenic quality that may link it to cancer.

Stevia seed is hard to germinate, so the plant is best grown from cuttings. It requires a moist, rich, loamy soil and a sunny, frost-free position. It is easy to grow in Northland's warm climate and is naturally resistant to aphids and other insects. The stevioside is concentrated in the leaves and tips, which are stripped from the plant, dried and then powdered. At the time of writing, New Zealand and Australian regulations permit the stevia plant – but not stevia extracts – to be used as a sweetener.

I spent two months wwoofing at Milmore Downs, a biodynamic sheep, beef and grain farm in North Canterbury, and had a real variety of work (see Chapters 20 and 21). My encounter with herbs there was memorable because it involved making dandelion 'coffee' – a favourite drink of mine. The job of digging over an old flower garden unexpectedly turned into a dandelion harvest. It was autumn, the best time of year for harvesting. These were not just any dandelions, but were anchored deep in the soil with roots as thick as three or four centimetres in diameter. There were so many of them, and they were so luxuriant, that, rather than chuck them in the compost or further away onto the high heap of invasive weeds, I decided to make dandelion coffee. The dandelion roots I'd managed to collect from my own garden had always been paltry, and it didn't really seem worth the time and effort to collect, dry and roast them. But these giants almost demanded to be used, so I soaked them overnight in a bucket of water to loosen the soil, then washed and scrubbed them, left them to dry for a day or two so the medicinal milky white sap didn't run, then cut them into thin slivers to continue drying on a hanging rack.

After a few days I chopped them up again roughly, and roasted them on low in the oven, jumping up and checking them every five minutes or so because I wasn't sure what temperature they should be at. With the aid of a coffee grinder the finished product was rendered into a perfectly palatable brew that was all the more flavoursome because of the effort taken to produce it.

Dandelion (*Taraxacum officinale*) is well-known for its beneficial effects on the liver, kidneys and gall bladder. Both the root and leaves are used, the latter being a good source of vitamin A. The leaves are best eaten when young, in spring before flowering, before they become bitter, but the bitterness is hardly noticeable if you chop them finely in a salad.

10
THE FIRST YEAR ENDS

I skipped down through the lower North Island, staying a night or two there with friends and family. The fertile Horowhenua, with its market gardens, was familiar territory for me. Many a Christmas holiday during my childhood was spent in Levin, with trips to the local berry farms to pick our own berries, and excursions to visit second or third cousins on the Kapiti Coast, in Manawatu or the Wairarapa.

Although I was brought up a city girl, my closest ancestral link to farming is no further back than my father. When Dad was five his family moved from Levin to a five-acre (2.02-hectare) poultry farm just south of the town in Weraroa. The family sold eggs and day-old chicks. As a boy, Dad fed the hens, collected the eggs and folded the hexagonal little boxes into which the day-old chicks were packed for dispatch. My grandfather invented some sort of incubator for eggs, which never actually got made. He died of a heart attack at 42 while digging the front garden, leaving my grandmother to raise the two boys and pay someone to help run the farm.

Vague images of the farm still hover in my memory, but by the time I was about six, Gran and Uncle Ian had moved back up the road to Levin. In keeping with my family's occupational focus on books and words, my uncle ran a second-hand bookshop. The house was a nondescript suburban bungalow, with a neatly mowed lawn, a few shrubs, dahlias and the like out the front, but out the back the garden was positively riotous, with small forests of potato foliage, sprawling pumpkins (kumi-kums, they called them, also known as kumikumi or kamokamo), currant bushes, silverbeet, lettuce, broad beans, and a straggling, struggling peach tree whose fruit seemed destined to fail, and formed hard unpalatable lumps that aged before their time. The broad beans in particular became synonymous in my mind with Levin and with the summer holiday period, and there were so many of them we always had to 'get through' them, as though they were some kind of penance.

Even with the addition of our family of five for a few weeks, we didn't seem to make that much of a dent in the bumper broad bean crops. Gran and Uncle Ian ate simply, and managed to keep themselves in a few staple vegetables for much of the year, with the aid of the freezer. My uncle saved his seed every year like a good old-fashioned subsistence gardener.

On my wwoofing journey I passed through Levin to visit. Gran had died a few years before at the ripe old age of 100 – testament, perhaps, to her simple living and natural health regime. Uncle Ian now had to manage the house and garden as well as his business, and if the garden had been a riot beforehand, it was now anarchy. I stepped outside the back door and saw the poor peach tree, looking skeletal but for a few leaves still hanging on for dear life. The garden was still producing; potatoes and pumpkin were on the menu that night, but not broad beans, somewhat to my relief.

I spent a few days wwoofing out at nearby Waitarere Beach, with Annmarie Coote, a friend who had recently become a wwoof host in order to get some help with her two sections. One section was slightly inland: one-and-a-half hectares in a sort of U-shape around part of a little lake that was home to a number of swans and ducks. A handful of sheep roamed around, keeping the grass down and helping themselves to any windfall fruit in the old orchard area, which had mainly apples, pears and plums.

Annmarie's beach bach was where I stayed and worked, within earshot of the sea. That November was punctuated by squalls and gusty winds. On the north-facing balcony was a profusion of plants in pots and containers, including herbs, and there were lettuces, silverbeet, rocket and carrots growing in slightly raised beds around the edges of the house.

'I want to landscape the backyard,' said Annmarie as we leant over the balcony with cups of tea, looking out into the garden.

'Three different levels,' she continued, indicating with her hand, 'with two or three steps between each level. What do you think?'

'Yeah, that would work well, I reckon. And you wouldn't have to bend over when gardening, because you'd do it from the next level down, where the bed would be raised.'

So the main work there was landscaping, creating the three terraces out the back from a gentle slope of sand with a thin crust of grass and a hint of topsoil. Digging was easy; it was giving the sand form that was hard, and it was clear that the three terraces were going to need small retaining walls of some sort to keep them from reverting to dunes. Annmarie also wanted to regrass part of the areas that had been disturbed, and had me ring around to find some grass seed of a type that was strong and would grow in virtual sand. It seemed to be quite hard to find something suitable. Buffalo grass was suggested by one nursery, but I hadn't found a source by the time I left. Could the dreaded kikuyu grass, scourge of many farmers and growers in the north, be a solution? Or would it go brown and die off in dry periods?

We went for walks on the beach with Olive the dog, down to the Wreck of the *Hyderabad*, the shipwreck that seemed so exciting and mysterious as a child, and therefore needed capitals. Where once it was a full boat shell that we had climbed up and into, and posed for photos on the prow, now it was almost completely buried in the sand and was more than skeletal – it was archaeological.

After six months in the North Island I had clocked up stays with no fewer than 19 WWOOF hosts, and at the end of the first year of wwoofing I had visited a total of 29 hosts. The South Island was calling me back again, and it was time to make a decision about my journey. In the planning stages, a year's wwoofing sounded like quite long enough, so it was the arbitrary length of time I had given myself, after which I presumed that the next phase of my life would evolve. But as that year was nearing the end it was clear I didn't want it to stop – I was on a roll. There was nothing else I would rather be doing than continuing my wwoofing journey, so why not carry on? My tenants were happy to stay on for another year.

I had become quite accustomed to this new lifestyle, to the stimulation of travel, meeting new people and learning new skills, and to the expansive sense of freedom and opening up of possibilities. Yes, I was poorer than I'd ever been, but my outgoings were small, as food and board were provided by my hosts. The biggest costs were associated with my car: petrol and maintenance, which wasn't very green, but there it was. Some people had suggested I try cycling around, but I just laughed at the image of me straining to pump the pedals up a hill in the pouring rain, laden down with my gear including my laptop and gumboots, review copies of books.

With my newfound spirit of adventure, I planned my trip back to the South Island. Someone had mentioned that there was a freight boat called the *Straitsman* that travelled between Wellington and Nelson, and it took a few passengers and vehicles if there was room. I booked onto it, since Nelson was to be my first port of call anyway, and the *Straitsman* was comparable in price to the inter-island ferry.

The ship catered to the dictates of the cargo first and foremost, leaving this passenger to hang around at the dock for a couple of hours while freight trains and trucks rolled in.

'Welcome aboard!' called a friendly crew member. 'You're the only passenger on this sailing, so you'll have the lounge to yourself.' He showed me the small but comfortable passenger lounge and the dining room. Lunch and dinner were included in my fare, and I ate and chatted with the crew while still in Wellington Harbour, asking them questions about their work. They in turn were interested in hearing about my experiences on organic farms.

'Organics, eh?' one of them said. 'You'd better talk to the chef about that.' Which I did, and it led to an interesting discussion on the pros and cons of genetic engineering.

'Feel free to come up on the bridge,' invited the captain. 'Just ask any of the crew to show you around.' I took him up on his invitation and went up to the bridge shortly after lunch, just as the boat was nosing out of the relative shelter of the harbour and into the wilds of the strait. The bridge loomed up a couple of storeys above the foredeck, where livestock was often penned, but the deck was empty today. We had great views of the surrounding harbour and hills and the South Island in the distance. The ship began to pitch back and forth as we hit the open sea, where the waves either smacked forcefully into the bow, or stood aside for the boat to tumble forward alarmingly into a mini-abyss.

'Sorry, I'm going to have to lie down.' Suddenly, being horizontal became imperative, and a combination of vertigo and queasiness sent me lurching to the passenger lounge. After dozing off for a while I then awoke to a change in the noise of the engine, and realised the ship had crossed the strait, and was now idling.

Due to a late sailing and being held up a little by the weather, we missed our chance to sail on the ingoing tide through the narrow channel that is French Pass, and we had to wait for the tide to change again as there was no point in struggling through against the ebbing tide. As we sat waiting, I strolled around on deck in the fresh air and the moonlight, feeling much improved, well enough to join some of the crew for dinner. Finally we arrived in Nelson after midnight – about 12 hours after we'd set sail.

As I set foot on the South Island again I could feel myself relaxing and slowing down, inwardly breathing a sigh of relief. The energy of the North Island had been buzzy and volatile, arising out of the volcanic landscape, while 'The Mainland', by contrast, felt more stable, settled, deeper and slower. The coming year was time to slow down and spend longer at each farm, I decided, rather than racing around trying to achieve a lot in a short time.

WAIHI BUSH

The occasional distant baa from a sheep was the loudest sound in the drowsy heat of mid-January in South Canterbury. I was headed for Waihi Bush Organic Farm, near Geraldine, after a break back in Dunedin over Christmas and New Year. It was the first farm on the itinerary in my second year of wwoofing, and already I could feel myself slowing down and going with the flow.

I turned off a side road and at the large, leafy oak that had been mentioned as a landmark, swung into the driveway of Waihi Bush, which was lined with gorse hedges and pasture on one side and a woodlot on the other. The drive opened out when it reached a weatherbeaten but sturdy-looking barn, around which gathered a couple of tractors, a ute, and various bits of farm machinery.

'Hello!' I called, as a man emerged through a sliding door from what looked like an office. I recognised him as the farmer, David Musgrave, a softly spoken man whose eyes had the far-away look of someone who was used to scanning the skies and distant paddocks. We had met briefly at a Soil and Health conference the year before. After a reintroduction he directed me to drive on and park by the house.

'If Lorina's not in the house, you'll probably catch up with her at the magic pond with some friends,' he said, instructing me how to get to this mysterious pool, down a track through the bush. David's wife, Lorina Harding, was a musician who had lived in Dunedin. I hadn't met her or heard her music but the name was familiar to me.

The house was a large, two-storeyed wooden place with stone-wall façades here and there, and some tall, arched old windows that looked as though they were from a church. Beyond that was a neatly mown expanse of lawn, and a paddock with a light sprinkling of sky-blue chicory flowers amongst the grasses. In the far corner was a gate into the patch of native bush, and a narrow walking track winding through it. After a few minutes I came across Lorina and her friends standing in the gloom of tall trees that surrounded a clear, deep pool held in a cauldron of rocks.

'Hi, Philippa,' said Lorina. 'You're just in time to hear about the magic pond.' Apparently eels had not been seen in the pond for a long time, but when a tohunga came to bless the pool, an eel had reached up out of the water to touch the tohunga's tokotoko (carved walking stick), which depicted an eel.

That evening I helped Lorina prepare the dinner, and felt an instant rapport with this warm, funny woman whose Canadian accent had softened after years in New Zealand. She was a musician and actor from way back, and a damn good cook. Lorina was capable of looking serious and serene one minute and then breaking out into laughter and cracking jokes in a variety of perfectly executed accents from her extensive repertoire. Another wwoofer arrived that day, Julia from Canada, and Lorina said we'd have to play croquenole (a kind of tiddlywinks played on a special board) in honour of Julia and Lorina's home country. One of David's sons, Oliver, and Lorina's daughter, Hannah, made up the current family complement around the dinner table. During dinner we adults discovered we all practised yoga, and got up early the next morning for a yoga session in the living room.

For my first day's work I drove not just one but two different tractors, having never driven one in my life. David wanted me to roll a recently sown paddock – to drive a tractor pulling a heavy roller in order to flatten out the ground. This was to ensure good and even germination of the seed (lucerne and other pasture species) and also to bury any stones that were sticking up. Much of the area was riddled with small stones, and on some neighbouring farms you could see stones piled up in heaps, having been removed for ease of cultivation.

I was hesitant about driving the tractor, but David was confident in my abilities.

'It's not really much different from driving a car,' he said. 'And you'll be going *really* slowly in a flat paddock. I'll show you first, and then make sure you've got the hang of it.'

He was right; it was pretty easy, just inching up and down the field, looking back and forth to keep a straight line and not roll over the same area twice. The tractor was a bright green John Deere, relatively new, with built-in cab, radio and comfy, well-sprung seat. It was a glorious day: a hot sun, a clear blue sky with just a few wispy clouds, and the mountains in the background were outlined with the sharp definition of an infinity lens. Later I drove another tractor with a trailer for barley that had been harvested, and then did more rolling.

I had seen Waihi Bush flaxseed oil in organic and health food shops, but there didn't seem to be any flaxseed grown on the farm. David explained that he had about a dozen contract growers to grow it for him.

David got into farming through discovering the health benefits of flaxseed oil. It is reputed to be the richest source of omega 3 essential fatty acids (EFAs). These are beneficial for allergies, asthma, arthritis, and skin conditions including eczema, heart attacks and for the prevention of strokes, and help lower cholesterol. The oil comes from the plant also called linseed (*Linum usitatissimum*), not from New Zealand flax (*Phormium tenax*). Linen flax is the same species as flaxseed, but has been bred for the fibre, which is produced from the stem. Generally the word flaxseed is used to denote the edible oil, which is pressed at low temperatures in the absence of light and oxygen, in order to keep its qualities. Linseed usually refers to the industrial quality oil used in paints and stains.

When David's son Oliver was two, he reacted severely to a measles immunisation. Within a few days of the injection he got measles, and really bad eczema. David and his wife tried steroids, but it only got worse. Then, after nearly three years of health problems, someone suggested flaxseed oil for the persistent eczema and, having exhausted other alternatives, David gave it to Oliver. The boy recovered almost immediately.

At the time, David was working as a plant breeder for Dalgety, specialising in pasture species, and before that he worked for 16 years as a scientist for MAF Research. He began researching flaxseed oil, and the more he read about it, the more fascinated he became.

No one was growing flaxseed commercially in New Zealand at that time (mid-1980s); it was imported from Canada, the world's major producer. David was so impressed with the results he'd seen with Oliver, he decided to give it a go at Waihi Bush, his family farm.

He started with a couple of non-organic crops, then switched to organic, and became Bio-Gro certified in 1989. The bulk of the flaxseed has always come from contract growers but, when I visited, David was growing some himself on a nearby site, although the Geraldine area is the wettest part of Canterbury and the weather can be very variable at harvest time. David's main business, Functional Wholefoods, did the pressing, bottling, marketing and distribution of the flaxseed oil from Geraldine.

At Waihi Bush, David was growing several crops, including oats, barley, triticale and spelt. He was very enthusiastic about spelt, which is an ancient variety of wheat that most gluten-intolerant people can eat, although it does contain some gluten. It's not especially high-yielding, but there is a strong demand for it both in New Zealand and for export.

When I wwoofed there, cattle and sheep were part of the seven-year crop rotation plan, and there was ample scope for David to use his knowledge of pasture species. There was also a white goat, Thelma, her young kid, Beejo, an elderly horse called Percy, a couple of guinea pigs, a Jack Russell terrier called Polly and a cat named Possum (which was a little confusing for Polly, who liked to hunt possums).

Thelma was milked morning and night, and provided a litre or two of milk each day. Milking her became one of my wwoofer chores, and she and Beejo became used to me heading towards them in the paddock, calling out 'Thel-ma!' They came running because milking time was also feeding time. Thelma leapt up onto the wooden milking stand, and I secured her head in a wooden frame so she couldn't get out. The bucket of scraps then sat in a tray so she could eat the contents, while

I positioned the milking bucket under her udder, and milked her by hand.

It took me a while to get the hang of milking, to know how and where to hold my hands, but eventually I got into the rhythm of a firm downward squeeze, and could squirt strong streams of milk into the bucket. But that wasn't the only thing to concentrate on. If you were on your own you also had to fend off Beejo, who would try to eat the scraps in the bucket, and you had to watch Thelma's tail in case it went up, which was a sign of imminent droppings, necessitating an immediate withdrawal of the milking bucket lest it be contaminated. And if you didn't milk fast enough, Thelma would finish her food and get restless, kicking with her back legs and sometimes upsetting the milk bucket. If there were two wwoofers, we sometimes did the milking together, so one of us could distract Beejo and pick branchlets off the nearby willows for both the goats to munch. The food bucket always had some nice fruit and vege scraps, and we put in some flax fibre (ground-up flaxseed). Banana skins were a real treat for them and were gobbled up in seconds.

An added attraction of the farm was that, every year around Waitangi Day in February, David and Lorina held the Waihi Bush Folk Festival at their farm. In fact that's how they met: Lorina came to play her music a few years before, and the previous year they were married at the festival. I had heard about the festival, and my arrival in January was a happy coincidence. Since I was enjoying my time there, and David and Lorina liked me as a wwoofer, they asked if I would stay for a while and help out with the folk festival as part of my wwoofing duties. I leapt at the chance.

There was a lot of preparation, as at least 200 people were expected to come to the three-day festival, and camp at the farm. To get the paddocks out the back a bit safer for the campers, Julia, the other wwoofer, and I, spent a couple of days working companionably together digging out a bit of blackberry and cutting the grass along the water race that snaked through the paddock. The water race had got a bit overgrown, and people needed to be able to see it so they didn't trip up. At the end of a hot day, we went skinnydipping in the Waihi River, which ran along the northern border of the farm, not far from the house. It was cold enough to make us gasp, but refreshing.

A few days later, Julia left and an American wwoofer called Daniel arrived. Daniel, Oliver and I were assigned the task of emptying the muck out of the toilets provided for the festival-goers. The toilets were simply large containers in the ground, and since the previous year's festival, the EM (effective micro-organisms to help break it down) had rendered the waste and sawdust into a compost-type mix. Daniel and Oliver did most of the dirty work, only calling me to help with one of the containers, which was not set in the ground but was a 44-gallon plastic drum sitting below a loo amongst some trees. The full drum was too heavy for the two of them to manoeuvre over rough ground and through the trees, so they enlisted my help to literally push shit uphill. Once up on the flat ground, Oliver lifted it up onto the tractor forks and took it away to empty.

Around this time a trio of Israeli wwoofers showed up unannounced on the doorstep just on lunchtime one day. I don't think they were WWOOF members; perhaps they had borrowed someone else's WWOOF book.

Lorina was put on the spot. She could either turn them away, or let them stay, and being a generous soul, decided on the latter, with a proviso.

'I'm not really sure how much work there is,' she said, 'so you can stay for one night and then we'll see how it goes.'

The young man had recently finished his compulsory stint in the Israeli army, and seemed surprised to learn that New Zealand did not have a similar arrangement. The two women were a little older and more worldly-wise. When it came time to discuss the sleeping arrangements, the women made it abundantly clear that neither of them was 'with' the man – they had just met him in New Zealand and were travelling with him because he had a car.

The next morning two of us were weeding near the vege garden and the others were doing some digging elsewhere. After a while the guy came over to me and asked if he could borrow my 'stick' – indicating a spade.

Later the three of them gathered under a tree for an animated confab in Hebrew. I got the idea that something had happened and they were discussing – and disagreeing – what to do about it. Then, just before lunch, the three of them gathered awkwardly in the kitchen, the two women pushing the man forward, urging him to say something, which I thought was odd since their English was much better than his, and he was stumbling over his words, hanging his head, saying that the three of them were going to leave now.

'Oh, but lunch is ready now,' said Lorina. 'You may as well stay for lunch.'

'Oh, no, we must travel now,' he said, and the three of them cleared out in a flash, leaving the rest of us looking at each other, puzzled.

'What was that all about?' asked Lorina. Later we discovered that the reason the guy had asked to borrow my 'stick' was that he had broken the spade he was using. In fact it had already had a crack in it and would have broken at some stage anyway.

We carried on with preparations for the festival, making hay and stacking the bales, which would be used for seating, by the marquee area behind the house. One evening shortly before the festival, Mark the Kiwi wwoofer arrived. He was tanned, with rugged good looks and a teasing manner, and had been wwoofing for about four years at that stage, hitching around with his backpack and his dog Dody, camping occasionally along the way. He was obviously a regular wwoofer here and festival attendee, and David was pleased to have another pair of hands. Mark was just in time to help with putting up the big marquee, which had two tall poles in the centre. He was in his element climbing up ladders and rigging ropes, or swinging a mallet or the blunt side of an axe down on the pegs.

The festival itself was busy for us wwoofers, but great fun. We helped with the signs, washing dishes, and all sorts of errands like emptying the rubbish and recycling containers, checking the toilet paper, and not forgetting to milk Thelma. There were workshops in the morning, including massage, singing and various kinds of dance, and music in the afternoons and evenings. A barn dance was held on the Saturday night, and we all had a rollicking good time.

A local with a digger came before the festival began, and scooped out a swimming hole in the river, which was a popular place for all the festival-goers, children especially. Down on the riverbank was a sweatlodge, which Mark organised the building of, using sycamore saplings lashed together in a half-sphere shape, then covered with old blankets and tarpaulins. Each night Mark forwent the live music concerts, instead tending the fire outside the sweatlodge and heating the fire bricks that he then carried inside on a spade to heat up the lodge. Those of us inside sat on our towels on hay that padded us from the stony riverbank, poured water over the red-hot bricks, and sweltered in the steam until we could stand no more and went out and jumped into the cold river. It was magic there under the bright canopy of stars, with the fire crackling and the trees standing like tall sentinels around us.

Some of us went from sweatlodge to river several times, and in the lodge we sang, meditated and shared our dreams in the steaming heat and total darkness. One man I met there was only known to me by his voice and his name, and it wasn't until about three years later that I met him in the light of day and was able to put a face to his name.

After the festival we had a big clean-up: we took down the marquee, took away the rubbish and recycling, restacked the good hay bales in another paddock, and rebaled the mess of hay that was left strewn around the marquee site.

The festival was such fun that I returned the next two years running, both times doing a short wwoofing stint as stage manager, as well as helping with the set-up and pack-up. The atmosphere was encouraging and supportive, and in the second year I plucked up the courage to sing at one of the blackboard concerts that was open to anyone to perform.

Wwoofing at Waihi Bush had extended me in lots of ways, had given me new skills, and above all some new friends.

12
FRUIT OF THE VINE

Travelling around the New Zealand countryside these days one cannot help but notice the wine boom. Where once there were sheep farms in the likes of Marlborough, Central Otago and North Canterbury, now a mini-forest of posts and vines has sprung up. A web of wires glints in the sun, and rows of vines flick past in the peripheral vision, offering split-second vistas up narrow avenues whose parallel lines converge in the distance. Baby vines are sheltered from rabbits, hares and wind by plastic sleeves of a particular shade of green that might be natural on a tropical fish, but here looks as artificial as a lurid shade of state house mint green.

Here and there are wineries and cafés: some conspicuously ostentatious, some tasteful, some built in a Mediterranean style. Of the hundreds of vineyards and wineries, there were only half a dozen or so that were certified organic in 2003, and only one of these, Sunset Valley Vineyards, was listed in the WWOOF book. Guessing correctly that it would be a popular destination, I made sure to ring a month in advance of the harvest to secure a place, and rolled up there on a beautiful autumn day, sun smiling gently, birds singing.

I drove past orchards and market gardens and vineyards on the plains near Nelson, and then at Upper Moutere the land folded itself into soft rounds and hollows, with vineyards on the sun-facing slopes, and the open country of sheep farms stretched away into the interior. Did I say the birds were singing? Yes. This is a rare sound in vineyards these days. More usual is the uncanny silence – sometimes punctuated in the harvest season by the startling shots of bird-scaring devices –

and the lack of bird habitat: trees. But plenty of birds were in evidence at Sunset Valley Vineyards, delighting and alighting in the thousands of trees that Ian Newton and Ros Squire planted.

Ian and Ros met while they were working for MAF as scientific observers on fishing boats, monitoring the catch on Russian, Japanese, Korean and Norwegian vessels. They were at sea for up to three months at a time, on separate boats, and hardly ever saw each other, so they started planning for the next stage of their life. Ian studied viticulture and oenology (they liked to say Ian-ology) – the science of winemaking – and Ros did a Masters in resource management. Then they looked for land with the express desire of growing grapes organically, and in 1993 found 25 hectares of bare land, formerly used for sheep grazing, with barely a tree on it. It had just what they were after: a nor'west aspect, plenty of sunshine and long hot summers. For the first few months they lived in the barn while building their adobe brick house, a simple one-and-a-half storey dwelling that is warm in winter and cool in summer.

By the time I visited in 2003 there were about three hectares of grapes: sauvignon blanc, chardonnay, riesling, pinot noir, cabernet sauvignon, a few merlot and gamay, and some shiraz that had just been planted the previous season. Ian worked in the vineyard and winery, and Ros worked part-time as a planner for the Tasman District Council and part-time at Sunset Valley. They had full Bio-Gro certification for both the vineyard and the winery, and sold to retail outlets, private customers, and from the shop on the premises in the summer.

Ros and Ian's commitment to organics grew out of their passion for the natural environment, and in 2002 they won first prize in the primary producer category in the Tasman District Council's environment awards. For several reasons, including shelter, aesthetics and biodiversity, they have planted thousands of native trees, grasses and flax. They have also planted some stands of exotics (acacias, eucalypts and cypresses) for shelter and eventually for timber. Their method was to plant the trees in blocks, mulch with thick layers of newspaper and cardboard, and then cover this with bark chips. This provided an effective weed barrier for the establishment phase, after which the trees began to provide their own weed protection in the form of shade as they grew bigger and bushier. This mulch worked so well for the trees they tried it on the grapevines and it proved very effective in suppressing weeds and retaining moisture.

The presence of so many trees is an anomaly in New Zealand vineyards, because of 'the bird problem', although nectar-feeding birds like tui and bellbirds are no problem; it's mostly the waxeyes, thrushes and blackbirds that share our taste for grapes. Like other grape growers, Ian and Ros use bird netting to cover the vines as the fruit ripens, but there is always the odd little hole or gap where the skirt of the netting doesn't quite trail down to the ground, and the wily birds sneak in. For much of the year,though, the birds are not a problem, and indeed contribute to the health of the vines by controlling the insect population, and donate their guano free of charge.

Within a short time of my arrival, the other wwoofer, a Danish woman called Liselotte, initiated me into bird scaring. This was one of the regular jobs at that time of year, done two or even three times a day. We would lift up the netting at the top end of a block of vines, then the two of us would go down the slope to the other end of the rows and flush the birds up and out of the netted block, scaring them with noises: loud clapping and the occasional yell.

The two children, five-year-old Kim and three-year-old Kate, some-times accompanied us on our bird-scaring expeditions, enjoying the chance to run around and make some noise. Maggie the dog also liked to come, but was sometimes more of a hindrance than a help, as she ran around barking like mad in hot pursuit of any bird in any direction. She didn't seem to have cottoned on to the strategy of working up from the bottom, flushing the birds out under the raised curtains of netting at the top of the slope.

The worst culprits were the waxeyes, and as soon as one got in it would chirp to all its mates, who would fly over to join it. They were also the hardest to flush out, hiding amongst the leaves until we were almost on top of them, then cheekily fluttering out and straight past us down to the bottom of the row so we had to retrace our steps and chase them out again.

The harvest was a bit delayed that year because of the changeable weather, but there was plenty of pre-harvest work to do. As well as the bird-scaring, there was leaf-plucking, which meant hand-picking selected leaves off the vines, for several reasons: to expose the grapes to more sunlight to help them ripen, to improve the air circulation thereby reducing the likelihood of fungus, and also to make the bunches easier to see when it came time to harvest them. It was somewhat monotonous work, but with Liselotte in the adjacent row things were never boring; we talked about everything under the sun, from relationships to politics to our respective royals. It was so relaxing to be out in the fresh air, in the peace of the countryside, with the distant baa-ing of sheep and the occasional somnolent drone of a tractor the only sounds rising out of the background chorus of birdsong.

One of the bonuses of leaf-plucking and bird-scaring was the accessible snack food: grapes straight off the vine. What a simple pleasure it was, popping the skin with your teeth to let the sweet flesh explode in your mouth. Any sour ones were promptly ejected.

That year the harvest was spread over about six weeks, which was good in that there wasn't a frantic burst of picking all at once, which would have meant long hours for all of us, for days in a row, most of all for Ian, who was often processing the freshly picked grapes well into the night. As it was, the harvest proceeded at a leisurely pace, with days off here and there, and a few rainy days to fill the water tanks.

The first day of the harvest we picked pinot noir from 8.30 in the morning, and came in after 6.00 that evening. With a lunch break, and morning and afternoon tea, of course. Usually wwoofers are expected to work four or five hours a day, but working the land puts you at the mercy of the weather and the seasonal task at hand, and both wwoofers and hosts have to be flexible. At Sunset Valley the longer harvesting days were balanced by days off to explore the area and do our own thing. Liselotte and I took off one day for a walk on Mt Arthur on the other side of the Motueka River, and climbed up through the forest and into a magical world of mountain neinei (*Dracophyllum traversii*), with their distinctive tufted foliage and awkward elbowed branches.

Another day I went to the popular holiday village of Kaiteriteri, where I visited Kimi Ora, a health retreat which has a vegetarian restaurant using mainly organic ingredients, including fresh fruit and vegetables from their own gardens. Sunset Valley wine was also on the menu. When I visited friends in the area for dinner, Ian generously supplied me with a bottle of wine to take along.

In my mind, the process of winemaking seemed at once scientific and mysterious. The winery was a cross between a chemistry lab, with its large steel vats and thermometers, and a sorcerer's kitchen, with fermenting brews bubbling away, and good old-fashioned oak barrels lined up in rows. We wwoofers didn't spend much time there as Ian said there was really only enough work for him to do, and much of the work needed a trained winemaker: someone who knew about brix (sugar) and acid levels in the grapes, when to add the yeast, how long to ferment the wine, and so on.

'I'm going to test the brix levels today,' Ian told us one day. 'Could you two go and pick some samples for me?' He instructed us which rows to pick from so he could test several different grape varieties, and asked us to pick a representative sample: bunches towards the top of the slope, from the middle of the row, and the bottom. He wrote on the buckets to identify the row and the variety, and when we returned, we squashed the grapes by hand so Ian could test the resulting juice. The brix levels weren't quite high enough to be ready that day. It was a balancing act to be able to harvest the grapes when they reached the peak of ripeness, while hoping that the weather would co-operate.

The picking wasn't onerous, but required concentration. We used sharp snips (or nippers, as Kate liked to call them) to cut the bunches off at the stem, and it was easy to nip your other hand, so they had a supply of bandaids at the ready. The best way to cut grapes is to loosely hold the bunch in one hand and cut with the other, while also watching out for bees and wasps lurking on the bunch or even inside an apparently whole grape. The renegade birds peck open little doors in the grape skin, allowing access to the sweet flesh inside for themselves and the insects.

Right from the start I made a deal with the bees: I wouldn't hurt them if they didn't hurt me, and I assured them that there would be plenty of grapes left over for them. Some of the others laughed at this, but the bees kept their side of the deal, and I escaped unscathed, while most of the others got stung.

We learnt the difference between 'first set' and 'second set' bunches. Second set grapes grow from flowers that have set fruit some time after the main crop, and are usually distinguishable by the small, sparse bunches, their green colour. If in doubt, a taste test will reveal their sourness. They usually grow higher up in the vines.

When picking, we started at the top of the slope, one picker to a row, with large blue plastic picking bins to fill. As we moved down the rows the bins got heavier and we had to drag them, and we left the full bins at the bottom for Ian to carry back to the winery in the ute and then load into the de-stemming machine before making into wine.

After that first day I felt a bit achy from the constant up and down of picking grapes high and low, and from lugging the heavy picking bins. Oh for a hot bath! But rainwater was the only supply here, plus a couple of small dams for irrigation. It hadn't rained much and the water tanks were getting dangerously low. The priority for water was for cleaning out the equipment: picking bins, vats and the press.

Ian had custom-built the press, and it seemed to work pretty well. He loaded red grapes into a metal cylinder with small holes all around it, and with a machine slowly pressed the grapes down, so that the red juice oozed out of the holes and into the vat that the cylinder sat in. The colour of red wine comes from the skins, not the flesh (which yields a colourless juice on its own), so to make red wine, the grapes are crushed, leaving the skins, pulp and juice together to ferment for a few days, then the wine press is used to separate the liquids from the solids. White wine is made by crushing the grapes and pressing them immediately to separate the juice from the solids. Ian made use of the discarded skins, stems and pips in a large compost heap, which, judging by the boozy aromas coming from it, was undergoing its own fermentation process, and would eventually be fed back to the vines.

There was many a talk about organic practices, often triggered by my questions, and Ian seemed happy to have a wwoofer to talk to who was really keen on organics. In keeping with the philosophy of biodiversity, there were several herbal ley species planted in between the rows of grapes, most obviously chicory, with its bright blue flowers on tall stalks standing out above the rest of the pasture species. Its deep roots helped aerate the soil and bring up nutrients. There were also a couple of pockets of buckwheat planted in between the blocks of grapes as habitat for beneficial insects.

Micro-organisms featured large in our conversations, whether it was soil microbes, fungi or yeasts. Yeasts and enzymes were used in fermentation of the wine, and for Bio-Gro certification Ian had to get confirmation from the suppliers that these were not genetically engineered, or manufactured using GE. Unfortunately Ian often had to spend time following up the suppliers to get written confirmation, only to receive frustratingly vague and ambiguous answers.

Grapes can be susceptible to various fungal problems. To prevent them, Ian used a fungus called trichoderma, which he bought and sprayed on the vines. Botrytis, or bunch rot, was a fungus that could affect the grapes during or after wet weather, and was easily recognisable by brown, shrivelled-up grapes. Generally these are no good for making wine. At Sunset Valley the riesling block had quite a bit of botrytis in it, but because of the mostly dry weather the dried-up grapes tasted like raisins, which would in this case improve the flavour of the wine, and Ian planned to make a special botrytised riesling, a sweet dessert wine.

Another fermented mix that Ian sprayed on the vineyard was EM – effective micro-organisms; a mix of beneficial microbes that make the nutrients in the soil more accessible to plants and counteract disease-causing bacteria.

After a while Liselotte left and a Japanese wwoofer called Sawako arrived. She was small but strong, worked at a horticultural training institute teaching people how to grow vegetables, and seemed to be quite at home doing the various tasks around the vineyard. We got into a routine of doing a bird scare around 7.00 a.m., before breakfast, and although Sawako was very delicate with her clapping, she was nevertheless effective.

One day she was about to have a shower (the bathroom had no door, so she modestly undressed behind the shower curtain) when someone realised that the gas bottles had run out, and we wouldn't have any hot water.

Sawako had just turned the shower on, and presumably was waiting for the hot water to flow through.

'Sawako,' Ros called. 'I'm very sorry but we've run out of gas, so the water won't be hot.' It was Thursday evening, the night before Good Friday.

'No hot water till Tuesday!' Ian sang out, with his usual deadpan humour, but a cheeky grin for those of us in the living room. Sawako was somewhat surprised but took this with good grace. Like many of the Japanese wwoofers, she was adaptable to changing situations, and never complained. Fortunately for Sawako, standing naked in the shower that Thursday evening, Ian found a small spare cylinder to use until more gas cylinders were delivered.

Autumn in a mixed vineyard like Sunset Valley is a colourful display, as the leaves of the red grapes turn red, and the white grapes' leaves turn yellow. The late afternoon sun would set the hillside ablaze with stripes of colour of the different varieties, the hues becoming more vibrant once we had harvested and removed the netting that protected the ripening fruit from the birds. The netting was sturdy white nylon, great long strips of it, attached to each other by plastic clips down the length of the rows. After each block had been harvested, we removed the clips in preparation for removing the netting.

Taking off the netting was at least a two-person job, or preferably three. Ian drove the tractor slowly, pulling behind it a trailer with a contraption of his own design and construction, with a ladder climbing up to two great metal arms that stretched out horizontally for several feet and were upturned at the ends. The netting on one side of a row was tossed over the metal arm closest to it, and fell down to the person standing on the back of the trailer (Sawako and I took turns). This person hauled the netting down hand over fist like a sailor pulling in a rope, and furiously stuffed it into wool bales that sat on the trailer, as the tractor crawled forward. These great high arms were the most effective way of lifting the netting up off the vines with a minimum of snarls and catching. The third person was the trouble-shooter, walking along the rows and making sure that the netting didn't catch on the vines or on any nails or staples in the posts, and that all the clips holding the netting together had been taken out.

Another harvest activity at Sunset Valley was gathering the hazel-nuts from a small grove with Kim and Kate. We made it into a game, a competition to see who could collect the most, and that held the children's attention for a while, until they suddenly were off, running wild and free down the hill on the next adventure of the day. I spread the hazels out onto a tray for them to dry out for a few weeks before they would be ready to eat, although I couldn't resist trying some. Most still had slightly soft flesh of a light pinky beige hue, and an unripe taste.

Near the hazels were some stone pines (*Pinus pinea*), a handsome pine with a distinctive rounded shape. This is the pine nut tree, whose nuts are often used in Italian cooking, and are fiddly and time-consuming to extract. I guess that's why they're expensive. There were also apples and pears to pick in the orchard, and the feijoas had just begun to drop their fruit. But best of all were the figs that grew on a spreading tree conveniently planted near the front door. The tree was laden with soft ripe fruit and had to be netted against the birds. Waxeyes were the main culprits, again.

Below the house there was a henhouse and vegetable garden. One day Ros seconded us to help her weed the garden.

'I know Ian wants you in the vineyard, but my vege garden is getting really overgrown and I'd love a hand with it,' Ros said one day. Some of the summer crops were finished, but the garden was still producing lots of green leafy vegetables. Beside the garden was a large drum surrounded by clumps of comfrey. Ros made a strong, liquid, comfrey fertiliser simply by continually adding more comfrey leaves to the drum – and NO water.

'How come you don't put water in it?' I asked. 'Doesn't it just make a sludgey mess in the bottom?'

'It smells if you add water,' she replied, taking off the lid. I bent over and inhaled. My comfrey and water brews always stank to high heaven. This was virtually odourless.

'Look, I've put a mesh screen in there, raised up off the bottom, so the liquid that comes out of the rotting comfrey collects in the bottom and then you just turn on the tap and take what you need.' She turned the tap and out came a thick, black liquid. It is very concentrated, but you can add water to it at that point before you fertilise the plants. The only trick to this pure comfrey liquid is to have enough comfrey; it requires several thick clumps, and regular pickings to keep adding to the mix.

Towards the end of my stay a young American wwoofer called Emily arrived, a slender slip of a thing, 20 years old, shy and softly spoken. She was wearing a stylish pair of cream-coloured jeans, which she continued to wear even when we were picking, although she was offered a pair of overalls.

It was routine at Sunset Valley for the wwoofers to wash the dinner dishes, and on her first night there Emily obligingly cleared the table, then began wiping the dishes with a cloth and giving them a brief rinse in cold water. I joined her, teatowel in hand.

'Um, I think it's probably better to do a proper hot wash,' I suggested.

'Oh, ah, what should I do?' she asked in a hesitant voice. It transpired that she had never washed dishes by hand at home before – she had grown up with a dishwasher.

Ros was the chief cook, and an expert at throwing together a nutritious and delicious meal in minutes. Every day or two she would mix up a batch of bread dough to rise overnight, and then pop it in the oven at breakfast-time, filling the kitchen with the yeasty smell of baking bread. We'd have fresh bread for lunch, or even for morning tea if we were particularly peckish.

More often than not we enjoyed a modest glass of wine with dinner, and a couple of times had blind tasting sessions. We had three or four unidentified samples set before us, to sip before eating so that the food flavours didn't interfere with our tasting. Which was the riesling? The sauvignon blanc? The chardonnay or, trickier to identify, the unoaked chardonnay? The more I quaffed the less certain I was, although after Ros or Ian had identified it, the answer seemed blindingly obvious.

One evening Ian issued us all with pencils and paper along with our wine to make tasting notes for the cabernet sauvignon. We sat on the verandah exercising our tastebuds and brain cells, but all I could come up with was 'rich' and 'plum pudding' – nothing especially poetic for the label. Though the plum pudding description wasn't used, the Sunset Valley label was now familiar and would jump out at me from a shelf full of wines at 50 paces. OK, five. And I would say to myself, or anyone that would listen, oh yes, the vintage of 2003, I picked some of those grapes.

13

DIY

Sometimes hosts ask you to do things that aren't strictly wwoofing type tasks, not gardening or farming, but DIY activities like building or painting. Some of these things are well out of my comfort zone – I'm not very experienced beyond a bit of painting, plunging blocked plugholes and banging the odd nail in the wall. Power tools? I've only wielded a chainsaw once.

Although the objectives of my journey were to learn about organics, farm life and self-sufficiency necessarily means building and making and repairing things, and using the old Kiwi ingenuity with number 8 wire. At one place, a discovery and an inspired suggestion of mine sparked a DIY project for the whole family.

Brett Hutchinson and Jane Bellerby lived 'up the One Spec' in a bush-clad valley near Takaka in Golden Bay. The One Spec Creek flowed through part of the property. One side of the farm bordered on the Anatoki River, with a pedestrian swing bridge over the river as one access way to the property. The other access was a road that ran through dairy pasture that gradually gave way to small orchards and native bush.

Golden Bay, on the north-western corner of the South Island, is a popular holiday spot and has a warm climate and plenty of rainfall. It's one of the few places in the South Island where you can grow subtropicals like feijoas and avocados. It was late autumn 2003 when I arrived, and the feijoa trees were dropping plump fruit on the ground. The method of feijoa harvest there was to drag them out from under the dense hedge-like bushes with a hockey stick. The mandarins were nearly ripe, and the persimmon fruit and leaves gave a glowing sunset contrast to the clear blue skies, and the distinctive angular elbow-like branches emerged ever more stark as the leaves gradually fell away.

Sitting comfortably and unobtrusively amid the green swathes of the garden and surrounding bush-clad hills was the house that Brett built, out of wood, which has mellowed with the years. Brett bought the land in 1981, and Jane joined him in 1984. For 10 years they grew avocados and tangelos biodynamically, and were Demeter certified, but eventually decided it was time to move on and try something different. They found that running an orchard involved a lot of hard work, and long hours. As well as selling to organic shops, they also took their fruit to sell directly at the Nelson market during the harvest season, driving two hours there and two hours back every weekend. The couple decided they wanted their life back, wanted time with their two children, and time to pursue their own interests.

When I visited, their income came from a diverse mix of activities. Jane worked from home as a journalist, writing for gardening and cooking magazines, and worked a few hours as a nurse aide at the local hospital. Brett made trugs: shallow baskets made of strips of wood that can be used for carrying herbs or flowers or vegetables, or as containers for fruit or nuts. They had removed most of the avocado and tangelo trees, converted some land back into pasture for lease to their neighbouring dairy farmer, and in other areas planted timber trees for future income: Tasmanian blackwood (*Acacia melanoxylon*), silver wattle (*Acacia dealbata*), and lusitanica (*Cupressus lusitanica*), a type of cypress tree a bit like macrocarpa. And they still grew a few avocados from seed to graft and sell as seedlings.

When I arrived, Brett was working with a young German wwoofer whom I'll call Sabine, filling up black plastic planter bags with potting mix to put some baby avocado plants in. There was a heaped trailer load of rich black potting mix, so I joined in, as did Jane when she arrived home. This communal activity was a good way to get acquainted with my new hosts, who were laid back and friendly.

Across the lawn from the house was an old, still functional though little-used long-drop toilet, camouflaged by rampant, jungly vines (mainly jasmine), which Sabine and I were deputed to cut back and remove the following day.

'Go easy with the loppers and pruning saws,' said Brett. 'There's a pile of bricks under there somewhere.'

We hacked and snipped and tugged at the stubborn vines that created a tangled web encircling the long-drop and surrounding bushes, anchored by suckers that had taken root here and there. The native forest had sent out a few emissaries to colonise this small patch of wilderness; there were self-sown mahoe in the midst. Gradually the pile of bricks emerged in the sunlight alongside the shack. They were large square terracotta fire bricks, the size of two ordinary bricks sitting side by side, that Brett had salvaged from a big old commercial kiln in Golden Bay that had been demolished some years before.

'Wow, these are great,' I said. 'We should move them, otherwise the vines will just grow over them again. Or how about making something with them?'

'Well, I've been saving them for something special,' said Brett. 'Have you got any ideas?'

'A seat? A path, maybe?'

'Yeah, a path isn't a bad idea because the lawn gets soggy ... but then again the bricks might just sink in.'

'How about steps?' I suggested. This idea took hold of our imaginations, and offered a practical solution to the rotting railway sleepers that were past their use-by date as steps up to the verandah.

Just as well we got to the bricks when we did. It wasn't just vines we had to hack back, but also the mahoe trees that had taken root in amongst the pile, rendering some of the bricks cracked and broken, or difficult to extricate without breaking.

We transported the bricks by wheelbarrow across the lawn and stacked them by the verandah. Cleaning them took some time, as many of them were not just muddy but nurtured their own little moss-based ecosystems. Sabine and I took to them with wire brushes, and as we cleaned, we sorted them into piles of whole bricks, half bricks and broken bits.

Building the steps was a family affair, with much discussion and consultation about the design to begin with. We had to measure and remeasure to work out how high they needed to be, get the depth of tread right, make the foundation, mix a concrete slurry to use as mortar, lay the bricks, and finally Jane put the finishing touches with a bit of landscaping on either side: native grasses, garden sculptures and a lemon tree. It was a Kiwi DIY masterpiece – a functional and funky set of steps up to the verandah, warm and earthy and rustic, fitting perfectly with the house and garden.

It's the sort of project that might be merely one of a number of changes on one of the ubiquitous television DIY makeover programmes these days, except that a TV programme would have supplied us with a 'Handy Andy', and possibly other minions beavering away in the background out of sight of the cameras. And we wouldn't have had to spend a day cutting the vines and trees, or another day cleaning the bricks – a pallet load of clean new bricks would be delivered by magic, as would the sand. In our case we had to bring the sand by wheelbarrow from the back paddock, after excavating it from a sandpit that was no longer used.

Nor would the TV programme be interrupted by the discovery of an escaped animal in the back paddock. At one point I went down to get another barrow load of sand, and Song the horse came trotting over to say hello.

'Come on, Song, I've got a treat for you today.' I held out an apple. But before she got to me she suddenly saw – or sensed – something, stood stock still with ears pricked, acting nervous, quivering and snorting and pacing up and down. I scanned the next paddock, not knowing what to look for, and finally spotted an emu among the young timber trees. I went to alert Brett and we tried to herd it through the gate into the next paddock, but our attempts were thwarted by the emu's swift stride and its stubborn refusal to be driven by our flailing arms and tentative hustlings. Brett immediately realised it must have come from the neighbouring farm across the river – somehow it had crossed the swift, roiling Anatoki, no mean feat. Perhaps, we speculated, it had come across on the swing bridge! Apparently it had been missing for a week but the neighbours hadn't thought to ring Brett and Jane because they didn't think it would be able to cross the river. They came over to take it back, and I went back and saw Song, gave her some apples, stroked her mane and talked softly to reassure her and calm her down.

The first set of brick steps was so successful that Brett put me to work on a second set, much the same as the first, also leading up to the verandah. There were plenty of bricks left over, but many of them had to be cleaned with a wire brush, and Sabine had left by then so I scraped away on my own. For the foundation, I laid down some flat stones, then some metal bars for strength, then Brett came by and we made a more or less level base for the bricks. I wasn't very confident about working mostly on my own, but Brett was just over in the trug workshop if needed.

'You're doing fine,' he reassured me. 'Don't worry, it's a One Spec job.' Meaning it didn't have to be perfect. We were up the One Spec, after all, out in the backblocks where things could be a bit rough and ready, as long as they were functional. For a time I worked away diligently until it became obvious, when putting on the second layer of bricks, that the cement mortar was like soup. Just then Brett came down to the house for a cup of tea with a neighbour.

'How are you going there?' he called.

'I've made the mortar too runny,' I said, staring at the gloopy mix that was sliding slowly off the tops of the bricks.

'Oh, well, you'll have to add a bit more sand and cement.'

So, more trudging down to the back paddock and scraping the last of the sand out of the old sandpit, removing bits of grass that were growing in there, as well as small plastic toys. Because there was more of the mortar in the barrow it was heavier and harder to mix. I strained with my puny arms to mix it evenly, scraping with the shovel right down into the corners of the barrow, but somehow it was still too runny, and not helped by the addition of my tears of frustration. Nothing was going right! I was out of my comfort zone and my perfectionism was showing. Time out was required.

'Time for a cup of tea,' I decided, removing my gloves. Brett came to my aid after morning tea, and I felt relieved to be working with someone who had done this sort of work before. My diary entry the next day reveals my lack of confidence: 'I just hope the steps don't collapse because I haven't put enough brick bits in the hollow in the middle.'

Then we embarked on a third set of steps. It was a more ambitious project, involving a sloping surface, and an existing paved brick area that the steps rose up out of. We had used up a lot of the good, whole bricks by now so we used cracked and broken ones on the underneath where it didn't show, and carefully saved the whole ones for the visible areas. By this stage my confidence was growing as I got my head around the measurements, and began suggesting ideas and solutions, but these steps weren't completed before I left. Rain held up the work from time to time, and we had to cover the project to protect it from frost and rain, using old boogie boards and tarpaulins.

My room at Brett and Jane's was a snug, private, custom-built wooden caravan that Brett had made, with a bit of a gypsy look to it. Inside were bunks, a double bed, shelves, and a little wood burner, which came into its own as the autumn deepened into winter. Although the mid-year temperatures in Golden Bay weren't as low as what I was accustomed to in Dunedin, there were several frosts and very chilly mornings. If the fire was banked up overnight it just required a top-up first thing in the morning to get it roaring again, making the small space toasty warm in no time. It made its own sort of music, a kind of percussion, with a dull thump of metal expanding or contracting, a constant tinkling sound of bits going up the chimney, and another higher-pitched cracking of metal.

There was no electricity to the caravan, only the wood fire for heating and candles for lighting, which I was super careful with, having heard about caravan fires caused by candles. There were windows on all four sides, letting the light of the moon and stars shine through right onto the bed. If I got up to wee in a secluded spot outside, I would linger and gaze in awe at the myriad bright stars cascading across the heavens, many more than were visible in the light-polluted cities and towns.

Brett and Jane were excellent hosts and gave us wwoofers at least one day off a week. When it rained we sometimes had enforced time off, or did indoor activities like stewing apples, baking and housework. One gorgeous day I asked Sabine if she'd like to go for a drive with me and visit a couple of places in the Bay. Most wwoofers would have jumped at the chance of a day trip, but Sabine seemed almost uninterested. In the end she decided to come, and we drove to Milnthorp Park for a walk. It was an area of bush that had been planted mostly by one guy, with various tracks through it, some going to the nearby beach. I was surprised by the number of gums and acacias in there along with native species until I read the blurb about the park's history, on the back of the map from a box in the carpark. Apparently the soil was so poor that many of the native species didn't do that well so they planted some Australian trees as well.

When we got to the beach the tide was way out and had created tiny lagoons around which the gulls and torea (oystercatchers) congregated. The bay was as calm as a lake, and the water such a pale blue you could hardly tell where sea met sky.

Then we drove to Pupu Springs (more properly Waikoropupu Springs). There were tracks through regenerating bush, and DOC information boards telling us that this is the largest springs system in Australasia. The crystal clear water bubbles up from an incredibly deep aquifer, forced up through the rock at something like 14,000 cubic metres per second. There are a couple of natural outlets out in the bay where fresh water from the springs comes up into the seawater. The whole place had a surreal, spiritual feeling to it, and indeed is wahi tapu, a sacred place for Maori.

Sabine was unlike most of the other wwoofers I'd met, who were generally extroverted and chatty – sometimes too chatty – apart from some of the Japanese who were shy. Maybe she was homesick, maybe she was depressed, but whatever it was she did not seem happy. She virtually never spoke unless spoken to, and conversation with her was an effort. Her English was very good, so that wasn't the problem. Brett,

Jane and I all endeavoured to talk with her and involve her in things as we were concerned about her. She worked away willingly enough, but when one task was finished she would just wait to be told what to do next, rather than asking, and when we'd knocked off for the day she often just sat on the couch, doing nothing, not even reading or watching TV. After a couple of weeks there she left, and I have to confess to being relieved. I only hope things improved for her.

One day Brett asked if I'd like to help him with his trug making. He was going down to the river to cut some willow saplings to make handles. It was a fine, sunny day, quite warm. We drove down to where the valley opened out onto a wide flat plain, and parked near the stony riverbank. Leafless winter willows fringed the river on both sides in dense thickets; there was no shortage of the main raw material for Brett's trugs. When he first started making them he was advised to use native trees, but found through trial and error that willow was a much better material. The trees were plentiful to the point of being a weed, and the wood was easier to work with. Brett referred to this variety as bitter willow.

We fell into a rhythm: he selected willow trunks about the diameter of my arm and cut them with his chainsaw, and I gathered them together in small bundles and carried them to the car. When we had 101 he declared that to be enough and we set off back to the workshop.

Brett made three different types of trugs. The most popular one was a shallow, more or less oblong basket made of thin – but wide – strips of willow that had been steamed and curved up at each end. The handle was made of a thin strip of willow that formed almost a square with rounded corners, and went right round the bottom of the basket. Brett left the bark on the handle as a rustic touch. The thin strip around the rim of the basket was also bark-covered, and nailed on with bright copper tacks.

The harvested willow first had to be cut into the correct length and width. We donned earmuffs and Brett did the measurements and operated the machinery while I fetched and carried and stacked. Then Brett inserted the handle lengths one at a time into a fat metal pipe where they were steamed, so they could then be bent around custom-made frames: a wooden base with pegs. Once wrapped around the pegs, the handles were then left to dry out and set into their new shape.

The other two types of trug he made were higher, more boxy looking baskets, all flat planes and angles. Brett sold the trugs to individual customers who drove up to the workshop (there were very few of these in winter), through some retail outlets, and also by mail order – often through word of mouth.

There were several trugs in use in the house, mostly as fruit bowls for avocados, mandarins, feijoas and so on, and there was also one filled with walnuts. It was here that my penchant for the humble brain-shaped nut began. I had never before regarded walnuts as anything special rather, they seemed like a lowly and common nut compared with more exotic nuts like cashews, Brazil nuts, even almonds. The flavour had never particularly appealed; they seemed woody and uninteresting. But the walnuts at Brett and Jane's were still in the shell, and were fresh and even sweet tasting. Now it dawned on me that I had probably never really tasted good, fresh walnuts, and that most of the walnuts I'd eaten up until now had been out of the shell for some time and were probably somewhat stale. I developed almost a craving for them, and was possibly self-medicating, getting doses of omega 3 essential fatty acids, which are present in only a few foods, of which the walnut is one. From then on I began to seek them out and have them on hand (shelled) as a snack in the car while driving from farm to farm.

Diary entry
Tuesday, 10 June 2003

Brett and I planted trees yesterday. *Acacia dealbata* and *Acacia melanoxylon* (Tasmanian blackwood). I walked up the clay track. It was raw as a wound, yellow clay and white clay and bare rock like bones showing through. Up at the top a flat boggy paddock, and a slope covered in debris – smashed up kanuka and gorse and bracken and mamaku, and acacias planted in between. I thought of European settlers and the rawness they would have created on this land, the chopping down, the devastation, the gradual taming of the wilderness.

The hillside was oozing, just like the paddock. There were wide ribbons of moss down the slopes, and acacias still surviving in the squelch. On the skyline was the most beautiful gorse tree, at least three or four metres high and well formed. We picked our way through the debris to find spaces for acacias, me gingerly in my sloppy gumboots, with my weak ankles. There were unexpected dips and holes and gaps between fallen branches, not to mention all the prickly gorse you could fall into.

I fell, but only onto grass. We planted acacias in little pockets and gaps, on a bank and on another slope further up above the very top paddock. I made the plastic sleeves, cutting small holes in them with Brett's excellent knife, a stout sturdy thing you can open and close with one hand, then threaded the bamboo stakes through the holes.

A tui is chattering again. I saw a couple of them in the persimmon tree yesterday, distinctive with their glossy black sheen revealing flashes of other colours – green, purple – and their white throats bobbing. There's a morepork that often comes round in the early dawn – I heard it hooting a while ago. I can also hear a rooster that's been crowing for ages. Now several other birds are joining in as the dawn light gradually pales.

We've got the power and phone back on again now (after a 24-hour cut) so life is 'back to normal', but it was kind of fun for a night to have it off. At least we could use the wood burner in the living room for heating and cooking.

As with everywhere else, there was weeding to be done. On the path to the swing bridge were a number of fruit trees, including some avocados, most of which were at least four or five metres high, thick with luxuriant growth. Underneath these sheltering canopies were veritable forests of weeds and young trees that I weeded out. There were dozens of seedling avocados; native saplings, including mahoe, totara and pittosporums; barberry and nightshade around the edges where it was lighter. The work was meditative and peaceful there under the protective umbrellas of the avocados.

Another weeding task was to remove the gorse and broom from around the edges of the pond. Many of the plants were quite small and could be removed roots and all, but the larger ones I had to cut at ground level, and then cover the stump with small squares of old carpet held down with stones to try to prevent regrowth.

Other winter jobs included pruning the nashis, digging over a bed ready to plant garlic, and one day we went to the beach to collect seaweed, mostly sea lettuce, which we put under citrus trees and on the vegetable garden.

Diary entry
Tuesday, 1 July 2003

I need to make a decision about where to next – sounds like Christchurch or Wellington for the select committee hearing [on the New Organisms and Other Matters Bill – to do with genetically engineered organisms]. I know my path will evolve but sometimes it's frustrating not always knowing where I'm going to be ahead of time, sometimes it's kind of scary and unsettling. Sometimes I long for a more stable life where I'm not having to make these decisions all the time. But at the same time I've grown used to, and indeed celebrate the freedom I have to move around. I feel sad that my time here 'up the One Spec' is coming to an end because Brett and Jane have made me feel very much at home.

14

HEIRLOOMS

There are six apple trees in my city garden in Dunedin, and over the years several people have hazarded guesses at what varieties they are. My fruit trees were used two winters in a row for pruning workshops run by the now defunct OGGO (Organic Gardeners and Growers of Otago) and, as well as being pleased to have people helping me with the pruning, I was thrilled to discover that the large cooking apples were apparently Peasgood Nonsuch. The name had a magical quality, an ancestral reverberation, a fairytale ring to it – echoes of Pease Blossom from *A Midsummer Night's Dream*, perhaps.

One tree is very obviously a Granny Smith, the fruit exhibiting the characteristic firm, shiny, greasy skin in that wonderfully vivid shade of 'apple green'. May to June is harvest time, later than the other trees, and there's often fruit still hanging on in July, when the birds start making a real go of them, and what appears to be a pristine whole fruit from below sometimes turns out to be hollowed out by hungry birds from above.

Tui and korimako are nectar feeders, or so I thought, until one morning in the orchard I counted about seven tui and a couple of korimako, several of them feasting on the Granny Smiths. The bellbirds, usually well camouflaged in the bush by their drab olive green plumage, stood out in the stark outlines of the leafless tree. They also disabused me of the notion that tui and korimako are never to be seen together.

I'm fairly sure one of my other apples is a Cox's Orange, bearing small fruit with an orangey red stripe and a tangy sweet flavour.

There's also a tree with three different kinds of yet-to-be-identified apples grafted onto it.

Anyone with the vaguest interest in apples must have noticed the change in what's available in the shops: the varieties of my childhood, like Gravensteins, Sturmers and Cox's Orange are barely to be seen, having been replaced in more recent years by Braeburns and Pacific Rose, but even these varieties are perhaps a little passé, and may be superseded by trendy young upstarts like Jazz, or the imaginatively named T22.

What is the effect of this constant innovation on the apple industry? Are there whole orchards of productive young trees being ripped out, nipped in the bud, as it were, to be replaced with the latest market-researched, patented, designer brand? Why is there such a trend to change (improve?) one fruit, when another, the grape, is much less subject to such trends, and the majority of wines are still made from the tried and true varieties.

In the early days of my wwoofing journey I'd stayed with Robyn and Robert Guyton on their 400 square metres of permaculture paradise in the pretty seaside fishing village of Riverton. The Guytons' garden was full of fruit trees, about 100, mainly apples, and some plums, pears and berries, and the delightfully old-fashioned-sounding medlar. In order to eat this latter mysterious fruit, it must be bletted, in other words become so soft it is almost rotten. Unfortunately, it was then too early in the season for the fruit to be ready, so this delight still awaits me.

The Guytons have collected fruit trees from around Southland and beyond, mainly from elderly gardeners with heirloom varieties that are now seldom, if at all, available through nurseries. One of these, an apple, was the Worcester Pearmain, an even bright red all over, with crisp, juicy white flesh and a heavenly sweet flavour and scent. They also had Keswick Codlin, recognisable by its trademark 'seam', a raised line (sometimes two), running from stem to calyx.

Another WWOOF host, Mark Lagerstedt, had an heirloom cooking apple called Warner's King, which lent itself very kindly to apple crumble. Mark, a ruddy redhead who had learnt the Gaelic tongue of his ancestors, was one of a number of migrants from the city who had heeded the call of the land. He had thrown in his city job as a draughtsman to buy a smallholding in the hamlet of Hampden, north of the Moeraki boulders.

On his wall was a detailed map of North Otago, with coloured pins to indicate known heirloom fruit trees. Mark was on the committee of a local horticultural network called Futuregro, which was cataloguing these trees for several reasons: historical interest, to find out which varieties grow well in the region, and to identify neglected or threatened orchards and trees in order that they might be protected.

He took me to see three old orchard remnants, two of which date back to the 1860s. Two were on farms, one in quite a bad state of neglect, with gnarled old lichen-encrusted trunks and straggly branches tangling overhead.

'Look at these trees – they're survivors,' he enthused. 'They've lived 140 years! Even if we don't save these trees, we can take scion wood from them, and carry on their genes. There's an apple culture just waiting to be brought back to life, a knowledge of the different types of apples and what they can be used for.'

(Scion wood is a cutting taken from a tree to be planted, or more usually, grafted onto rootstock.)

In tune with the worldwide movement of Slow Food (dishes prepared from scratch, from fresh, locally grown, preferably organic ingredients), Mark's vision was for the development of regional cuisines around New Zealand, so that North Otago apple varieties can be promoted alongside other local products, such as Whitestone cheese.

Mark also put me on to an apple expert, Jim Dunckley, of Palmerston, and I got inspired to write an article about heirloom apples for *Organic New Zealand* magazine. Jim was clearly the repository of a great deal of knowledge about apples, and in particular, how to identify them. Palmerston was once a fruit-growing district, but this became uneconomic when the Central Otago railway opened, allowing easy transport of Central fruit to Dunedin and beyond. When Jim moved to the town, there was an old fruit tree in the paddock across the road that he couldn't identify, so he sent them to a man in Christchurch, who identified the tree as Majetin, and also sent Jim a blow by blow account of how he had come to that conclusion, which got Jim's attention, and he's been fascinated ever since.

Identifying apples is an art. Jim had been interested in apples for more than 30 years, but only became serious about identification after the late 1990s. He was collecting specimens of known cultivars and photographing them to aid him in his identification. He took photographs of the apples on a black velvet background, with a Kodak grey card so the colour reproduced accurately, and with a tape measure for size. He photographed them from the top, bottom and side, and two cross-sections (vertical cut and horizontal cut). Colour, shape, core structure, details of the stalk and calyx, the flavour and cooking properties of apples all came under his close scrutiny.

To test the cooking properties of an apple, he put slices of apple into a shallow dish, covered it with foil close to the slices, put the dish into the oven at 200°C for 15 minutes, then lifted the foil to observe: was it a fluffy purée, ordinary purée, or in soft or firm slices?

Then of course, came the taste test. Dessert apples are often insipid and tasteless when cooked. Dual-purpose apples also have a good flavour, but pure cooking apples have the best (strongest) flavour. Yellow Bellflower, from the Catlins, he was warned, would lift the lid off his pot if he more than half filled it, so much would it fluff up in the cooking.

Jim was aided in his identification by a number of specialist books on apples, including Ragan's classic compendium, *Nomenclature of the Apple*, a 1904 catalogue listing a staggering 14,000 varieties.

We were seated in his comfortable living room, with cups of tea and biscuits, and as Jim chatted away he dropped names of apples into the conversation as though they were dear friends; Lady Sudely, Annie Elizabeth, Ingrid Marie, Gloria Mundi, Mother. Some names revealed geographical origins: Irish Peach, Devonshire Quarrendon, Kentish Fillbasket, Reinette de Canada.

During the course of the afternoon two boxes of apples arrived from Oturehua for Jim to identify, and to see if he was interested in scion wood from them. He immediately opened one of the boxes and picked out an apple, quickly describing it as round to conical in shape, slightly ribbed, a conspicuous calyx with erect sepals, greasy skin and lenticels (that's spots, to you and me).

'But as to narrowing it down to a particular variety, that could take hours of poring through my apple books,' he sighed. Old nursery catalogues were invaluable in his quest, as they gave helpful clues as to the varieties sold in different areas.

Jim was also a keen apple grower and grafter. He took me out into the garden and showed me several of his apples, including one espaliered tree that had 26 different varieties grafted onto it. He was encouraging about grafting.

'Anyone can do it,' he said. 'Get the scion wood when the tree is dormant in winter. Take a cutting about the thickness of a pencil and wrap it in damp newspaper and a sealed plastic bag, put it in the fridge, and most importantly, label it with the variety name. Then in spring, graft it onto the rootstock, when the rootstock's buds are just beginning to move.'

He advised using grafting tape or plastic insulation tape, light-coloured so it doesn't heat up. Completely seal it with grafting compound, which you can buy or make yourself out of melted beeswax and heavy grease.

Since my visit to Jim he has been using the internet to help with apple identification, and has discovered several useful websites, including:

www.webvalley.co.uk/brogdale/collectionapples.php
www.ars-grin.gov/cgi-bin/npgs/html/taxon.pl?104681
www.ronnieappleseed.co.uk/variety.html
library.wur.nl/speccol/fruithof/dnb1/BgCdEng/Start.htm
www.pometet.kvl.dk/Aebleliste.htm
www.keepers-nursery.co.uk/search.aspx

Another heirloom apple expert I was recommended to contact was Dieter Proebst of Treedimensions near Motueka, the Demeter certified orchard mentioned in Chapter 5. At the time of writing, the orchard has about 3000 trees, 700 different fruit varieties, about 200 of which are apples. Until 2000 Dieter also had a nursery selling his own grafted fruit trees. Now he focuses on the fresh fruit and has branched out into fruit leather and juice. He grows mainly apples and pears, but also plums, prunes, quinces, berry fruit, grapes, citrus, feijoas, peaches and others.

My wwoofing stint at Dieter's was in late spring, when there were very few apples left from the previous season's harvest. The following autumn, when I was wwoofing nearby at Sunset Valley Vineyards, I jumped at the chance to visit Treedimensions again for Dieter's annual Easter open day. My fellow wwoofer Sawako and I took the day off from wwoofing and drove over to the other side of the Motueka River. We arrived slightly late, but followed the voices down into the orchard where Dieter was showing people around, talking about the different varieties of apples, and answering questions.

When it came to apples, Dieter was a walking encyclopedia, and was happy to share his knowledge, which was grounded in the practical experience of growing so many different varieties and finding out which ones performed well. Some heirloom apples aren't really worth keeping except for interest's sake, he told us – not all of them are particularly tasty, for example, or they may not store well. But heirloom apples have stood the test of time and are reasonably disease resistant. It's a matter of selecting the right varieties for your climate and soil.

Then we had lunch – his wwoofers had prepared a feast on an outdoor table. As well as savouries, there were plenty of apple dishes: pies, cheesecake and loaf. We all sat under the pergola in the warm autumn sunshine and chatted.

Finally came the apple tastings. There were 110 varieties to sample: four or five of each kind all arranged on neatly labelled plates. Some of them must have been kept in the coolstore, as surely not all of them would be ready at the same time. Dieter had prepared tasting notes, listing all the varieties alphabetically, their harvest month, and whether he thought they were 'winners' or not.

We sampled tiny slivers so we could try as many as we could, and there were compost buckets for spitting into if we didn't want to swallow – like wine tasting. It was just as well we had eaten already, otherwise an overdose of apple might have resulted in a bit of a sore tummy. My favourites were Cornish Aromatic, Egremont Russet and Merton Russet. Lots of the apples were tart and flavourful – my tastes tended towards these, whereas Sawako preferred the blander, sweeter ones.

Dieter Proebst has a list of about 45 apple cultivars he reckons are worthwhile growing in New Zealand. Here are his top ten (for his own orchard):

Cultivar	Boskoop (or Belle de Boskoop)
Harvest time	April
Characteristics	discovered in Holland around 1850, cooker, large russeted fruit, tart, highly flavoured, sweetens in storage

Cultivar	Cox's Orange Pippin
Harvest time	April
Characteristics	one of the most popular dessert apples, firm, tart, juicy, essential pollinator

Cultivar	Cornish Aromatic
Harvest time	April
Characteristics	originated in Cornwall in 17th C, crisp, aromatic, rich flavour, good keeper

Cultivar	Discovery
Harvest time	February
Characteristics	old English variety, crisp, juicy, disease-resistant

Cultivar	Egremont Russet
Harvest time	March
Characteristics	creamy, dense flesh, nutty flavour

Cultivar	Laxton's Fortune
Harvest time	April
Characteristics	developed in England, 1904, scab-resistant, sweet, crisp, juicy

Cultivar   Reinette de Canada
Harvest time   April
Characteristics   cooker, good bearer with large fruit, keeps well

Cultivar   Sturmer Pippin
Harvest time   April
Characteristics   dense flesh, good juicing apple, flavour develops
                  in storage, high in vitamin C, excellent keeper
                  (till late October)

Cultivar   Telstar
Harvest time   March
Characteristics   crops heavily, crisp, rich, sweet flavour

Cultivar   Tydeman's Late Orange
Harvest time   April
Characteristics   classic tight clusters, needs to be thinned, firm,
                  juicy, keeps well, flavour intensifies in storage

While the apples nourished my body, another, spiritual dimension
came into play: I felt an affinity with this land and with the apples,
having tended to them the previous November. This direct connection
with land and food has an immense impact. When we grow our own
food using natural methods, we are part of nature, part of the cycle,
nourishing the plants that will in turn nourish us. How much more
satisfying this is than to trundle down brightly lit supermarket aisles,
tossing plastic packaged, processed food into our trolleys: food that
exudes only a ghostly shimmer of its former vitality.

Little wonder that Farmers' Markets are catching on here – people
like to have a connection with their food, to know where it comes
from, and if they haven't grown it themselves, to know who has. Little
wonder, too, that the market for organic food is growing at an estimated
50 % a year in New Zealand; people want food that is healthy for them
and the environment, without cancer-causing chemicals; food that is
grown in tune with nature.

GROWING UNDER GLASS

In my second year of wwoofing, when spring was teasing winter, I arrived at Clean Greenz glasshouse business on the outskirts of Blenheim, in an area where orchards are being ripped out to make way for subdivisions and vineyards, and much of the surrounding countryside that once was a quilt of sheep paddocks is now measured in grids of posts and wires that prop up grapes, with nary a tree in sight.

Steffan Browning and his partner Astrid Brauksiepe were my hosts. We had met at the Soil and Health Association conference in Christchurch three months before, and then again at a field day at their property, so they weren't complete unknowns as many of my hosts had been, and that initial politeness of first meeting was out of the way.

When I rang to arrange my stay, Steffan was friendliness personified. 'Philippa!' he boomed. 'We've been wondering when you were going to come and wwoof with us. When are you coming? How long can you stay?'

'Next Monday, if that's OK with you. And I'm not really sure how long for. A few weeks?'

'That's fine. Stay as long as you like. Astrid's away in Germany for another six weeks, so it'll be good to have an extra pair of hands.'

First impressions of Clean Greenz: concrete yards, a great pile of coal, the fiery furnace and smokestack – an industrial atmosphere, albeit on a small scale. But step inside the glasshouses all this was forgotten, and if you stood still enough you could almost hear the vegetables growing in the reverent hush. The prolifically fruiting tomatoes and beans, shiny cucumbers and eggplants, vibrant capsicums and chillies were all testament to Steffan's abilities as a grower, honed over 20 or more years.

Clean Greenz was the largest organic heated glasshouse operation in New Zealand and consisted of seven large glasshouses covering 2400 square metres. The glasshouses were made of wood and glass and were missing the odd pane, but otherwise were in remarkably good shape considering the oldest ones were built in the 1930s and the most recent in the 1970s. A coal-fired boiler heated water that circulated through metal pipes, which ran the length of each row in each glasshouse, held just above the ground by bricks here and there.

The irony of using fossil fuels to produce organic food had not escaped Steffan, and the boiler room door sported a faded Greenpeace sticker that pictured belching smokestacks, and exhorted the reader to 'Stop Incineration'. Polluting the atmosphere was to Steffan one of the most troubling aspects of his business, and he had thought long and hard about other heating methods, and about more efficient energy use. Because he was renting the glasshouses, he took on the whole set-up as it was, organised to use coal, and it would have been a massively expensive undertaking to convert the glasshouses to another form of heating. Coal was quite simply the cheapest and, given the set-up, easiest option. Most heated glasshouses in New Zealand use it.

To go some way towards remedying his impact on the environment, Steffan had taken the initiative of paying a voluntary carbon tax each year, and donated money to the Marlborough branch of Forest and Bird to spend on reafforestation projects. Since my stay, he lowered the temperature in the glasshouses slightly to reduce the environmental impact, not to mention save money. Then in 2005 he stopped heating altogether when his resource consent ran out, and wound up the business to focus on political lobbying for organics, and consulting work. Since he stopped growing, he has left a real hole in the market for organic glasshouse-grown produce, as there are few others growing on such a scale and with his expertise.

Steffan started out small, growing a few vegetables in tunnel houses at his previous place in the Marlborough Sounds. In 1989 he moved up a notch, gained Bio-Gro organic certification, bought his trusty second-hand ute (still going strong), and started taking wwoofers. Since then he has become one of the movers and shakers in the organic sector. At the time of writing, he is spokesman of the Soil and Health Association of New Zealand, the world's longest-running organic organisation, founded in 1941. Soil and Health has a diverse membership of home gardeners, commercial growers and farmers, and consumers concerned about the environment and the quality of their food. It publishes the magazine *Organic NZ*, and is also a political lobby group, issuing media releases and writing submissions to the government on things affecting organics. Branches around New Zealand organise field days and other events.

Steffan has also been a board member of Bio-Gro, the Biological Producers and Consumers Association, which was established in 1983. The organisation is not-for-profit, and is the certifying agency for hundreds of organic farmers, growers, processors, retailers and suppliers of inputs (for example, fertilisers). Steffan was also involved in setting up Organic Aotearoa New Zealand (OANZ), an umbrella body that aims to bring together the various organic organisations that have proliferated in recent years.

During my stay Steffan was constantly busy, wandering around the glasshouses checking the crops and supervising wwoofers and paid staff, stoking up the boiler, or working in the office in the living room on various environmental campaigns or on business management. The portable phone was invented with people like Steffan in mind. If the phone wasn't stuck to his ear it would be poking out of his pocket as he roamed around. More than once I saw him juggling two ringing phones – his land-line and his cellphone. His openness, ready smile and joking manner instantly put me at ease and within a short time I felt like another member of the family.

My attributes – including fluent English, gardening experience, cooking skills, and a New Zealand driver's licence – all added up to a very useful CV for my hosts. If Steffan was busy, he dispatched me to pick up wwoofers from the bus station, give them a tour of the place, and instruct them in some of the main tasks. I stayed for two months, and met Steffan's partner Astrid towards the end of that time when she came back from her trip to Europe. She was a lively but laid-back German who came to Clean Greenz as a wwoofer, and stayed on when she and Steffan fell in love – a not uncommon story. As well as the passing parade of wwoofers, there were four workers: three young men working full-time, and one woman who came in two or three days a week mainly to do the orders.

Steffan was a congenial host and engaged in friendly banter and jokes with everybody. Even Wilma, a somewhat reserved Dutch wwoofer, came out of her shell and joined in the fun, teaching us the phrase '*Goedemorgen, lekker ding!*', which roughly translates as 'Good morning, you sexy thing'. It just so happened that the next wwoofer to arrive was also Dutch, an ebullient redhead called Ocky, and we tried out our new language skills on him, to his great amusement. During my stay, a total of eight other wwoofers passed through, usually just for a week or two, or only a few days, although one, an ethereal young American called Sky, stayed less than a couple of hours before telling us that he felt he was called to go somewhere else.

Four days after my arrival, Steffan asked me to look after the place for a weekend while he went away. Fortunately I didn't have to load the boiler up with coal – one of the workers would do that. My task was to regulate the boiler temperature and listen out for the alarm. At that time of year, late August and into September, the temperature fluctuated between frosty nights and soft warm days. If the temperature in the glasshouses fell below 7°C, an alarm would sound in the house, and Steffan would have to dash out in the middle of the night and turn up the boiler. Fortunately the alarm never disturbed us during my stay; Steffan kept a sharp ear out for the weather report, and was a good judge of how low the temperature might go. He would set the boiler accordingly, checking it before going to bed and again first thing in the morning. He impressed on me how crucial the temperature was, and I followed his instructions to the letter.

Of all the plants, the tomatoes were truly a wonder to behold. They were the tallest, or perhaps longest, tomato vines I'd ever seen, but the method used to stretch them out and keep them growing and fruiting is the norm in glasshouse operations, conventional or organic. The plants grow twisting up around strings that hang from overhead wires. Once the tomato plant reaches the wire, the bottom few leaves are stripped off and the lower part of the stem is laid down horizontally across some large metal staples stuck into the soil, so it's held a foot or so off the ground. The upper part of the stem, still growing up around its string, is just moved along a bit so it's hanging further along on the wire. Thus the stem emerges from the ground to grow vertically for a foot or so, then extends horizontally – eventually up to an astonishing five or six leafless metres – before going up again in a profusion of green leaves dotted with tomatoes in varying states of ripeness and shades of green, yellow, orange and red. This method extends the life of the tomato by several months, ensuring more or less year-round production. What efficient capillary systems these tomatoes must have, to get all the water and nutrients from the soil along and up these lengthy stems to the growing tips and the fruit.

The main picking days were Mondays and Thursdays, unless there were urgent orders at other times, or so much ready to be picked that we had to begin the day before and store the vegetables in the large, walk-in chiller overnight – except tomatoes, which were never chilled. Picking was all done by hand, with no tools needed. We picked the tomatoes with the calyx (the green five-pointed 'collar') still on, because they look better, and the condition of the calyx is a good indicator of freshness.

If the tomatoes had been recently sprayed with sulphur to get rid of the pernicious russet mite, it was OK to pick them without the calyx, for ease of washing any sulphur residue off. Sulphur was used only occasionally, and is allowed under Bio-Gro rules as a restricted input. It was one of two sprays Steffan used, the other being neem tree seed oil, which was the backstop when his biological controls failed to keep the various pests in check.

There was little kink in the stalk, about a finger's width above the tomato, where it snapped easily if you pressed it with your thumbnail. The sap of the tomatoes turned our picking hands a dirty shade of greenish yellow, which then became a lurid chartreuse when we washed our hands. It was hard to get rid of the discolouration under the thumbnail, and I became resigned to a semi-permanent stain.

The green runner beans came in all sizes, and we had to discern which ones were big enough to be picked, and which were too big, or too far gone, and were destined either for seed production or simply for the compost heap. Fardenlosa was the main variety, shiny and very long, growing up to 20 centimetres or so. At the end of September we 'strip picked' one glasshouse full of beans: we picked everything, no matter how big or small or dried and shrivelled up. The guys then went through and pulled all the plants out to make way for a new lot. We spent the next couple of days grading the beans into five categories: tiny 'gourmet' beans, first grade, second grade, seed beans that had already dried on the vine, and seed beans that needed more drying.

Cucumbers were perhaps the easiest of the vegetables to harvest. They were the Telegraph variety, and were large and obvious amongst the tall vines. Determining whether they were ready to pick was mostly a matter of judging their size, as with the beans. One could almost feel the cucumber vines breathe out a sigh of relief as another weighty burden was plucked from them.

Eggplants, on the other hand, had rather more subtle clues as to their ripeness: colour was not necessarily an indicator, as there were six or seven varieties in different colours. Some were small and round in creamy parchment white (hence the name eggplant); another variety (Machiaw, sometimes called Asian eggplant here) bore long thin fruit in a pale to vibrant purple occasionally streaked with white; some were white streaked with purple; and some were what most New Zealanders probably think of as the typical eggplant: large and lustrous, in a deep aubergine hue. When ripe, the eggplants developed a swollen 'shoulder' up at the top of the fruit, as though they were trying to burst free of the calyx.

There were several varieties of chilli: habañero (also known as Scotch bonnet), jalapeño, serrano, bird's eye, and fireflame (the only hybrid variety), plus sweet chillies: anaheim, ancho and Hungarian hot wax. Steffan was disappointed with the pollination of the habañeros that year; many were only a centimetre in diameter, too small to be worth picking. He thought that it was probably due to not having enough bumblebees in the glasshouse at pollination time. When picking the chillies, we had to be careful not to rub our eyes – or indeed touch any sensitive membrane – especially when picking the habañeros, which are the hottest chillies in the world. Steffan and Astrid made a delicious chilli chutney from a mixture of chillies, minus the notorious habañero.

All the glasshouse plants were grown in soil with compost added, and more nutrients were piped to them in the 'fertigation' system (irrigation plus fertiliser), including liquid seaweed and EM (effective micro-organisms). Steffan swore by EM, and put it through the fertigation system once a week.

When I first heard about EM it had an aura of mystery, as though it were some sort of magic potion. Then Ian from Sunset Valley Vineyards explained it to me in scientific terms. At the Clean Greenz field day I mentioned before, Mike Daly from the Nature Farming Society, which sells EM mixes on a not-for-profit basis, was there to talk about how it works. It was the discovery of a Japanese horticultural chemist, Teruo Higa, whose work with chemical fertilisers and pesticides in the 1970s involved studying different strains of micro-organisms. He threw out several test batches on the lawn outside and later noticed that one patch of the lawn was doing particularly well. He then studied how different mixes of microbes work together to improve the microbial balance in the soil. Out of this research came EM, which consists of a specific mix of microbes in a solution with organic matter and sugar. According to Steffan, EM gave his plants a real boost; the difference after he started using it was visible. He also sprayed it on his large compost heaps out the back, to assist in the breaking down process.

Despite the extension of life granted by the glasshouses, by early spring many of the plants were beginning to lose vigour and succumb to pests (like whitefly, aphid and mealy bug) more easily. The tired old plants would soon make way for new crops, with a specific rotation system so that each glasshouse got a different crop, which helped against build-ups of pests and diseases. Capsicum, chillies and eggplant were seen as one crop type, and a glasshouse was planted with 700 of these (mostly capsicums), alternated with 700 cucumbers (ie. every second plant was a cucumber). Cucumbers are fast-growing but relatively short-lived, lasting only a few months. When they were finished, the first of the green capsicums were ready, the old cucumbers were removed and capsicums had a growth spurt since they were no longer shaded by cucumbers. The capsicums, chillies and eggplants would last for up to two years, and then when prices were at their low point (autumn), the plants would be taken out.

The next crop would be tomatoes, which were planted every second hole (700). As they grew, Steffan would train two leaders up the strings in the summer, and a single leader in the winter because of the low light. When the tomatoes began to falter, Steffan's small flock of black Cayuga ducks were let in to clean up any pests, and every second hole would be planted with beans until it became predominantly a bean glasshouse. Beans have a reasonably long picking period with two main flushes. When the beans were finished, the houses were emptied out again and cleaned up, and then the cucumber/capsicum combination would start all over again. The tomato/bean combination would be over in a year, while the capsicums lasted two years. A few other crops fitted in between the capsicums, eggplants and chillies, including basil, loofahs, squash and bitter melon (or karela, used in Asian dishes, and apparently a very acquired taste).

Twice we all gathered, workers and wwoofers together, to clean out an entire glasshouse and prepare it for recomposting and replanting. Those were the only times we all worked as a gang; generally we all worked away on different things: planting, harvesting, grading, washing and packing. First, all the plants were taken to the compost heap, then we turned the heating taps off and removed the radiator pipes to one side. These long metal pipes were as thick as my forearm and required three or four of us to lift them. Next, we carefully rolled up the long lengths of black plastic weedmat that covered the entire ground surface in a patchwork, making sure we knew where to replace them; if we put them back the wrong way the holes for plants wouldn't line up with each other or the heating pipes. Then, we made sure the fertigation taps were off and removed pipes and whiskers, and any stray stakes, pins and strings, and let the flock of ducks in overnight for pest control (they were particularly fond of slugs and snails). Finally, the glasshouse was ready for a fresh layer of rich, dark, sweet-smelling compost. One of the boys scooped up loads of compost with the front-end loader and delivered them to the glasshouse door, while the rest of us toiled like the seven dwarves, spading compost into wheelbarrows and tipping it all round the glasshouse, and finally raking it evenly all over before replacing the weedmat and all the pipes.

Almost all of the plants at Clean Greenz were grown from certified organic seed, either saved on the premises, or procured at some cost. Much of the bought seed, although sold by seed companies in New Zealand, was imported from Europe, in particular the Netherlands. The main crop tomatoes were Palmiro and Excel (both are hybrids, and are typically grown in conventional glasshouses). Steffan also grew open pollinated varieties including Big Rainbow, Evergreen and Roma, and just a few plants of other varieties, like Black Krim, which some of his customers at the farmers' market in Blenheim would specifically ask for. Roma, a long Italian cooking tomato, was prone to blossom end rot, although those with only small patches of brown on their bottoms didn't go to waste; we took them into the kitchen and cut off the ends – the rest was usually fine. Evergreen was the next most prevalent to blossom end rot.

While I was there, we planted two different kinds of tomato seeds, which would later be grafted together. We planted several types of chilli seed and Fardenlosa beans, both of which had been saved on the premises. And we planted cucumber seeds, on their sides, as though they were fish swimming. I had had limited success with growing cucumbers from seed in my own garden, and perhaps this was why; I'd always planted them either lying flat, or vertically, hazarding a guess at which end would root and which would shoot.

Steffan didn't always graft the tomatoes as he was not fully convinced that grafted tomatoes were better than non-grafted. Quite often he propagated tomatoes from laterals that he plucked out. According to some organic glasshouse growers, grafting definitely can help reduce soil-borne diseases because disease-resistant rootstocks are used.

The Palmiros were grafted onto a sturdy rootstock (Beaumont) to produce a superior plant. Steffan grew both the rootstock and the scion varieties from seed, one of each in small containers, carefully marked to identify which was rootstock and which was scion. Then when the plants were only about eight centimetres high, Ocky and I grafted the two together in a painstakingly delicate and time-consuming operation involving a razor blade, a steady hand, and a tiny grafting clip to hold the two plants in place until they grew together. When we finished, the two plants were each still rooted in the one pot, but now leaning towards each other, joined in the middle, and with only one set of leaves up top, as we cut off the rootstock's top. Later the scion would be snipped from its own roots, when it had successfully grafted onto the rootstock.

Trays of various seedlings in small pots were thriving in the moist warmth of an improvised plastic tunnelhouse within a little side glasshouse. There was the snake bean, which had a slender pod, smaller than that of the main crop runner bean, twisty like strands of DNA, and with occasional purple marbling over green. The snake bean didn't grow as tall as the runner beans, so we planted it along the sides of the glasshouse where the roof angled down to meet the walls. There were Armenian Yard-long cucumbers, which sounded great but looked like any other cucumber at the seedling stage. There were seedlings of squash, gourds, watermelons and basil. We also took cuttings off some fig boughs that had recently been pruned, and planted them in boxes to be individually potted later and sold at the farmers' market.

Although the glasshouses were the main focus for growing, the whole property was a model of biodiversity and efficient land use. In the strips of soil between the glasshouses there were vegetables like celery and kale, and herbs including thyme and parsley. One strip was a long asparagus bed, and when the tips began to pierce through the soil, picking was a daily chore as the spears shot up with phenomenal speed. If they were left for more than a day or two, they would sneak up, long and leggy, and start their fern phase. Harvesting wasn't an onerous task at all, but required balance, patience and a certain tolerance of cold. One had to squat down most of the time, or bend over the bed to reach spears in the middle, all the while trying to avoid standing on any barely visible baby tips that were just emerging from the earth.

It was often a chilly business, as we did it first thing in the morning to fit in with deliveries, and even if we moved fast, it wasn't exactly an activity to get the blood flowing. We followed the asparagus stems with naked fingers just under the surface of the cold earth, where we cut them at the base with sharp scissors.

Washing and grading took place in the packhouse, in a room with a huge sink with only one tap: cold. Even the cold water felt warm when it first hit my chilled hands as I rinsed the gritty earth off the asparagus. The spears varied from the short and fat to the hugely tall – as long as elbow to fingertip – and skinny. A few were stunted by frost and had whitish, sickly looking tips, often growing in odd shapes like mutants. We couldn't sell the rejects (mainly those that were too tall or skinny) but apart from the frost-damaged ones, most were still edible, and we took them back to the house for a tasty pre-dinner snack.

There was a patch of daffodils that ran the length of one glasshouse, and for two or three weeks we had to pick this small-scale crop every day or two, selecting blooms that hadn't yet fully opened. It was a much easier and more pleasant job than picking asparagus, as our hands didn't touch the earth. Out the back behind the glasshouses there were about 200 cherry trees, and while I was there they slowly, shyly began hanging out their blossom like pretty pale pink bloomers.

There were more vegetables out the back: silverbeet, broccoli, kale and Chinese cabbage, mainly. Most of these were past their best and there was little left to sell, but we got plenty for our own use. Although unaware of it at the time, I had become very anaemic, and was probably unconsciously self-medicating by eating large quantities of iron-rich kale every night. The house recipe for kale as a side dish was simply to chop it up, lightly sautée it in butter with garlic, and add salt, cracked pepper and a dash of lemon juice over it when serving.

Oh, and make sure to remove the thick stalks first. We were eating Raggedy Jack, also known as Russian kale, and Steffan also grew a tall Tuscan variety called palm-tree kale because of its shape.

Down one side of the property there were several chooks in a large run. They were let into the soil strips between glasshouses in between plantings, for weeding, pest control and light tilling duties. In exchange for their work and their eggs, they were fed with organic grain, leftovers and spoiled vegetables. The ducks lived on the other side of the property near a small pond. They were also part of the pest control system, as already described.

Pest control was a major issue, because there aren't so many predators present in glasshouses – no birds for a start – and the lack of wind and the constant warmth can contribute to certain pests increasing exponentially in a short time. Steffan used neem spray, sulphur on the tomatoes occasionally, and had yellow sticky strips hanging here and there for whitefly – although these trapped pests and predators indiscriminately, and occasionally stuck to my hair if I wasn't careful. Biological pest controls at Clean Greenz included predator wasps to control aphids and whitefly, and three different predatory mites to control a range of mites and thrips. Steffan also got in two kinds of ladybirds, one (*Cryptolaemus montrouzieri*) whose main prey was mealy bugs.

Another insect that was crucial to glasshouse production was the bumblebee, and Steffan had to buy some every couple of months in small cardboard box hives. They were critical to the pollination of the tomatoes, capsicums, chillies and aubergine, because low pollination means small fruit, and it appears the higher the seed count, the bigger the fruit. Bumblebees, rather than honey bees, are used in glasshouses because they operate in a wider range of temperatures, are easier to manage, and work well in the confined space because they naturally forage much closer to home.

The produce from Clean Greenz was all sold on the domestic market, and was distributed to organic shops around the country, including the local Casa Organica in Blenheim. Every Saturday from November to March, Steffan also had a stall at the local farmers' market. He and Astrid used to own the Blenheim organic shop with two others, then they sold that business, and Astrid now spends much of her time travelling around New Zealand as a guide for parties of German tourists, and teaches self-defence to girls.

After a couple of weeks, Steffan asked me if I'd like to help with some of his environmental work. Specifically, he wanted someone to organise files on his computer, and put together a couple of email lists. The thing about working in glasshouses is that you can always work in warm and dry conditions, unlike many other farms, where the activities are more dictated by the weather. So it was good to have a change of scene for a bit, and do something familiar. I also helped Steffan organise an organic sector rally against genetic engineering, held outside parliament in Wellington, with a number of speakers including Steffan on behalf of Soil and Health.

The rally was held a couple of weeks before the government was due to lift the moratorium on the commercial growing of genetically engineered crops. Activists against GE from around the country were in overdrive with last-ditch attempts to keep the ban or, at the very least, use the landmark date to highlight the problems we could face if transgenic organisms were released into the environment. Their arguments were compelling: that there was mounting evidence of detrimental effects of GE organisms on the environment and on human health; that co-existence of GE and GE-free crops was a non-sense; and, no matter what the science, that consumer perception and demand would rule the day, with the possibility of New Zealand losing its clean, green reputation and millions of export dollars along with it. Many people also raised ethical and spiritual objections to humans tampering with the building blocks of nature.

The day of the rally dawned overcast and cool, and the crowd wasn't as big as we had hoped (around 200) but there were farmers and growers who had taken time out from the busyness of their spring work, and had come from as far afield as Auckland and Timaru. Some beekeepers turned up in their white suits and veils, complete with smokers (for pacifying bees). There is concern among beekeepers that GE crops could pose a greater threat to bees than the varroa mite does.

Some MPs emerged from the Beehive to address us: not unsurprisingly two Greens, co-leader Jeanette Fitzsimons, and agriculture spokesperson Ian Ewen-Street, who gave us plenty of reasons for keeping New Zealand GE-free; Environment Minister Marian Hobbs, who said any applications for the release of GE into the environment would be closely scrutinised and monitored; and Winston Peters, leader of the New Zealand First Party, who read a statement opposing genetic engineering in the environment. The rally finished on a light note with a humorous speech from a Helen Clark impersonator, complete with a sash proclaiming her 'Monsanto Woman of the Year'.

When the moratorium was lifted it was rather an anti-climax, and to date no-one has applied to grow GE crops commercially, which is a relief to those involved in organics, and probably also to the majority of New Zealanders who expressed opposition to GE crops in poll after poll. I suspect that the ongoing debate about GE in New Zealand, and continued opposition from a majority of the public, has created an unfavourable environment for companies who wish to grow GE crops. There have been field trials, though, and a number of lab experiments with plants, all of which is fairly pointless unless there is an intention to grow GE crops commercially.

After the heady rush of organisation for the rally, it was good to go back to the glasshouses and destress with the repetitive but calming tasks of picking, washing and grading vegetables. It was peaceful there in the still warmth, with the lazy droning of the bumblebees in the background, the faint rustling of plants growing, the barely audible squeaks of glossy eggplants jostling and swelling, and the long, slow blush of ripening tomatoes.

16

KAIKOURA

'We've got a bit of rock picking to do; would you be happy about that?' Doug Eaton the farmer asked me when I rang to see if I could come wwoofing at his place. There was a pause. Had I heard right?

'Rock picking?' I queried blankly. This was supposed to be a dairy farm.

'It's not that bad,' he assured me, laughing. 'There are a couple of paddocks I'm improving by picking out all the rocks so there's more pasture and it's easier on the cows.'

'Ah, sure, I can do that,' I said, with 'try anything once' bluster.

'They're not that big,' he promised.

Doug's farm, Woodgrove, was on a terrace set up and back from the Kaikoura coast, the gently undulating pastures still sprouting a few renegade native trees, notably kowhai. The farm looked out over pastures and a narrow ribbon of sea to the distant eastern horizon, and behind it the foothills of the Kaikoura ranges, thickly clad in scrub, rose sharply. No pre-dawn starts for the wwoofers here. Doug had sharemilkers to do the milking, though he always got up early himself as well to do various chores. Most of the farm was run conventionally, but the large home garden, which included vegetables, fruit trees and a pond surrounded with native plantings, was organic.

Helen, a physical education teacher from England, arrived just in time to become part of the rock-picking brigade. The three of us would go over in the mornings, Doug driving the tractor and Helen and me jolting along on the huge flatbed trailer. The work wasn't too onerous, and in fact gave my arms a much-needed workout.

'Who needs the gym?' I asked no one in particular, pumping a rock up and down in each hand, and then hurling them onto the trailer. On a fine spring day, with such a grand view, fresh air in the lungs and the body feeling fit and healthy, there was nothing better than picking rocks. But after five days of it, when a bleak sea fog rolled up, my imagination hatched a story about stone pickers on some far-flung, desolate island, like the Shetlands of my Jamieson forebears, destined for generations of back-breaking work under the lash of cruel feudal overlords.

Doug's cellphone trilled, startling me out of my dismal reverie.

'Hello … yes … where are you?' Doug's voice frowned, and I could hear the tinny jabber of what sounded like a foreign wwoofer on the other end of the line.

'I'm out on the farm right now,' he said carefully. 'You ring me later when I come home.' And then slower: 'You telephone my house tonight.'

More painful sentence fragments, and the voice on the other end rose in pitch and volume, until Doug finally understood that there were two wwoofers from the Czech Republic who were actually at his house right now; they'd just bowled up without ringing beforehand. Doug glanced at his watch.

'I suppose it's lunchtime anyway,' he said. 'Let's go and check out these Czechs.'

He seemed a little doubtful, perhaps on the back foot by having been ambushed, as it were. There to greet us at the gate were two burly blokes and their wheels: a car towing a caravan, and a motorbike. As soon as our host clapped eyes on them his face lit up. They were two good keen men, one of them especially big and brawny. Doug's face was easy to read: a new team of rock pickers!

It was good timing indeed. Despite my newfound muscles and Helen's pre-existing occupational fitness, the two of us were quite ready for other duties, and were happy to weed the vege garden, mow the lawns, mulch the fruit trees with lawn clippings, and make marmalade out of the surfeit of grapefruit. There were a number of citrus trees and even a couple of banana trees – the only ones I'd seen growing in the South Island.

Jakob and David, the Czechs, seemed to have boundless energy for work, and set off cheerfully in the mornings tanked up on porridge for a few hours' stone picking. In their 'afternoons off', they mowed the lawns, hosed the outside of the house and washed the windows, and tidied up the woodpile and the flotsam and jetsam that might one day be useful that had accumulated on the back porch. They weren't the least bit interested in the tourist activities of the area: whale watching, swimming with dolphins or visiting the local caves, winery or lavender farm. The only trips they made off the farm were to go and buy beer, or take it in turns to ride Jakob's motorbike cross country up into the hills and valleys above the farm.

'What did you do today?' Jakob enquired, after they had been stone picking for two or three days, and Helen and I had been doing a variety of tasks around the house and garden.

'Well, I made marmalade, did some weeding, mulched some of the fruit trees ...' I trailed off. It didn't sound like a great deal, and there wasn't much to show for it apart from a few jars of rather stiff grapefruit marmalade, and a slightly tidier vegetable patch, not that anyone probably noticed. But one could spend a whole day weeding. And Jakob hadn't seemed to notice that Helen and I did the dishes pretty regularly and helped with meals. Why did I feel the need to justify myself, anyway? As long as we worked our hours and Doug was happy, that was all that mattered. But it remained a source of tension between the 'workaholic' guys and us 'slackers'.

In contrast to the Czech boys, the English wwoofer Helen was keen to fit in as many tourist activities as possible, and I was happy to be her companion and explore this part of the country properly for the first time. Just south of Kaikoura on the main highway is a large sign saying simply 'Cave', which I've passed dozens of times, but never even been curious about, let alone visited the cave. Now that I had all the time in the world, there was no ferry sailing to catch, no impending dusk keeping me on the road, I could stop and check out those places I'd been meaning to go to, and come across others I didn't even know existed. The cave was nothing outstanding, but was a good example of a limestone cave, with the usual formations like stalactites and stalagmites, was handy to the road, and for our $10 we got a knowledgeable and personable guide.

One day Helen and I arranged to take the day off to go whale watching. I'd never seen a whale, and got up at 5.30 with a childlike sense of excitement. We drove down to the whale watch centre in the clear blue dawn of what promised to be a glorious day. The centre is a modern building, run by the local Ngai Tahu people and employing several of them, and has all the things we've become familiar with since tourism has become New Zealand's major industry: shops with postcards, souvenirs and the latest range of possum-merino garments, a café with a noisy coffee machine, and in a darkened alcove, a video that was compulsory viewing for all whale watchers, containing safety information as well as some background on the whales and other wildlife.

After the video we were bussed to South Bay where we boarded the boat, a launch with comfy seats inside. Those who were prone to seasickness were advised to sit near the back, so Helen and I, not feeling terribly confident about our stomachs, made our way down the aisle. There was a state-of-the-art screen that showed the location of the boat relative to the shore, and the depth of the water, which increased rapidly as we sailed over the shallow strip of seabed close to the shore, and found ourselves suddenly above the deep trench that makes this area a good place to see whales. As the guide rattled off all sorts of fascinating facts, I was mesmerised by the screen, and watched as if from above as the boat inched steadily south and then out to sea. While we sped away from the shore, the guide advised us to stay inside; another crew member was assigned to whale-spotting duty and would let us know as soon as there was anything to see.

For ages, nothing much happened. We just kept heading towards the horizon: a thin line of deep blue that separated the forget-me-not colour of the sky from the cobalt sea. The occasional seabird glided past the window and I got the distinct and strange feeling of being a captive animal being curiously observed by another. Then the spotter saw a whale quite a distance away and the captain accelerated to pursue it. The launch was no match for this whale, unfortunately, so we gave up after a while. It was October, a time when the few whales that are around are mainly adolescent males ranging far and wide in search of girlfriends.

My stomach, which until now had been quite settled, so that my fear of seasickness had subsided, now began to protest. The speed of the boat over the choppy waves, which were bigger now that we were further from the shore, were starting to create internal waves, and that hideous feeling, that doomed certainty of vomiting. The seat pockets in front of us were well stocked with sick bags, and I clutched one in anticipation. Helen was looking rather green, and succumbed to seasickness shortly before I did. Relief was immediate, and at that point the launch slowed right down and we were all allowed out on deck for a welcome breather. There was little to see except for some low-flying mollymawks, perhaps the same ones that had been peering in at us before, and a few seagulls. Apart from that, the sea seemed strangely empty, a blue desert stretching to the far horizon. On the shore side we had a spectacular view of the Kaikoura Ranges, their snowy peaks glinting in the sun.

We had travelled much further from the shore than most whale watch trips, and spent the best part of an hour out there before the captain decided it was time to give up. There were simply no whales to be seen. Most of the passengers were resigned to the fact by now, and judging by the numbers reaching for the sick bags, a good many were keen to get back on shore. The journey back was subdued, and the guide apologised and said we would be refunded 80 per cent of our money.

Back at Woodgrove Helen and I both had a nap to recover from that horrible shakiness of motion sickness. The Czech boys were still full of beans, choosing that afternoon to clean the entire outside of the house by hosing it down, so that I woke groggily to the sound of spray on the windows, with the impression of still being afloat.

'You no work hard,' said Jakob later on. He seemed almost scathing of us taking a day off to do something as frivolous as whale watching.

I tried to explain to him that the wwoofing deal generally only required wwoofers to work four or five hours a day, and that we had worked extra hours on other days so we could take the day off to go whale watching, but he still shook his head at our monumental laziness.

Jakob was keen to cook a Czech meal for us all, and the next day was fossicking around in the large chest freezer, trying to find some suitable meat. He gradually lowered his large torso into the frozen depths, tossing out meat, bread and unidentifiable packages in his search for the perfect meat. When he had almost disappeared, and nothing could be seen but his legs, we heard a muffled cry of triumph, and Jakob emerged from the freezer, victoriously holding aloft in both hands a large piece of meat. It took me a minute to identify it, partly because it wasn't what I had been expecting: a pig's head.

'This good!' Jakob enthused. 'I make very good roast pig's head for dinner.'

'It's been in the freezer for a while,' said Doug, 'but I'm sure it will be OK. I've been wondering what to do with it.'

I reminded Jakob that I was a vegetarian.

'You not try my meal?' he asked.

'Sorry, but no. I don't eat meat.'

'Neither do I,' chimed in Helen, who seemed to have become an instant convert to vegetarianism since pig's head was on the menu.

'It sounds delicious,' Doug reassured Jakob, not that he seemed to need reassuring, as he approached the task of cooking with his characteristic ebullience. He set aside the head to defrost overnight, and roasted it in a slow oven all afternoon the next day, filling the house with the overpowering smell of meat cooking: a hearty, savoury aroma, but to me, almost sickening. He deputised David to wash and peel potatoes and chop garlic for an accompanying dish, while he created a stuffing, and occasionally opened the oven to baste the head with its own juices.

As dinnertime drew nearer I popped into the kitchen to see how things were going, and decided to cook a separate dish for us vegetarians, using some leftover chickpeas in a simple curry.

'What you doing?' demanded Jakob. 'I make dinner tonight.'

'Well, Helen and I can't eat the pig's head so I'm making a vegetarian dish,' I replied.

'No, I make something special for you. You wait and see.'

'Thanks Jakob, but look, I've nearly finished making this now, so we can have it as well.'

Dinnertime was unforgettable. The menu consisted of a yummy fried potato and garlic dish, a watery concoction of boiled apple and cabbage (the 'special' dish for us vegetarians), my chickpea curry, red wine or beer. But the centrepiece (and talking point for months afterwards, according to Doug) was of course the pig's head, the crowning glory an apple stuck in its mouth. Jakob proudly carried the head to the table, and the men tucked into the pig's cheeks with relish while Doug's teenage daughter Claire, Helen and I just looked at the thing with bug eyes, our mouths zipped firmly shut. No morsels of this delicacy would pass our lips, nor would we say anything negative about it. After all, Jakob had slaved all afternoon to prepare this Czech feast for us.

The next day was my last at Woodgrove, and as I was packing things into the car Jakob stomped about, scowling.

'Why you no respect me?' he demanded.

I was taken aback. 'I respect you. What do you mean?'

'We cook a meal for you and you come into kitchen while we are there. You should leave us alone.'

'I'm sorry ...' Was there some cultural rule operating here that I was unaware of?

'You no like our food.'

'Yes I did. It was delicious.'

'Why you cook something? Is insult to chef.'

'I wanted to contribute to the meal too. And to have some protein in my dinner.'

He grumbled for a while but eventually, after apologies on my part for any unintended offence, we came to a truce and shook hands on it. I felt relieved; I didn't want to leave on bad terms.

17
HAZELS

A cloudless day in late spring. A soft breeze. A road winding up through bush to the Geraldine Downs, a small plateau above Geraldine township. Vistas of the Canterbury Plains stretching out below, of the sea merging into the horizon in the far distance, and inland the snowy peaks of the Southern Alps glistening, picture postcard clear.

I drove slowly, muttering the instructions of how to get there under my breath: right, right again, then left. There was the usual collection of rural letterboxes on the corner of the road, large, sturdy, no-nonsense affairs, one big enough to house a small dog, if it cared to jump that high.

Further down the road was the driveway I was looking for. The words 'Totaranui Farm' were carved into the wooden farm gate, although age and lichen had rendered them somewhat indistinct. The driveway was lined with native trees and curved up to a house built of Oamaru stone, the limestone common in the South Canterbury and North Otago area. A golden retriever hurtled towards me, all bark and wag, colliding into me with the clumsiness of a puppy. Not far behind, his human strode across the yard.

'Hello Philippa!' Jim Jolly hailed me. He was a friendly fellow with twinkling, crinkling eyes, a neat beard and an amused smile.

'I see you've met Sam,' said Jim, pulling the overly enthusiastic dog off me. 'Please excuse him – he can't see very well so he tends to bump into things. And people. Well, come on in. You're just in time for morning tea.'

I had met Jim and his wife Eleanor at a Soil and Health conference in Ashburton a couple of years before, and they'd been on my 'must visit' list for some time. I wanted to get some experience on a nut farm, and Totaranui seemed to be the only certified organic farm in New Zealand that concentrated solely on growing hazelnuts.

Jim led me inside and introduced me to another wwoofer staying there, a Japanese man called Oto, and then after a quick cup of tea Jim excused himself – he was off to an Environment Court hearing on behalf of the Tree Crops Association.

'Sorry, but I'll be back in a couple of hours. Oto will show you around,' said Jim as he put on a tie. 'Would you mind working with him weeding and mulching the hazels?'

'Of course not! That's what I'm here for,' I replied.

Jim left and then Oto showed me to the barn to get some tools and gloves. The garden tools were neatly stacked in a 44-gallon drum, and there were workshop tools hanging in their designated places on a large wallboard. A couple of empty outlines gave away the identity of the missing tools: a spanner and a pair of pliers. Lengths of used baling twine hung like a smooth fringe from a rafter.

'Wow, it's really tidy,' I commented, thinking of some of the archaic sheds I'd come across, packed with years of accumulated bits and pieces that might one day be useful, if they hadn't rusted, ossified, or spontaneously composted in the meantime, and didn't require an archaeological dig to retrieve them.

'Yes,' Oto agreed. 'Jim and Eleanor are blood type A.' It seemed to be a non sequitur, and I looked at him blankly for a second, then remembered that the Japanese look to blood types rather than astrological signs as an indication of personality type.

'Blood type A people are tidy and organised,' Oto explained. 'Type O are friendly and everybody likes them. Type B are *wagamama* – they do whatever they like.'

When we'd gathered together the tools we needed, Oto took me to the block of hazels where he had been working. It was a large, gently sloping paddock, with a nor'west aspect, and row upon row of four-year-old hazel saplings stretching down the slope towards a shelterbelt of gums and native trees. The hazels were about one to one-and-a-half metres; most were sturdy and strong, but the odd one was still rather spindly. By this time of year, November, they were in full leaf, although here and there the leaves bore dry, brown patches of windburn from the ravages of the notorious Canterbury norwesters.

In this block there were several hundred of the popular Whiteheart variety, and every seventh row was a pollinator variety. Hazels have male and female flowers on the one tree, but by some mysterious quirk of nature they never flower at the same time, so other varieties that flower at the right time must be planted nearby to ensure fertilisation.

Our main job was weeding around the hazels, a springtime task to get rid of the first flush of weeds that would be competing with the trees for nutrients (affecting the younger trees particularly as they had small root systems and were still becoming established), followed by mulching to suppress further weed growth and keep the ground from drying out from the scorching norwesters. We pulled up the thick grass and weeds mostly by hand, although with the likes of dock or thistle we used a hand tool to dig them out roots and all if possible, or cut them off at the base if they proved too tough, or were so close to the trees that digging them out might disturb the hazel roots.

A few weeks before, Jim had mown between the rows; the cut grass and herbal ley was flung to the sides of the rows where it had dried out and now we used it as mulching material around the hazels. Like other organic tree croppers, Jim and Eleanor sowed a mixture of species in the avenues between the hazel rows: chicory, red and white clover and lucerne. There were also various grasses and weeds, including plantain, dock, thistle, nettle, mallow and willow weed. Their practice was to mow the rows alternately, leaving every second one to grow as habitat for the beneficial insects like hoverflies and lacewings that eat aphids. In some seasons aphids proliferated, but the Jollys relied on their 'beetle banks', and on their herbal ley to encourage predator insects, and have never sprayed the aphids.

Most of the four-year-old trees still had their protective plastic box-type sleeves, anchored with bamboo stakes, which we removed from all but the puniest trees, as most of them had big enough trunks to stand firm in strong winds. The routine was: pull out the stakes, unhook the flaps on the box, open it up like a coat and take it off, strip off any leaves growing on the trunk, check for scale insects and use digital control (thumb and fingers) to eliminate them, snip off any suckers growing from the base of the tree, weed around the tree, and then mulch.

Scale insects were one of the few pests. They are cute little purple bugs about the size of a ladybird that live on the trunks and branches. When you squash them they explode in a puff of white powder, leaving behind a reddish shell. It's like popping miniature bubble wrap, and quite satisfying. My usual qualms about killing animals dissolved because of the size of the insect and the fact that they were a pest and could affect my hosts' livelihood. If there was a bad infestation, they seemed to inhibit the growth of the trees slightly, and cause some damage to the bark, but the digital control was very effective in getting rid of them.

When Eleanor came home that first evening from her job in Timaru she breezed into the kitchen, laden down with shopping, her blonde hair windblown. She welcomed me warmly, offered me and Oto a glass of wine, then immediately set about preparing dinner, chatting as she worked, and eliciting our help with the preparations. A consummate multi-tasker, Eleanor was never idle, and always had a number of projects on the go, including sowing seeds and planting vegetables in the home garden, packing and dispatching hazelnuts, working alongside us wwoofers amongst the hazel trees, and at that time of year, making the Christmas cake and organising presents.

That night she cooked a delicious vegetarian stew with hazelnuts – it was the first time I had eaten hazels in a savoury dish. Dinnertime was a good time for a catch-up on the day's events and for lively discussions about organics. I didn't want to pester my hosts, but my curiosity and thirst for knowledge inevitably burst out into questions. Fortunately, like most of my hosts, Jim and Eleanor were happy to share their knowledge and were interested in my wwoofing experiences too. They told me how in 1993 they had left their city life in Wellington to pursue a life closer to the land. Initially they had other crops, including strawberries and garlic, but found that the hazels were enough to concentrate on. Not all of their income was off the farm; Eleanor worked part-time as a librarian, and Jim, a former DOC scientist, continued to do environmental consultancy work.

In keeping with the philosophy of organics, there was a great deal of biodiversity on the farm, despite there being one main crop. Jim and Eleanor planted a eucalyptus woodlot, and hundreds of native trees along their boundaries and as shelterbelt strips between paddocks. They had a small flock of 27 sheep, a few geese and their own home vegetable garden and orchard.

Their approach to farming clearly involved much careful planning, starting with the selection of the site, which was slightly sloping and north-east-facing. They had about 2000 hazelnut trees on their 81-hectare property. In 1994 they planted the first block of hazels, three years later the next paddock was planted, and in 2000 the third and last lot were planted. Expanding gradually like this was invaluable for management, allowing Jim and Eleanor to get used to their new lifestyle, and learn from each planting so they didn't make the same mistakes with the next lot. And as their growing, harvesting and marketing experience increased, so did their crop yield as each successive planting started bearing. First they planted several varieties: Butler, Ennis, Lansing and Madame Thompson. The last planting is all Whiteheart, a variety selected in New Zealand that is the most popular variety in this country, particularly in demand as a roasted hazel, and for baking. And there are also the pollinator varieties, which produce nuts too but they're small and not as tasty as other hazels, and of no value commercially.

The soil at Totaranui is a heavy clay, which becomes wet in winter and hard and dry in summer. The Jollys humped and hollowed the ground at first and put in some ditches for drainage. Because the soil held moisture well there was less need for irrigation, but they had to be careful of compacting the soil, and wait until it dried out before using the mower, for example.

Oto and I began work every morning by 8.30, working through until lunch at around 1.00, after which we'd sometimes go back and do a bit more work, or have the afternoon off. Later we'd pitch in with the dishes after dinner, or help cook the meal. One night Oto and I made sushi, and it turned out that he'd only made it a couple of times before so he had to be the sushi sous-chef and follow my instructions.

When Eleanor wasn't working in town she would often busy herself with household chores or vegetable gardening first thing in the morning, then bring a picnic basket down with morning tea and biscuits for us all to eat in the shade of a shelterbelt. After morning tea she'd carry on weeding and mulching with us until lunchtime. Jim would be around doing various tasks like fixing the irrigation, spraying one of the hazel blocks with a mixture including fish fertiliser and EM, or working in the office. One or other host was usually around if we needed to consult them about our work. No matter how explicit a host's instructions are about any particular task, as soon as they're out of sight and earshot, there are inevitably questions that come up as the wwoofer begins work. If the host is nearby, they can answer questions and keep an eye on the wwoofers to start with and make sure they are doing things right.

Harvest time is in the autumn, from March to May, varying a little from year to year. The Jollys laid down long strips of netting to catch the nuts, which were then dried in a custom-built loft in the barn on shelves of wire netting. The Jollys mainly sold a mix of their different varieties of nuts, generally in the shell, as table nuts for eating rather than for further processing. There were plenty of customers: organic shops and wholesalers, and some individuals who bought in bulk.

A few times I helped Eleanor pack up sacks of nuts for dispatch. We brought the sacks over from the barn to the nut-packing room to do a quality control before packing.

'Could you go through this lot, and take out any that have cracked shells?' Eleanor asked. We spread out baskets and containers to hold the nuts. The shells were glossy and handsome, with fine stripes in several shades of chestnut, gold and brown. Only the odd one needed to be discarded.

'Here, crack some open and check the kernels,' she said, handing me a sturdy wooden nutcracker that resembled a large stapler with the jaws of an alligator and two shining rows of metal teeth.

'These are all fine,' I pronounced, after sampling a few nuts. Eleanor liked to maintain a high standard of appearance as well as taste, and preferred to err on the side of caution when it came to quality. Almost all of them seemed to be fertilised; Eleanor, with some kind of sixth sense, picked out just a couple that were empty shells. We worked on quietly for a while, the only sound being the percussive roll of each new handful scooped up for inspection. The task became mesmerising and I had the strange sensation of seeing both the wood and the trees – seeing each nut as an individual, but also as one of the mass of golden brown woody marbles.

The typical shape is more or less spherical with a peaky point on top, but there are differences depending on the variety. Butler is longer rather than round, almost oblong. The Lansings were the largest nuts, with some shells as big as small chestnuts. The Whiteheart nuts were usually the smallest.

Eleanor tried to educate me about the flavour differences too, but that would have required a longer apprenticeship than the two weeks I stayed there. Most days I ate some hazels fresh from the shell, cracked with the alligator nutcracker. Eleanor used the nuts occasionally in meals, and kept a tall jar in the kitchen stocked with crunchy, flavourful roasted hazels. She had a number of hazel recipes, including a delicious homemade ice-cream, and roasted hazels coated in a mix of sugar and spices, which she made as a Christmas treat.

Over the past few decades it has become more common to buy shelled nuts (i.e. nuts out of the shell). Perhaps this is due in part to commercial pressures: shelled nuts take up less space, and the quality of the nuts is more obvious to the eye. The Jollys preferred to sell them in the shell, to keep them fresh for longer, but shelled them if asked, using their electric shelling machine. Nature has provided nuts with their own protective cover to keep them airtight and away from moisture, mould spores and other things that would deteriorate the quality of the nut and the freshness of the oil within. Hazels contain vitamin E and folate, and are good for the heart.

As well as hazels, there were a few chestnut trees at Totaranui. One of them was being affected by phytophthera, a fungus present in most soils, which causes dieback, so Jim injected it with a solution containing phosphorous acid. I thought that wasn't allowed – certainly the organic avocado growers can't inject it into their trees the way non-organic growers do – but Jim said it was permitted as a restricted substance on application to Bio-Gro. Fortunately for the Jollys, hazels are generally resistant to phytophthera.

One day Eleanor was working in the vegetable garden, with Sam for company. The two rams had been in the next-door paddock for a while and she decided to let them into the small orchard block between the paddock and the garden, so they could hoe into the cow parsley, which they loved, that grew wild underneath the fruit trees. The fence between the orchard and garden didn't run all the way along; there was an open area at the bottom of the garden, but Eleanor thought she could keep an eye on them while she worked. I was nearby weeding and mulching hazels, and for a while a bucolic peace reigned.

Then all of a sudden a yelping and a yelling broke out.

'Help! Stop! Get off!' I heard Eleanor's voice above the barking and squealing and came running to see what had happened. The rams had come through into the vegetable garden and one of them was butting Sam. Eleanor rescued Sam, who had obviously got a real fright, and we spent the next quarter of an hour tracking the rams through the tall cow parsley and orchard undergrowth to try to flush them back through into the yard.

'Poor Sam,' said Eleanor. 'He probably didn't see them and got a real fright.'

Several times I took Sam and his mother Abby for walks, usually just up the road to the mailbox. Sam had a ball that he liked to play with, or rather, he had several balls, all the same chewed rubber, bright orange or pink, but the colour meant nothing to him. He could only see the ball while it was moving, and once it stopped, he relied on his nose to find it, even if it was right in front of him. He wasn't very happy without a ball, and liked to take one with him wherever he went. But he was forever losing balls so we had to keep a sharp eye on them.

Abby was a bit of a liability in the hazel blocks. She liked to hunt lizards in the mulch underneath the hazels, which would have been fine, except that there were irrigation hoses running the length of the rows, often slightly buried and therefore not visible. Abby had already punctured pipes several times and we had to be vigilant if she accompanied us into the hazel blocks.

On the odd rainy day we couldn't carry on with the weeding and mulching, but there was plenty to keep us occupied until the weather cleared up again. One wet day we were assigned to clean up the barn. And I thought it was already tidy! We started sorting out all the bamboo stakes and plastic boxes that we'd removed from the youngest hazels. The stakes came from Jim and Eleanor's own stand of bamboo. Many could be saved for reuse, but quite a few had to be thrown out, as they had begun to split or rot, or had snapped into smaller pieces, which could be used as kindling. We also sorted the plastic tree boxes into keep, throw-out and to-be-repaired piles.

What looked like neatly stacked bales of hay in the back of the shed had in one corner, on closer inspection, been home to some rats – no wonder Abby had been sniffing around in there. There was a smelly mess of scraps of paper, short twists of twine and other unidentified nesting material that we swept up and chucked out. Several bales were falling apart. Eleanor and I used them as mulch around some of the older hazels, transporting them one or two at a time in a wheelbarrow, then pouring some sweet molasses-scented EM on each bale before pitchforking it out around the trees.

The two older plantings of hazels were mulched using a system that Jim and Eleanor had perfected over the years. The rows were covered in long strips of black plastic weedmat, a strip on either side of the trees, overlapped down the middle to make a strip more than a metre wide, and held down against the wind by tyres, and pinned around the edges. The weedmat suppresses the weeds by blocking out the light, and even burns potential weeds and seeds by absorbing the sun's heat.

One row in four is covered with weedmat, which is rotated every few weeks to prevent the ground underneath becoming dried, cracked and lifeless. We weeded and mulched the exposed rows and then put the weedmats from the next-door row on top of the mulch. This system made weed control much less labour-intensive under the established trees, compared with the young trees that had not graduated to that system yet.

Another morning dawned drizzly with no sign of clearing.

'It's a bit wet for you to be weeding and mulching today,' said Jim. 'But it's not too bad out there. How would you like to count all the trees for me? I need a tally of each block.'

'Sure,' I said. 'I'll just put on my gumboots and raincoat.'

Jim explained that he was going to be applying some boron, and needed to know the number of trees so he could accurately work out how much boron he needed. Since his last count there had been the odd tree that had died, particularly amongst the young saplings.

I set out into the grey day, quite content to have a morning walk through the trees, confident that counting was an easy task. But as I soon found out, it wasn't as simple as standing at the top of each paddock and counting the trees in the rows that stretched down the slope before me. The further away trees seemed to merge into each other; certainly their foliage became one indistinct green mass, and even the trunks presented a distant thicket. To be absolutely sure of the number, I had to stand in the middle of each row and count the trunks above and below, and make a careful note of the numbers.

Having forgotten to put on waterproof overpants, I tried to avoid the long, bedraggled grass of every second row, but still managed to come back to the house with my jeans absolutely soaked. What a simple joy it was to return to a cosy house where the woodstove blazed and pumped hot water through the radiators, and a pot of tea awaited me on the table.

THE STAFF OF LIFE

The Canterbury Plains: a vast expanse of flat land, covered in rich alluvial soil deposited over millennia by the network of braided rivers that weave their way from the Southern Alps to the Pacific Ocean. Hot summers, cold winters and a dry atmosphere, sheltered from the prevailing westerly rain by our highest and longest mountain range, which runs like a backbone down the South Island.

Canterbury has been called the bread basket of New Zealand, because the environment is good for growing grains, although in recent years the grain-growing area has diminished in favour of dairy farms, in particular, and we are increasingly importing grains and flour, notably from Australia. This is madness, I think, because it moves us in the opposite direction from self-sufficiency, and puts our food security at risk because of the ongoing drought conditions across the Tasman.

I had heard of just four organic grain farms in New Zealand, only one of which was listed in the WWOOF book: Milmore Downs, a 320-hectare farm tucked away amidst rolling hills near the hamlet of Scargill, roughly midway between Amberley and Cheviot. In winter the freezing mountain air pools in this frosty pocket and the thermometer plummets several degrees below zero, but in summer it's battered by nor'west gales and the temperature soars to the late 30s. I arrived in late April, when the weather was still sometimes mild and sunny but increasingly turning cold and frosty.

Milmore Downs was well known in the organic farming community, and the owners, Ian and Gita Henderson, were stalwarts of the biodynamic movement in New Zealand. The farm had belonged to

Ian's father, who ran it as a conventional sheep farm. Ian and Gita converted it to biodynamics and the farm became Demeter certified in 1983. As well as running sheep and cattle, they also grew grains: wheat, barley, rye, oats and spelt (which Ian and Gita called by its German name, dinkel). They also grew lentils, various green crops for fertilisation or stock feed, and smaller-scale crops just for the family, like potatoes and apples. By autumn the grain had all been harvested and stored in silos, in sacks in a large shipping container, and in bins in the mill.

Ian took me on a drive around the farm to show me around. Winter crops of rye and dinkel were already up and sprouted, several centimetres high, clothing the earth in soft, lush green; there were paddocks sown with green manure, and others in herbal ley with chicory, plantain, clovers, crane's bill, shepherd's purse and various grass species, including tall fescue, brome and cocksfoot.

One paddock was covered in lucerne stubble, and the whole field was strung all over with spider webs: thin threads crossing horizontally between the plants. They were shimmering, moving and shining in the westerly sun, looking like row on row of fence-wire stretching off into the distance. It was magical. Ian stopped the ute so we could get out and see it. Two other paddocks were sown in green manure: one in oats and lucerne, and another in oats and tick beans (which Gita also had a patch of in the home vege garden). The green manure would later be ploughed in, the oats returning carbon, and the lucerne and tick beans fixing nitrogen from the air into the soil.

The Hendersons didn't use compost at all, except in the home garden, relying instead on their rotation of sheep, cows and grains, on animal and green manures, and on the biodynamic preparations for fertility. On one part of the farm where the soils were richer and heavier it was a seven-year rotation, with four years in pasture and three years in grains. On the other part of the farm, with lighter soil, the rotation was even longer – 10 years – with seven years in pasture and three in grains.

There were several houses and buildings on the farm. One house was occupied by a farm worker, Ian's mother Ngaire lived in another house, Ian and Gita lived in a two-storey wooden house they had built, and Gita's mother was in a small house nearby. Their son Matthew, in his early 20s, was at home at that time and helping out on the farm. The wwoofer quarters were near the yards, and consisted of three bedrooms in one building, next to another building that was the remains of the old farmhouse, now reduced to just a kitchen/living room and bathroom, with a long-drop toilet out the back.

The area around the yards was the hub of farm activity. There were sheep yards and a shearing shed, a large implement shed, grain silos and mill rooms. Nearby were the tractor shed, hay barn, chook house, dog kennels, killing shed, cow bail and storerooms. The building closest to the wwoofers' quarters housed a large hulling machine and, in an adjacent room, one of the Zentrofan mills. The advantage of the Zentrofan was that it could grind whole grains very finely, so one could get the nutritional benefit of the whole grain as well as having a flour that was light and suitable for baking.

The other millhouse had the rolling machine in one room, to roll the oats in, and the room next-door housed another Zentrofan mill, plus bins of grains and flours, and all the weighing and packing equipment. All these areas had to be kept clean, tidy and mouse-free. Doors shut at all times! Mouse-hunts at the slightest sign of a dropping! Fortunately, this was seldom. Sweeping, vacuuming and wiping down surfaces had to be done from time to time to keep everything clean, as a fine film of flour would build up. There were white lab coats to go over your clothes if you didn't want to be dusted with a fine layer of flour, masks to prevent 'miller's lung', which I wore if I was in there for any length of time, and earmuffs to wear while any of the milling machinery was going. Gumboots and shoes had to be removed at the door, and there were clogs or slippers to wear inside.

Gradually I became used to the different sounds: the rhythmic pulsing of the Zentrofans, and the loud crushing sound of the rolling machine, which fortunately was only on for short periods of time.

Twice a week orders of grains and flour were dispatched, to organic shops and individual customers. Weighing out the different grains and flours, packing, labelling and stacking them ready for the courier to collect were satisfying jobs, appealing to my liking for order and precision. It was good to have a change of scene from outdoor work, and could be done when it was raining, but on cold mornings I preferred to be outside doing something active to get my blood moving, like feeding out to the animals.

The mill was lined with posters in German and Dutch promoting biodynamics, and in the wwoofers' living room was a poster with different types of labelled grain attached to it. Gradually I came to distinguish the different grains as I scooped them into bags or poured them from sacks into storage barrels: the golden colour of dinkel, the paler barley, the longer, pointed kernels of oats.

A truck came by one day to collect a large grain order. This was transferred directly from the silo to the back of the truck by way of a long tube with an auger inside. As the auger rotated, its corkscrew form drew the grain up the tube and deposited it out the top onto the truck.

It was autumn, and time to spray the biodynamic preparation 501, a silica spray, made of finely ground quartz crystal that had been packed into cow horns and buried for six months or so over the summer. While preparation 500 is used to enliven the life forces within the soil, as described earlier, 501 increases the effectiveness of the forces of light from the sun and other heavenly bodies, thus stimulating plant growth and health. It also has a particularly beneficial effect on the seed, improving it with each generation. Of course grain is the seed of the plant – and the main crop of Milmore Downs.

Mixing and spraying was done in the morning, as long as it was fine. Because of the size of the farm, it made sense to do the mixing by machine, otherwise we would all be tired out hand-mixing for several mornings in a row. There were two 44-gallon copper drums of water standing side by side on a platform near the yards. Above each drum was a horizontal wheel with mixing arms coming down off it, and the wheels were fitted with belts attached to a machine (powered by electricity) that made them rotate first one way for several seconds, and then the other. This created the desired vortex in the mixture, and then chaos as it changed to the other direction. Ian got up before dawn to heat up the water, which was done with gas. According to biodynamics, the water into which the preparations are stirred should be lukewarm, preferably rainwater, and should not be heated by electricity, but instead by fire, gas or the sun.

On the first morning of spraying, I was awoken by a new noise: the hum of the mixing machines. While the machines did their thing I helped Ian clean out the spraying gear, by hosing water into the tank and spray lines to get rid of any residual gunk and traces of the previous spray (500). When the mixing was finished, Ian siphoned the 501 into the spray tank, which was hooked up to the tractor, and set off to spray a couple of six-hectare paddocks. For several mornings in a row Ian continued this procedure until he had sprayed the whole farm. It was a sight to behold him driving slowly up and down the paddocks, silhouetted in the early morning sun, the light making rainbows in the fine spray mist.

After the morning's chores, there was lunch to look forward to: Gita's freshly baked bread, made with their own dinkel milled in the Zentrofan, not as light and fluffy as white bread, nor as heavy as ordinary wholemeal flour, but just the right combination of soft and springy. For the two months of my stay I ate it every day and never tired of it.

19

THE HUNGRY SOIL

In these lush temperate isles, many of us take for granted the fertility of our soils. This land gave us rich timber resources and then, after we cut down most of the forest and started farming, it gave us meat and milk, much more than our small population could eat.

Sheep and cows eat grass, which is produced from soil. Then we go and export their meat. What are the effects of this, of what amounts to the wholesale export of our topsoil? Where is the gain to our land? What are we putting back into the land? Of course, we've been using someone else's topsoil, too, by importing large amounts of Nauru's phosphate to enrich our soils, and now that island looks like a pock-marked moonscape. Hardly sustainable.

Ideally to grow organically one has either a system that is completely self-sustaining, or at least has a roughly even amount of inputs and outputs. Being able to produce all your fertilising needs from your own property is not always feasible. And it's not simply a matter of putting on the nutrients that plants need. Farmers, conventional now as well as organic, are increasingly realising that it is the soil that must be fed in order to produce a good crop. Organic and biodynamic farmers have for years been talking about the micro-organisms in the soil and the roles they play in plant health, and conventional farmers are realising that the old formula of NPK (nitrogen, phosphorus, potassium) is not the answer. Rather than seeing the soil as an inert medium in which plants grow, and to which nutrients can be added, the organic view is that the soil is an ecosystem, and that healthy soils teeming with life are essential to growing healthy plants.

With all this in mind, I was interested to see a listing in the WWOOF book for a farm that made vermicast and liquid seaweed compost in commercial quantities.

I had rung from a phone booth at Hot Water Beach in the Coromandel to say I'd be later than expected. Spending time with my old mate Lizzy relaxing in our own freshly dug hot pool in the sand was too good an opportunity to pass up.

Several hours later, aided by the light of the nearly full moon, I reached my next destination: a Bio-Gro certified farm near Te Puke in the Bay of Plenty, a major kiwifruit growing area. I pulled up by the farmhouse and went inside to meet my new hosts, Graeme Reid and Gaye Erickson, of Eco-Logic Concepts. It was a Friday night and they were sitting having a drink in the kitchen with a friend, and called out a friendly greeting.

'Oh, I forgot to tell you on the phone,' said Gaye, as she poured me a glass of wine. 'We've got a birthday dinner to go to down at the local. You'd be welcome to come along if you want.'

'Sure,' I said, 'Why not?' And shortly I found myself whisked into their car and driving down the road towards the nearby seaside settlement of Pukehina. Graeme and I soon became engrossed in a conversation about biodynamics, and planting by the moon.

'It just seems like common sense to me,' said Graeme. While not fully biodynamic, he used some of the preparations and followed some BD practices like sowing seed and fertilising according to the moon calendar.

At the pub I was introduced to all their friends. It's a small world, and especially so in New Zealand where we seem to have only one or two degrees of separation: it turned out one of their friends knew someone I'd gone to school with. I didn't see the beach that night, but went for a walk another day, right to the end where the dotterels live, and there were people gathering shellfish on the sandbank on the other side of the estuary.

The farm itself was an interesting mix, and the work was varied. There was a small flock of sheep and a few cows, and on the second day of my stay we attended to the stock, unwrapping silage, and putting up a new electric fence for the cows, which were being break-fed, munching their way bit by bit across the paddock as the electric fence was moved every few days. The two children came to help Graeme and me round up the lambs into the yards, all of us in a madcap caper dodging around old farm machinery as the wily sheep tried to outwit and outrun us. Once the lambs were in the confines of the yards, Graeme cut off their tails with a sharp knife and put rubber rings around the boy lambs' testicles to neuter them. My job was to hold onto the lambs while these operations were going on, and I felt both squeamish and, at the same time, a sense of horrid fascination.

Up the hill there was a plantation of paulownia trees, under which were planted golden seal and black cohosh, medicinal herbs native to North America that are not commonly grown in New Zealand. There were also tamarillos and table grapes, a small orchard of pipfruit and stonefruit, herb and vegetable seedlings in a large glasshouse, and while I was there several of us set up the irrigation system and laid out weedmat in a plastic hothouse and planted 1500 tomato seedlings.

But the most intriguing and distinctive thing about Eco-Logic Concepts was the organic fertilisers they made. Graeme made liquid seaweed extract in a huge flowform with a pump that kept the mixture circulating non-stop for six to eight weeks. The flowform is often used on biodynamic farms, and there are several different shapes, but this one is perhaps the most common: a structure down which water cascades, swirling around in two opposing bowl shapes on each level before going down to the next. The visual effect is of a series of figure eights with a central channel running down the middle through the narrow part of the figure eights. The idea is to aerate, agitate and energise the water, or in this case the liquid fertiliser, and imprint in it a sense of rhythmic movement, which, when the fertiliser is applied, will improve plant growth and health.

'Where do you get the seaweed?' I asked, mesmerised by the lively motion of the water.

'I import it from Canada,' Graeme replied. 'You just can't buy enough dried, powdered kelp here in New Zealand, and anyway, this Canadian seaweed is one of the best in the world.' How sustainable is that? the organic police in me queried, but then it set me wondering where the rock phosphate comes from that many organic farmers use, and I reminded myself that my favourite organic chocolate comes all the way from Germany, so who was I to talk?

Machinery was also employed to make vermicast on a large scale. Graeme, who used to be a mechanic, had an ingenious custom-built worm farm set up in the barn that consisted of a box 16 metres long by two metres wide, something like a giant cheese grater. Once a week it was moved up and down and the vermicast filtered through a screen to a lower level, helped by someone like me with a stick to make sure it fell through. Then it went up a conveyor into the tractor bucket, where it was transferred to a rotary machine that screened it again. The final part of the process was me, the wwoofer, hand-screening the rich, dark, crumbly mix through a sieve.

Graeme was particularly keen on his organic fertilisers, and outlined his plans to start making compost tea. At the time of writing, he had upgraded and expanded his vermicast system, was practising the Soil Foodweb ideas of soil microbiologist Elaine Ingham by making compost teas, and was also extracting humic and fulvic acid from the vermicast by using hot water. Compost teas are poured around plants or sprayed onto the leaves, in order to inoculate microbial life into the soil or onto the foliage, and to add nutrients to help feed the plant.

The humble compost bucket is a daily reminder of our connection with nature, of the need to give back to the earth. Everywhere I went there was a compost bin in the kitchen, generally immediately under the sink. Sometimes there were two bins: one for the chooks or goat, who got the choicest scraps; and the other for the compost or worm farm. Scraps for the worm farm often excluded citrus skins and onion skins, as these are not favourite foods of worms – but they do like coffee grounds. A couple of farmers buried their compost directly into the ground in an area to be converted to vege garden, reckoning that it would have broken down sufficiently by the time they planted there.

In Hampden, North Otago, Mark Lagerstedt had a row of compost heaps, in various stages of maturity, in several large square, slatted wooden bins of the kind that has been traditional in New Zealand backyards. One of the heaps was decomposing at a rapid rate and was pretty hot inside – a great way to warm up the hands on a chilly autumn morning. We did some turning of heaps that had got past the hot stage, and were full of worms, and we made a new heap: a wonderful layered creation that resembled a huge lasagne, including a whole trailer load of half-rotted, slimy kelp that we collected from the beach. Once we'd unloaded the kelp, Mark introduced me to a new plant that he used in the compost heaps.

'Here, take the rake,' he said, passing me one of his beautiful, hand-made wooden implements. 'And skim off some of the azolla in the pond.'

'What does it look like?' I asked.

'It's the reddish-green weed that's floating on the surface. Get as much as you can – it'll grow back soon enough.' This was my introduction to azolla (*Azolla filiculoides*), a freshwater weed, actually a fern, that grows on the surface of still or slowly moving water, and is either green or, if growing in strong light, red. It reproduces at a phenomenal rate, and can form a thick mat on the surface of the water.

It's an excellent source of nitrogen, due to its symbiotic relationship with a blue-green algae, *Anabaena azollae*, which fixes nitrogen and passes it on to the azolla to use. It can be added to the compost heap or simply used directly around plants as a mulch. In Asia it is widely used as a fertiliser in the rice paddies.

Armed with this knowledge I was able to pass it on to some more WWOOF hosts. Debbie Strachan and Michelle Cecile lived with their baby daughter on a lifestyle block subdivided from a dairy farm south of Whakatane. The farmer still leased parts of the block to run his cows on. The property was an unusual shape, with a few hillocks, and a pond.

One of my tasks was to make a compost heap. Michelle and Debbie had already amassed some piles of rotted-down grass clippings, food scraps, clippings of tagasaste (tree lucerne) and newspaper, and my job was to put them all together in a layered heap, with the addition of some cow manure. While scouring the slopes for cowpats and scooping them up into a wheelbarrow, I realised that the pond had a fair covering of azolla on it.

'That pondweed would be a good addition to the compost heap,' I suggested. 'I've used it before with another WWOOF host.'

'Go for it,' said Michelle. Back and forth with the wheelbarrow I went, tipping out my bounty onto the freeform compost heap, forking on layers of the different ingredients, and then covering the lot with old carpets and tarpaulins.

Michelle and Debbie had done quite a bit of planting already, mainly tagasaste for its quick growth and nitrogen-fixing abilities, eucalypts for firewood, native trees, a number of exotic specimen trees and an orchard. I planted several more native trees in and around the tagasaste trees, which were already well-established, and fair humming with bees, as they were some of the few sources of nectar in early spring.

My hosts asked my advice on planting fruit trees, and showed me their plan, which included several citrus trees, feijoas, apples, pears, plums, hazels, macadamias and a walnut. I suggested a little more spacing in some places, and replanted a few trees to give them a bit more room when they were fully grown. I weeded and mulched around all the orchard trees and dug holes for some new trees, mixing in a bit of compost in the bottom of the holes before planting. Debbie weeded and mulched too when the baby was asleep, and Michelle worked with me on the weekends.

The compost came from a simple black plastic bin of the type often found in home gardens, and consisted mainly of rotted-down food scraps and lawn clippings. It showed just how easy it can be to make good compost; the finished product, which was removed from the bottom of the heap through a little trapdoor, was a rich, black, sweet-smelling stuff that was probably delicious to all the trees.

Later, I realised that instead of the azolla, what really would have been a better addition to the compost heap I made would have been some bulky carbon material like hay or straw, as there was plenty of nitrogen-rich material already.

The more I learnt about organics, and about growing, the more I realised that the answers really do lie in the soil. Compost, compost teas, EM and the biodynamic preparations are all different ways of doing the same thing: enriching and enlivening the soil. If we get the balance of the soil right, and teeming with micro-organisms, then the plants and animals will flourish. The Soil and Health Association motto puts it perfectly: 'Healthy soil, healthy plants, healthy people.'

20

SHEEP

Sheep. They're ubiquitous in New Zealand, but actually are decreasing in number quite noticeably as dairying, in particular, has become more popular. And vineyards. In 1982 there were 70.3 million sheep, and by 2002 the number had dropped to 39.6 million.

There's something comforting to me about a paddock of sheep browsing peacefully, the occasional drowsy 'baa' in the distance. Something that tells me all's right with the world. It's part of the New Zealand landscape of my childhood, even though I had almost no direct contact with sheep and knew very little about them. Woolly maggots, a friend of mine calls them, and if you see them roaming a distant hillside they can look like plump well-fed maggots. But perhaps it is we humans who are the parasites. Our economy has been built largely on sheep, though they are no longer quite as important, as wool battles with synthetic fabrics and people eat less sheep meat.

At the Jollys' hazel farm I helped out with the small flock of sheep, shifting them to a fresh paddock every few days. One day another farmer came to drench and crutch the sheep, which we'd put in the yard the day before. I discovered that she was a vegetarian, which surprised me.

'I know what happens to the animals, and I wouldn't want to eat them,' she said. She also told me that in her experience, organic sheep didn't look as healthy as non-organic sheep, and were perhaps a bit smaller.

I acted as the assistant, opening gates, sweeping up the dags, handing her tools and keeping Sam the dog under control. The drench the Jollys used was cider vinegar and ground pumpkin seeds, though some organic farmers use cider vinegar and garlic. Both pumpkin seeds and garlic are also used to get rid of worms in humans.

Sam was both visually impaired and excitable. He sniffed the sheep all over and tried to lick the drench out of the corners of their mouths; all the while the poor sheep were held in the most ungainly position, legs splayed, rolling their eyes. Sam was a rambunctious young thing and wanted to mount anything on four legs (including his mother who had recently been on heat), and presented the most comical sight when he did actually manage to get himself in more or less the right position on a ewe, and took off across the yard with her, jumping in tandem on his hind legs until he could no longer keep up.

It's not true. Sheep are simply not the docile, follow-the-leader animals many people think they are. Like fishing, there's often 'the one that got away'. Rounding up sheep is an art that I was still learning about well into my third year of wwoofing.

At Waihi Bush near Geraldine six of us set off one day in two vehicles to part of the farm that was about 10 kilometres away. Our mission was to round up a flock of sheep and bring them back to the main farm block. There were no dogs in our team, only humans: David the farmer, his wife Lorina, his son Oliver and three wwoofers: Mark and myself from New Zealand and Daniel from the USA. The first four had experience in rounding up sheep and the other two of us had really no idea what we were doing, and little knowledge of sheep beyond their cottonwool presence as part of the New Zealand farming landscape, safely behind fences, chewing contentedly.

We arrived at the paddock and confidently, innocently strode in, dividing up so that some went down one side and some down another so we'd meet at the bottom of the paddock and push the sheep up and out. It sounded easy enough but, as we walked on, the paddock seemed to grow larger and turned into an obstacle course. There were uneven lumps and hollows that reared up or sank giving my unstable ankles a free physio session; a few patches of scrub offered hide-and-seek opportunities; and in case we hadn't already had it, the adrenaline factor was provided by a collection of beehives.

We managed to get most of the sheep up towards the gate but a few rebels had evaded us. It was then I discovered the swamp, an area of boggy ground with strong suction qualities on one's gumboots, riddled with small runnels and Dr Seuss-like grassy towers that looked firm but toppled unpredictably. There was a rugged old fence that fair sailed across a creek, leaving an inviting escape route below for a few unruly beasts.

If it was a game it might have been fun, for a while, until we realised we were losing to a creature that was meant to be dumber than us – that was, in fact, renowned for being simple. These few wily buggers had outwitted us in every section of the obstacle course, and were now grazing nonchalantly, not even out of breath. Meanwhile, I was bent over, panting hard, squelching in my gumboots, voice ragged from shouting at the others and at the sheep.

'Over here. I've found one over here!' I yelled. Daniel came to my aid and we bore down on the beast, turning it around in the direction of its peers with a skill we hardly knew we had. It was more probably luck.

'Down behind the beehives, Oliver,' said David. 'There's a couple down there.' Oliver ran off. Grunts, silence.

'Have you found them?' I called. No answer.

'Have you found them!' Yelling louder now. Pause.

Oliver emerged, walking, no sheep in sight.

'Where are they?' I asked.

'Oh, I thought you said you'd found them.' Back down the paddock to try again.

Eventually we cornered four of the miscreants in a corner fenced off on three sides, with a few trees just to make things interesting. There were four of us humans – David and Lorina were holding the rest of the flock up near the gate.

'Right, it's one sheep each, then,' said Mark, issuing his challenge with a grin, and promptly caught one to show me how it was done. One by one the blokes successfully tackled their targets. Even Daniel, as inexperienced as I was, managed to throw himself on top of one. Unfortunately my sheep, the smallest, evaded my grasp like butter through my fingers.

'Never mind,' said Mark. 'We'll let you get another one some time.' I had no doubt he would, and smiled grimly, totally exhausted.

Finally we had them all up near the gate, bar a couple that we had given up on, but would they go through the open gate? No way. They acted as if they hadn't even seen it, which was possible, or that they had no intention of leaving. After all, who would choose a paved road over a paddock of rich grass?

Soon a farmer appeared from a nearby house. He had probably been watching us running around like mad things during his lunch break and decided to give us a hand. He brought a large roll of green windcloth, which he instructed us to unroll, and three or four of us held it up to create a visual block for the sheep. It worked a treat. He suggested we keep it to use at intersections on the way back to the farm.

Horse whispering I've heard of, but sheep whispering, well it sounds more underhand, somehow, like rustling. This farmer showed us some rounding-up tactics, very gently urging the sheep with the slightest of breathy whistles and 'sh-sh' noises, only going forward when they had their heads pointed in the right direction, or when one or two had already set off towards the gate. Then we pushed them up, but not too close so they didn't feel pressured and try to break out back into the paddock behind us.

Finally they began to simmer towards the gate, and then shot forth onto the road like a head of steam. We all breathed a sigh of relief. The hardest thing had been rounding them up in that confounded paddock.

Walking them 10 kilometres back to the main farm was the easy part, if long. Some of us went ahead to warn any traffic (although it was pretty quiet), and to close gates so the sheep didn't stray off the road, and the others went behind, pushing the flock along. Because it was quite a distance, we took our time and even stopped for lunch, which Lorina, being the perfect hostess, had packed that morning. We slowed down and let the sheep graze the longacre, and we ate too.

One morning at Milmore Downs I awoke to an unfamiliar noise, a susurration surrounding the wwoofer cabins. It wasn't the whisper of a light wind, or the tiptoe of a misty drizzle. As I dozed, my ears picked up another sound, a quiet ripping. In the grey dawn, all around the cabins were dozens of sheep eating, softly wrenching mouthfuls of grass and then chewing them, the sound of a thousand butterflies. When I got up the whole paddock rustled as they scattered.

A few days later I was relaxing in the cottage, just about ready for bed. It was only 9.00, but the next morning was a 7.00 start in the shearing sheds, all hands on deck. I'd be trying out my skills as a rousie. There was the hum of a car pulling up outside, and then someone burst into the cottage without knocking, bearing a large chilly bin.

'Hello!' he said cheerily. 'I'm Edwin.'

'Hi.' Who was this guy?

'I'm staying for a few weeks doing some shearing in the area,' he said, plonking down the chilly bin.

'Oh … OK,' I said, a little put out that no-one had told me anyone was coming.

'Have you met the resident rat yet?' he asked, as he began to unpack some of his food. It was clear that he'd been here before.

'Ah, no. We've caught a couple of mice though.' For the first time in my life I had set a mousetrap, and I wasn't sure which was worse: the gnawing of the mice on the wooden spoon, which although washed and scrubbed no doubt still bore the imprint of a tasty curry, or the gnawing of my conscience about killing another being.

'Actually, there have been some strange scuttlings and scratchings, but I thought they might be possums on the roof.'

'Are you putting your compost in the heap out there?' Edwin asked.

'Yeah, they must be attracted to that. The chooks come over every day to check it out, and Dark fossicks around in it too when he's let off his chain. There'll be no chance of it rotting down with all the animals eating it!'

Edwin carried on settling into the kitchen, checking out what was there and organising his food in rat-proof jars and tins.

'Oh, and by the way because of the rat we usually put this lid over the cutlery container,' he said, 'and don't use the top plate from each pile, just use it as a cover to keep the others clean.'

Fortunately, despite some very suspicious scratchings, there was no visible evidence of the rat while I was there, though it was plenty cold enough that May for rats and mice to head inside to the warmth of human-inhabited buildings. One morning at 10.00 the thermometer was still sitting at only –3°C.

'Well, we're shearing tomorrow morning, so I'd better go to bed,' I said, getting up and heading for the door.

'Oh, there's no shearing tomorrow. Sorry, Ian told me to let you know. He can't get the shearers.' Great! Now I could sleep in.

Although he had interrupted my peace and solitude that night, I quickly got over that and began to enjoy this impromptu flatmate. Edwin Foord was about 50, with an open face and a ready smile, a lively, youthful energy, and an interest in healing and things spiritual. He and his partner had done the one-year biodynamic course in Havelock North and were looking to buy a farm. Meanwhile he was carrying on shearing as he'd done for much of his adult life, travelling around a bit depending on where the work was.

Most days, weather permitting, he'd be out and about shearing at other farms in the district, and if there was no work on, he'd help out at Milmore Downs with whatever needed doing – feeding out, moving sheep and cattle. Over the next few evenings we had lots of long talks and, among other things, he began to unravel some of the mystique of shearing for me.

One night he came home with red spots on his wrists and forearms, and rubbed them distractedly while he had a beer.

'What's wrong with your arms?' I enquired.

'Grease boils,' he replied. 'The grease from the sheep's wool gets into your hair follicles and it gets a bit irritated and inflamed. It'll go down after a while.'

Every night he cleaned the combs from his shearing handpiece, and told me about the characters he'd met in his many years of shearing, both shearers and farmers. I was lined up to work in the sheds for a day or two as a rouseabout, when the rain let up and the sheep were dry enough to shear, but had no idea of what was involved.

Edwin stood up and physically demonstrated the shearing process, bending over an imaginary sheep and patiently explaining the shearing process step by step, and also what the rousie had to do.

'First the shearer shears the belly. You pick it up, rip off the frib and throw that in the frib pile, and chuck the belly in the belly pile. Then the shearer does the crutch, which you sweep away. Then –'

'Hang on, what's the frib?'

'Well, it's a bit of wool on one end of the belly that's sort of yellower, more dense and curly. Then the topknot comes off. After that the shearer starts on the fleece.'

He demonstrated roughly how the shearer stood and moved about while shearing, and then how I'd have to pick up the fleece and throw it on the table.

Shearing day drew nearer, and finally after two-and-a-half years' wwoofing I got to spend a day in a shearing shed, picking up fleeces and sweeping dags.

'Now, you know you'll have to be ready to work on the dot of seven,' Edwin warned, knowing I wasn't an especially early riser by choice.

'Yeah, yeah, I'll be there.'

'Good, because we keep strictly to time, and we need you rousies there from the word go,' he said with a grin.

He needn't have worried. At 6.55 I crunched my way through the frost over to the shed, up the steps, retracting my fingers from the frozen railing lest they stick. Inside, the lights were on and a sense of anticipation hung in the air. Soon the electrics were humming and the shearers were straight into their work. Into the holding pen, grab a sheep round the chest and drag it out backwards, the wooden gate banging shut. Grab the handpiece and start shearing, the electric blades whining, follow the same pattern, set steps like a dance, a wrestling match with an unwilling opponent and a guaranteed win.

It was full-on, non-stop work, and even though that first day I was just sweeping and picking up bellies and topknots and all the bits and pieces, and trampling the wool down in the big wool sacks, I was exhausted by the end of the day. Monotonous though it was, the work was too flat-out to be boring, and was broken by the occasional yell from one of the shearers.

'Black wool!' This was the signal that there was a tiny patch of black wool in an otherwise white fleece, and one of us rousies had to come and remove it pronto and put it in a bag with other bits of black wool. It was important to keep it completely separate from the white wool. Small tufts of black wool were often obscured by dirt and grease before the sheep was shorn, but when the shearer's blades revealed the pure clean wool close to the skin, the black stood out unmistakeably.

'On the board!' meant that a yet-to-be-shorn sheep had come through from one of the holding pens onto the 'board' where the shearers were working, and it had to be put back immediately so it didn't get in the way. It didn't happen often; the sheep were generally not keen on getting close to the noise and bustle.

Morning tea was a substantial snack of sandwiches with our cup of tea, brought over by Ian's mother Ngaire, who also cooked lunch. Shearers need to be fed so much: they really put their all into it, working up a real sweat and changing singlets from time to time. Ngaire was in her late 70s and had lived on the farm for most of her life. She did numerous jobs: feeding and walking the dogs, feeding the chooks, the house cow and her calves, and collecting the eggs.

At lunchtime a car pulled up and it turned out to be some people from the shearing ITO (industry training organisation) who were checking out the work of the shearers. If shearers have done a course with them, the ITO people turn up unannounced occasionally to check their work, and that day the guy gave the two shearers some tips while they were working.

There's an art to it all, even to sweeping, which is done with a special broom that has no bristles, just a flat triangular piece of plastic on the end of the broomstick. One of the ITO women showed me how to hold and manoeuvre the broom. 'Here, hold it like this, and use your wrist to flick it,' she instructed, wielding the broom like a wand and magicking all the bits of wool away in a trice. Of course it looked effortless when she did it. I felt like a total klutz in comparison, but after all, it was my first day. Marinus La Rooij, who was my fellow rousie, soldiered on stoically, despite his sciatica.

By the end of the day a hitherto unknown muscle group in my inner thighs was aching from constantly crouching down to pick up wool and springing up again. It was a good physical workout, but I wouldn't want to do it for days on end. As my head hit the pillow that night I had visions of the repetition of sweeping.

The next day I swapped jobs with Marinus and picked up the fleeces. This was the more demanding job, as the fleeces were heavy and had to be picked up a certain way so they could then be flung out on the tables for the classer. And all in double quick time, of course, before the shearer had dragged the next sheep out. Flinging out the fleeces is highly satisfying when you get it right. It's a bit like throwing a blanket out on a bed, up into the air so it billows out and lands exactly where you want it.

A fleece is heavy, and you need to pick it up with two of the legs held tightly between the thumb and forefinger of each hand, the other two legs gathered in by the rest of your fingers, and the bulk of the fleece bundled and scooped up into your arms. You then turn around from the board and fling the whole bundle out across the table, keeping hold of two of the legs between your thumbs and forefingers, so you can control it and the whole thing doesn't go flying off.

We had only two shearers and two rousies (although a good rousie could have easily done the job that we two novice rousies were doing). Ian did most of the classing and pressing, and his son Matthew made sure there were always sheep in the holding pens, and helped with classing and pressing. The shed was a hive of activity, and there was no time to talk. Even if we'd wanted to, the constant drone of the shears was too much to talk against. At lunchtime and tea breaks the silence rang in our ears and we sat, subdued, in the welcome peace.

There's no difference between shearing organic sheep and non-organic sheep, except that organic sheep are more prone to lice, which can reduce the quality of the wool, depending on the severity of the infestation. Organic certification rules don't allow the use of synthetic chemical dips that non-organic farmers use to control lice. Instead, controls include pyrethrum (a commonly-used organic insecticide made from the pyrethrum daisy) and a pyrethrum-garlic mix, but neither of these is completely effective. That year Ian was a little disappointed in the quality of wool, some of which was yellow and cotted because of the lice. Apparently they had had quite a good year the year before.

The main lice control at Milmore Downs is winter shearing. We were shearing in May so the sheep would go into winter with short coats and the lice wouldn't survive exposure to the cold and the light. Another reason to shear in winter is that the ewes, who were due to lamb in August, would seek better shelter for themselves and their lambs, giving the lambs a higher survival rate. At that time of year, the shearers used cover combs, which left a thin layer of wool so the sheep weren't completely bald. After shearing, the sheep were turned out into a paddock with good shelter for a few days while their skins thickened up a bit before we took them back to the hill block.

Ian doesn't even drench his animals for internal parasites, but relies on the pasture mix to give the sheep and cattle good health overall.

Diary entry
7 May 2004
Milmore Downs, North Canterbury

We were going to move the sheep from the hill block back to the home block at 6.30 yesterday morning but it was raining and windy and Ian called it off. With a nor'wester the sheep's instinct is to turn their backs to the wind, which would have meant they were facing the wrong way and we just wouldn't be able to get them to go. But it cleared later to a fine day, still a bit windy, and we herded the sheep back in the afternoon. I was driving the car in front. Pretty easy.

Matthew picked up four sheep in the back of the ute, two with flystrike and two older ones that didn't have much go in them. One of the flystruck ones had a big cape of wool hanging down over his rear end, but it was easily removed. The other flystruck one Matthew shore and saw that most of the flystruck patches had healed, and there was not a maggot to be seen, which was baffling. I put some hypercal lotion (hypericum and calendula, made by Weleda) on the raw bits while Matthew held her. She was pretty frisky. I let her through to the neighbouring paddock and she went running over to the other sheep there. They crowded around her. Then she went to greet another sheep that was lying down, then went to check out a gate and they all followed her.

'Would you mind just popping into the next paddock and getting that ewe and lamb through into the creek paddock?' Ian asked. He had visitors to show around and everyone else seemed to be busy.

'You'll have to open the gate in the far corner first,' said Ian. 'Skirt right around them, don't get too close.'

It sounded like a breeze after rounding up mobs of sheep, so I happily agreed, and went off with Tip the sheepdog to help me. As instructed, we made a wide arc around the mother and baby, who were contentedly grazing along the fence line. Opening the gate was easier said than done. It didn't look as though it was used very often, as it was held together by wire, rope and barbed wire on top, which required some wrestling in order to untwist. I dragged it open on its sagging hinges, then circled back around behind the sheep.

The pair had been left in this paddock because of the lucerne stubble that would be good nutrition for the mother during the early suckling stage. The lamb had been born out of season, in May, along with a set of twins in another paddock. Ian was wondering how it had happened, and thought perhaps that the cryptorchid that had been allowed to run with the ewes was perhaps capable of siring after all. Cryptorchid? I'll explain that later.

'Right, Tip, all we have to do is edge these two gently along the fence line and through the gate,' I said. We started walking slowly behind them, a little out from the fence. Tip got into stalking mode, head down, with his eyes fixed and unblinking, pacing slowly and deliberately towards the sheep. There were several sheep that had been grazing on the other side of the fence, in the creek paddock, keeping their sister and her baby company. Now they took off, heels kicking up, down the bank and out of sight. One of them stayed behind and somehow squeezed through onto our side of the fence. Uh-oh, Tip was getting restless, going too close, hounding them. I called him back.

'Get in, Tip!' Meaning 'get in behind', or more or less, 'come here'. It was one of two main commands they used with the dogs. The other was 'get outside!', meaning get right out of it, away from where you are.

The sheep were starting to stumble along the edge of the fence line now, and Tip barked, startling them into a trot. The lamb nipped under the fence, and didn't seem to know how to get back through. Its mother threw herself blindly at the fence several times in an unsuccessful attempt to join her baby. Tip was getting restless, going closer and closer to them and I kept calling him back.

'Get in, Tip!' I warned. He wasn't listening. I didn't want to frighten the sheep or separate the lamb from its mother. But Tip just kept on going, running now towards the aunty sheep that had taken off up the fence line.

'Get in!' I shouted. 'GET OUTSIDE!' Tip was running level with the sheep now and looked as though he was going for the jugular. I screamed at him at the top of my lungs, thinking he was going to maul the poor frightened animal, but at the last minute he came back. I scolded him severely and we waited a few minutes while everybody calmed down.

Then we set off again. This time I held Tip's collar firmly all the way, and moved the trio slowly up the fence line. Finally the two ewes went through the gate, where mother was united with baby, and they trotted off into the creek paddock while I wrestled with the wire. around the gate.

Ian had mentioned this 'cryptorchid' a couple of times and I wasn't sure if I was hearing right. It sounded like flowers in the basement of a church.

'What's a cryptorchid?' I asked.

'Well,' said Ian. 'Usually the boy lambs are either left intact to become rams, or we turn them into wethers by putting a rubber ring around their testicles so they drop off. But you can put the ring on so it's just around flesh, pushing the testicles up inside, and they keep growing inside. That way they still have a bit of testosterone but their semen isn't viable because it's too hot inside the flesh.'

The phrase comes from the Greek, crypt meaning secret or hidden, and orchid meaning testicle. At Milmore Downs the one and only cryptorchid was allowed to run with the ewes all the time, as he was unable to father lambs. He stood out from the rest of the flock because of his greater height, a slight dusky colouring in the wool, and a more assertive personality.

One day I was walking back to the yards from the eastern paddocks, and saw a lone sheep strolling nonchalantly through an open gate towards me. It was the cryptorchid.

Hello, I thought, what's he doing? A sheep on its own is an unusual sight. He had apparently escaped from the sheep yards, and Matthew came around the corner looking for him. I ran in futile circles around the paddock after him, trying to push him back through the gate. He was a faster runner than me, and much more agile, and it was only after I gave up, panting and wheezing, that he teasingly retreated back through the gate, as if to say, 'what's all the fuss about?'

Matthew wanted him back in the yards, but given that claustrophobic option or two other enticing open gates, the cryptorchid chose one of the other gates, and tore off through the orchard down towards the house. Matthew gave chase, eventually finding the bugger way down in the creek paddock.

'I'm going to shoot it,' he fumed. I had no doubt he would. He had been out with his mates several times in the early mornings, shooting ducks up by the dam. That was the last I heard of the cryptorchid, and I can only imagine that he met his fate and found his way into a freezer.

21

BOS TAURUS: THE DOMESTIC COW

The domestic cow is one of those species that people often refer to by the female name, unless they know for certain that it is a bull, a steer, a heifer or a calf. Farmers use the neutral 'cattle beast' or cattle as the generic term, but still refer to dairy farmers as cow cockies, even though those farmers may well have some bulls or steers in addition to a dairy herd. There are other species in which the female name is used exclusively as the word for both genders: duck has eclipsed drake, and goose has overshadowed gander. Is it because the females of these species are more useful to us, and therefore more numerous when in our captivity?

My father, who grew up in Levin, liked to tell us that when he was a kid their milk came from bulls. With a capital B, of course, as in the Manawatu town up the line from Levin. My sister Helen and I thought it was uproarious. Although we were city kids and had nothing to do with animals except the family pets and the birds in the garden, we knew that bulls couldn't give you milk. We knew that milk came from cows, and not just from the milkman.

Most years we used to drive from Dunedin to Levin to spend Christmas at Gran's. In those days the roads were much quieter, and occasionally one still encountered stock being moved on some of the main highways. One time when we were quite young, we found ourselves in the midst of a large herd of cows. It was a thrilling and slightly scary experience to be among these large beasts, with their liquid eyes peering inquisitively from only inches away, and their nostrils snorting steam onto the windows, but ultimately it was fun in the safety of the car. Later my sister and I tried to recreate the experience by hiding under a blanket in the back seat of the car and mooing loudly, pretending to be cows, and it became something of a family joke.

My only other childhood memory of a cow is the house cow at my uncle and aunt's farm in Australia. We were encouraged to try milking her, but I took one look at the cow's great bulk and chickened out. Helen, being more adventurous, mucked in and gave it a go.

A few years later, as a student, I was walking on the Otago Peninsula with a friend, and we'd got halfway across what we thought was an empty paddock when we heard a noise, and realised with a start that there was a bull cantering towards us. He was quite possibly just curious, but we weren't about to hang around and find out – we dashed for the nearest fence and jumped over, adrenaline pumping, hearts pounding.

So when I set out wwoofing, I had virtually no experience of cattle, and still felt wary of these large beasts. Sheep and goats were small enough not to be scared of, horses were an unknown quantity, but bulls were to be avoided at all costs.

[Names and some details have been changed in this passage for privacy]

Liz and Bill Brown were the parents of a schoolmate of mine, although I didn't really get to know them until 20 or so years later, when I began to bump into Liz at Taste Nature, the organic food shop in Dunedin. She was always friendly and interested in what I was doing, and one day had some exciting news.

'Philippa! Hi!' Liz called out. It was almost a statement from this diminutive yet somehow imposing woman. She directed the concentrated energy beam of her eyes and smile towards me.

'Hi Liz, how are you?'

'Wonderful! You know Bill and I have just bought a cattle farm in the North Island?' She exuded enthusiasm.

'Wow, really?' was all I could think of to say. It was totally unexpected. The Browns had always seemed like city folk.

'Yes, we're moving up there next year. We're doing it completely organically, of course. You should come and visit,' she offered.

'Ah, yeah, that'd be great,' I said somewhat lamely, thinking anywhere in the North Island was a long way away, far from anywhere I was likely to be in the near future. But it was only a couple of years later that I rang them up to see if I could come wwoofing at their farm.

'Of course we'd love you to come!' exclaimed Liz. 'We don't usually have people 'til a bit later in the season, because it's still quite cold here, but since it's you, of course you're most welcome.'

The farm was in a valley, about an hour from the nearest town. In this part of the North Island there were still occasional frosts in October. The area could have been almost anywhere in New Zealand. It was a valley with mainly cattle and sheep farms, pockets of native bush in the gullies, and a series of one-lane bridges on the road to their farm. There were two gates to open (and close, of course) on the drive up to the house, although I couldn't see any stock except for some up on the hills.

Liz and Bill came out to greet me. Liz's energy seemed undiminished by the wide open space of the farm, and Bill was his usual quiet, understated self. It felt good to be staying with hosts whom I knew; I could relax and be myself and skip the initial period of politeness that generally happened for the first two or three days with a new host. During my stay I got to know Bill a little better and came to appreciate his wry, dry sense of humour. He was a fantastic mimicker of accents, switching seamlessly from one to another. This mild-mannered man had me in fits of giggles with his imitations, which were usually performed totally out of the blue, the surprise factor adding to the fun.

'Guid morning. Wuid ye like a wee but of porridge?' he might enquire in a Scots brogue when I came into the kitchen first thing in the morning. Later, perhaps when I came in from collecting the eggs, he'd startle me with 'Kia ora cuz! Haven't seen yu fo' ages.' German,

French, Russian, Chinese, South African, Irish, Scots, a broad selection of American and English accents: you name it, he could imitate it, his personality changing accordingly. Oh, and Australian, did I mention Australian? Bill loved the TV comedy programme *Kath and Kim*, and would quote from it verbatim in a nasal Ocker whine, complete with a rising tone at the end of every sentence, leaving me in paroxysms of helpless laughter.

The farm was over 100 hectares, and comprised river flats and hill country, most of it paddocks, although there were also orchards, a vegetable garden, a house garden and patches of native bush. There were a couple of hundred cattle, a donkey, a horse, a dog, two cats and a litter of newborn kittens, eyes still closed. Liz employed a local man as her stock manager, although she did a fair amount herself, checking the stock on foot, or on horseback up in the hills. She also attended cattle sales, and had bought two bulls of which she was very proud.

When Liz and Bill first arrived, the place was covered in thistles, mostly Scotch and variegated milk thistles, with the odd nodding thistle and patch of Californians. The milk thistle wasn't so much of a worry because the cattle would eat it when it was smaller. There was also the possibility of harvesting this thistle and selling the seed, which is used in herbal medicines for people with liver complaints. At the time of my visit, milk thistle seed was imported from California, which seems crazy when it grows wild here. It would have been relatively easy to harvest; a matter of bagging the thistle heads – a good job for wwoofers. Both companies Liz contacted were interested in buying it, but only one would process it, and in the end never came back to them, and Liz never followed it up. She probably had enough on her plate managing the stock as well as the home vegetable garden and orchard.

The conventional way of getting rid of thistles was spraying with some synthetic chemical or other, but Liz was totally committed to using organic methods, which in this case was manual weeding: grubbing the thistles by hand. Whenever she went walkabout in the paddocks to check the stock, she routinely carried a grubber to strike down any thistles that dared to get anywhere near flowering. And then there were the specialist thistle slayers: wwoofers like me, who would happily spend a couple of hours here and there in heavily infested areas. I enjoyed the physicality of the work, and gradually found a rhythm in the swing of the grubber. My technique and aim improved to the point that I could whack out all but the largest thistles with a single forceful stroke. It was a good workout for the upper body, but after a couple of hours or so it was time to have a cup of tea or change to another chore to avoid aches in the arms or shoulders – and by then it was also time to sharpen the grubber.

Regular chores at the Browns' included feeding the chooks and collecting their eggs, and also filling up the water troughs for the heifers in a temporary strip of paddock running alongside the river. This was the only paddock without automatic refilling water troughs (or small dams), and we had to go down to the river and haul up a few buckets by hand, lug them up the bank and pour them into the troughs. Doing this laborious task made me realise how much cows can drink, although fortunately it was only for a few days and then we moved them into another paddock.

In a paddock close to the house there was a mournful, skinny, three-legged cow and two bulls for company. On closer inspection I saw that the cow did have a fourth leg, but it was held up at an odd angle, with the section below the knee held parallel to the ground. She limped around very slowly. Apparently she had broken her leg and the previous owners had left it like that. I was a little nervous with the bulls so close to the house, with only a wire-and-post fence between us. They were proud specimens: a white Charolais and a black Angus, and their muscles rippled as they sauntered across the paddock.

Spring was in the air. The plums were sprinkled with blossom like stars, and we counted an astonishing total of 18 tiny Paradise ducklings swimming around in the dam up on the hill. The bulls were getting restless in their small space. They spent most of their time over the far side, communicating with the cows in the adjacent hill paddock, or the heifers in the river paddock. Liz was worried that they'd jump the fence and get in with the heifers and get them pregnant, so she decided to let them run with the cows, and they happily trotted up the slopes to enjoy some female company. Then one afternoon the two of us set off on a thistle-grubbing mission all around the hill paddock.

'So that means we'll be in the same paddock as the bulls, doesn't it?' I queried, just out of interest, you understand.

'Yes, but it's a huge paddock. They probably won't be anywhere near us,' Liz assured me.

'But they could just appear out of the bush, or over a rise ...' The terrain was varied, with plenty of dips and ridges, and I had visions of a bull appearing over a hill, nostrils flaring, bearing down on me at top speed.

'Don't worry, we'll get plenty of warning by their sounds. Anyway, the bulls will be far more interested in the cows than in us.'

Still, my bull-phobia had me on the alert, aware of the nearest fence to jump over, or a handy tree to climb up. For some time we worked away quietly, with no movement but the whoosh of the grubbers as they flew through the air, and the whack as they struck the stalk of a thistle, severing it cleanly at ground level from its roots and leaving it to wilt and die. The only sounds were birds twittering happily, and the distant bellowing of cows like rural foghorns. At one point we disturbed a pair of Paradise ducks, who came flapping out of some bush towards us and then away, probably in an attempt to distract us from their nest. Their distinctive honks, one high-pitched and one low, call and response, echoed through the still air.

We worked our way up the hill, coming to the dam where we encountered a cluster of cows bent over the water, their long tongues parting the floating meniscus of red-tinted azolla weed so they could get a drink. Another pair of Paradise ducks forged an easy path through the azolla, and yes, there were still 18 ducklings following along in their wake. Further along the hillside there was a large patch of milk thistles, which I grubbed and then tossed over the fence to some cows and calves on the other side. They all gathered to inspect this offering and then savoured the sweetest, smallest and juiciest of the thistles.

When we finally did see the two bulls, one black, one white, they were strolling along the crest of a hill with some cows, all silhouetted against a clear blue sky. It was such a breathtaking sight I forgot to be scared, and simply admired these serene beasts that were peacefully going about their lives without the least interest in me.

Diary entry
18 May 2004
Milmore Downs, Scargill, North Canterbury

Yesterday Marinus and I went to move the elderly (16-year-old) cow and the arthritic steer from the bull paddock. Armed with pretty but useless plumes of pampas grass to make us look larger than we were, we approached the bull paddock, me with some trepidation, explaining to Marinus my fear of bulls.

'I'm not scared of them, but I do have a great deal of respect for them,' he said.

'Do I have to go into the bull paddock?' I enquired. It was really a rhetorical question.

'No, I will,' said Marinus. 'You can stay on the other side of the fence and open the gate when necessary.'

The bulls, Herman and Eveready, were sitting right by the gate, in just the wrong place. Eveready (the black one), didn't even bother to get up, but just sat there peacefully, like the placid bull, Ferdinand, in that favourite old children's book of mine. Herman (the red one) got up when Marinus went in, probably just wondering what was going on. Marinus tried to shoo him out of the way, and Herman deigned to move but a few steps.

Marinus fetched the old cow and steer and herded them down to the gate, which I tentatively opened, but then Herman decided to come out with them and I panicked and tried to shut the gate as the old cow was coming through.

'Open the gate! Let her through!' called Marinus. I managed to let her through and pull the gate to, keeping Herman from following, but of course the steer shied away and had to be brought back again to repeat the procedure. Fortunately Herman got the idea that he wasn't leaving, and moved out of the way. Phew!

A few days later all the cattle were scheduled to be tested for TB. That morning I didn't start till about 9.00, by which time Ian and Marinus had already been down to the hill block, rounded up the steers into the yards there, then rounded up the cows and calves into the yards at the home block. We separated out the cows and calves, and Matthew went to get the bulls while I rounded up the old cow, the arthritic steer, Sadie the house cow and her calf and the two orphan calves that were part of her entourage.

Ngaire brought over morning tea and scones in a basket. We all stood around the ute, eating and drinking, reading the paper and chatting, with Herman and Eveready grazing only metres away. I was acutely aware of the lack of distance – and fence – between us, and positioned myself cautiously on the other side of the ute. Then as we walked down past them to the yards, I used Edwin as a human shield, just in case. The guys had started to tease me about my phobia, and suggested I go to the next bull sale at which there was a steak dinner offered – and of course I'm a vegetarian.

The TB tester, a cheerful young woman called Sam, came at 11.00 to test the herd, hill block first, then home block. I counted the cows and calves again and got 66 and 63, respectively. Four days before I had counted only 48 cows. How could I have missed so many last time? It would be an astoundingly fertile herd if 48 cows could give birth to 63 calves.

Meanwhile, the bulls had got a bit excitable. Eveready decided that the lass on the other side of the fence was keener and stepped through the wire, snapping it like a thread, unwittingly also demolishing my illusion that a fence was any protection from these creatures. True to his name, Eveready displayed his amorous intentions to Sadie from time to time, despite the fact that she was already in calf again. Then we (with me as moral support behind the high fences of the yards) put the two bulls in a pen together where they jostled and butted each other.

Sadie and co. were dutifully lined up in the race, and Ian and Marinus were trying to separate the bulls from each other. Perched up on the 'catwalk', I could see Eveready eyeing the opening between two of the pens provided by the catwalk, albeit a metre or so above the ground. I steeled myself, flapped my arms nervously and raised my croaking voice to scare him off from coming through. Either he was humouring me, or I really managed to put him off.

'Don't let them out the front!' Ian yelled, as Herman came charging through the open gate into the pen I was in. Huh? Adrenaline surged through me as I hovered on the catwalk between the two pens – between the two bulls. Did he want me to shut the gate on the bull that was charging through at that moment? No way was I jumping off the relative safety of the catwalk and down into the pen with Herman. But he was talking about Sadie and co. in the race. No worries about that. I couldn't have moved even if I wanted to. Besides, Sam hadn't finished examining them for TB.

When all the cattle had been tested (none of them were positive), the guys were teasing me about my bull-phobia, and daring me to take the bulls back to their paddock. I'm afraid I didn't have the ovaries for it. Instead I took the soft option and helped herd the calves up the drive and down through three paddocks to put them in paddock number 16. They were being weaned. Both cows and calves had been bellowing for each other off and on during the day, though, fortunately, it wasn't too noisy overnight.

According to Ian, most beef farmers wean their calves in time for the main calf sales in March, but he found that giving them a couple of extra months of mother's milk gave them better health, weight and immunity to worms.

When I first arrived at Milmore Downs, the job of milking the cow was offered to me, among several other possibilities, but nothing more was mentioned about it when I didn't jump at the chance. The usual starting time of 8.30 was early enough for me – as it was I was often still gulping down my porridge when we all converged on the yard to sort out the day's work.

Milking the cow was a daily ritual that I hadn't yet witnessed, though the cow bail was visible from my cottage. The cowshed was a no-nonsense concrete-block affair, beyond another shed that was in a magnificent state of collapse, like a lean-to with nothing to lean on, an impossible-looking M.C. Escher kind of construction, all odd angles and distorted perspectives. Going from the wwoofers' sleeping quarters to the cottage for breakfast, or dashing out to the long-drop, I often cast my glance over in the direction of the cow bail, but only ever saw Sadie before or after milking. And yet here would come Ian, striding up the drive with a cheery 'Good morning!', swinging the shiny steel milking bucket, now mysteriously full.

Like a kid staying up to catch Santa Claus, I determined to get up early one morning and get a piece of the action. A thick frost lay over the grass, clinging, stinging my bare fingers as they fumbled with the gate. Sadie raised her head as if to say, 'What are you doing up so early?', her hot breath fogging the air as she sniffed me for treats. No apple forthcoming, she snorted and went back to grazing.

To make the most of an anticipated wait, I had slung my camera around my neck, and busied myself taking photos in the fresh clarity of morning light, as streamers of sunshine unfurled themselves across the paddock. Black and white cow. Crazy falling-down shed. Close up. Further away. Crouch down for arty angles. The cold was biting me now and I stomped over to the farmhouse. Time to come out now, Santa, the game's up. I knocked and went in. Ian and Gita were having breakfast.

'Philippa, you're up early,' said Ian's eyebrows.

'I wanted to have a go at milking,' I offered.

'It's my turn today,' said Gita. 'I was going to do it a bit later, but since you're here … '

Seeing my sudden interest in this mundane chore, she obligingly grabbed the milking bucket and another bucket of hot water and we walked back to where Sadie was patiently chewing the cud. 'What's the hot water for?' I asked, but needed no reply as Gita was already using it to wash off Sadie's own shit she'd been lying in, to reveal the udder, smooth and pink.

'I think she does it on purpose,' said Gita, 'to keep warm.'

Bran to keep Sadie happy, milking stool and bucket ready. Finally I got to milk a cow. Sadie had become familiar to me over the previous month, which helped my confidence. The action was similar to milking a goat, making a tourniquet of sorts with the index finger and thumb, trapping milk below it, squeezing and pulling down and out into the milking bucket with a satisfying squirt.

It's certainly a lot better feeling than hooking up suction cups in an automated cowshed, though not as efficient or lucrative, to be sure. At dairy farms, you can't engage with the cow, only with rows of rear ends, flicking tails and testy hooves. It's like a factory. The house cow, on the other hand, is more like a member of the family and, depending on the farm and the season, gets treats at milking time: apples and bran were on the menu at Milmore Downs. Sadie would probably have tolerated a human leaning into the warm bulk of her side while milking. Then, as some semblance of a rhythm manifested – squeeze, swish, squeeze, swish – the novelty disappeared as quickly as the wrapping off a present, and I let Gita take over the milking again.

As autumn turned into winter, feeding out to the animals became a daily chore at Milmore Downs. One of us would clamber up the huge stack of hay bales in the barn and toss some down onto the back of the ute to feed out to the sheep. Peeling off the flat 'biscuits' of hay from each bale and throwing them off the back of the ute was pretty easy. Feeding out to the cows was a little more involved.

Ian encouraged me to have a go at attaching the large prongs to the tractor, then driving over to the huge round hay bales and spearing one onto the prongs. Easier said than done! The bales were lined up in the lee of a shelterbelt, and I had to make a tight turn to get the tractor right up against the fence while concentrating on getting the prongs at the right level to plunge them into the bale. Then, with the bale speared and tilted back a little so it didn't fall off, I drove cautiously over to the ute and fiddled about with the controls to get the bale to drop fair and square on the back of the ute. With a bit of practice I'm sure my confidence would have been boosted and my skills improved, but even I got frustrated with my own slowness and caution, and after two or three goes I let Ian or Marinus fetch the bale while I mixed up molasses and hot water in a couple of pails.

Down in the paddock we unwound the hay from the bale like a giant roll of thick paper, as one of us drove along at walking pace. Then we sprinkled the molasses mix onto the hay, with a watering can, to make it tastier for the cows and give them a few extra nutrients. The cows would come running up and the cheekiest of them would try to slurp the sweet liquid from a pail or watering can with their long, pink tongues.

I was quite happy to drive a tractor in other circumstances – with nothing on the front to manoeuvre. One day after we had shifted the cows from one paddock to another, Edwin rigged up the harrows onto the back of the tractor and drove it into the recently vacated paddock. The harrows consisted of a heavy metal frame about twice as wide as the tractor, to which several old tyres were attached with chains. Edwin showed me how to drive the tractor slowly around the paddock so that the harrows were dragged over all the cowpats and any remaining clumps of hay. This was to ensure more even grass growth and fertilisation. Even in what appeared to be a more or less flat paddock, the slow inward spiralling drive revealed humps and hollows that weren't immediately obvious. After I'd done all I could in the tractor there were still a few clumps of hay to spread about more evenly with a pitchfork.

Cows have a habit of crashing fences, generally when you've just sat down to a meal. One day at Waihi Bush we'd just sat down to lunch when my host's (David's) son Oliver came in. He was a lanky teenager who had recently left school and was employed on the farm while he worked out what he wanted to do next.

'The cows have got into the bush,' he stated in his quiet, no-fuss way. Immediately there was a clattering of knives and forks, a scraping of chairs, as we all rushed out, lunch forgotten, waded through the long grass of the orchard and climbed over the fence into the bush.

This is not just any bush, but a rare remnant of South Canterbury virgin forest, after which the farm is named. It's about 15 hectares, has a QEII covenant on it, and contains some majestic trees, totara and matai in particular, many hundred years old, possibly a thousand. A heavy snowfall a couple of years before had broken through the canopy here and there and created some exposed areas on the margins where the light had allowed the growth of weeds like blackberry and Chilean flame creeper, but as we penetrated deeper it became darker and more mysterious. My host David reverently showed me the twin totara trees ('the props of Tane') and we paused to pay homage to these forest giants, one of which was over eight metres in circumference. From there our paths diverged, and we fanned ourselves out through the bush to flush the cattle out to the western boundary. We relied on shouts and cooees to pinpoint our location and keep moving forward as a phalanx of sorts.

'Oliver! Where ARE you?'

'Over HERE!'

'Can you see any cows?'

'Have you seen a cow?'

'NO! Have YOU seen any?'

After a while we just gave up, and blindly crashed through the bush probably much the same as the cows were doing, although I never spotted so much as a hoof print, let alone a glimpse of a beast through the undergrowth, until we were almost at the fence line, where all the cows were nonchalantly trotting through the gate as though nothing was wrong and they hadn't wasted the best part of an hour of our time.

At Woodgrove near Kaikoura, four of us wwoofers and our host Doug had just sat down to dinner, when a phone call came from one of the neighbours to let us know some of the cows had got out on the road. Doug and I jumped up immediately and dashed out to the car.

'Here,' he said, thrusting his car keys in my hand. 'You drive down the road and keep them from coming this way, and I'll scoot round the back way on the bike to head them off.' It was the dimmest part of dusk and I drove slowly with just the park lights so as not to frighten the cows. Once their black-and-white rumps loomed up ahead I pulled over, turned the lights off and got out. They were contentedly grazing the longacre, that succulent strip of roadside grass that must have tempted them out of the paddock. There was an open gate a bit further along – perhaps that was how they'd got out.

An engine's roar broke into the silence in a crescendo of rising gears. Some local yokels hooning around the back roads? Damn, I should have made the car be a roadblock, and put the hazard lights on to announce something amiss. Risking becoming roadkill, I stepped out in front of the oncoming vehicle, waving my arms wildly.

'Stop!' I called. 'Cows up ahead!' The car screeched to a halt, its lights dazzling my eyes, and two dark figures leapt out and strode towards me, shouting incomprehensibly. I was frozen to the spot, stunned as a possum in headlights, the only movement being that of my thoughts, which in a split second had invented feral inbreds on a murderous rampage, and headlines to match. In another split second the two silhouetted figures revealed themselves as my fellow wwoofers from the Czech Republic, who had sped up in their car to help.

'Turn your lights off!' I admonished. The cows had already kicked up their heels and fled from the lights and the gunning engine. Fortunately Doug had reached the other end of the road and the herd filed obediently back into their paddock. On close inspection, the gate latch was loose and easy to push through, especially for a big-boned, hefty Friesian who could tell, even in the dark, the greenness of the grass on the other side of the fence.

Halfway home we came across the fourth wwoofer, Helen, in a state of distress and consternation.

'What's going on? You left and then the two Czech boys took off without me,' she wailed, 'and I didn't know what to do, and I've been walking up the road in the pitch black, and I can't see a thing, and I was scared of bumping into a cow, and ... ' It was all I could do not to laugh and suggest she could have just stayed at home in the warm, helped herself to pudding and put her feet up in front of the telly. But a light turned on in my mind, a realisation of how much I had learnt in nearly two years of wwoofing, and I felt some empathy with her when I recalled my own fear, ignorance and naïvety not so long ago.

HOHEPA

Mid-February 2004 and it was a hot summer's day as I drove to Hohepa Farm just outside of Christchurch, with the windows down, clad in just shorts and a t-shirt in the dry heat. There was hardly any farmland left between Christchurch and Halswell, and the latter township was slowly spreading out over the adjacent paddocks, with new houses going up here and there. I sped past a short stretch of green, but hardly had time to breathe in the country air before arriving at the entrance to Hohepa, which was indicated by a sign on the letterbox.

Hohepa had been on my list of must-go-to farms, because it was biodynamic (and in fact Demeter certified), and also because it was not just a farm, but was run as part of a larger community of adults with learning disabilities (these we used to call intellectually handicapped) and the wwoofing work was to include working with the residents.

I drove slowly over the cattle stop and along the drive, taking in the various buildings: houses, a big barn, several outbuildings and numerous established trees. The drive led up to a workshop and a larger building that was the hub of Hohepa, and which housed the office, kitchen, dining room, coolstore, packhouse, potting and tool sheds.

Several people were wandering around, and some of them came over to me as I pulled up.

'Hello,' I said. 'I'm looking for Vimbai.' She was the farm manager, whom I had spoken to on the phone to arrange my stay. A chorus of voices responded.

'Vimbai, where's Vimbai?'

'Don't know where she is.'

'Maybe in the office, try the office,' someone suggested, showing me to a small room inside. No-one was there.

'I'll find her,' said a woman, who was one of the caregivers or 'house mothers'. 'And in the meantime why don't you make yourself at home in the cottage?' She pointed to an old white wooden house that I found out later was the original farmhouse. The accommodation was different from most of the places I'd been to, in that the wwoofers and other volunteers (there was usually at least one volunteer who worked as a caregiver in one of the residential houses) were all put in the cottage together, and we did all our own cooking and cleaning, functioning like flatmates. When I arrived, there was a German wwoofer called Achim, who slept in a nearby building, and two German sisters, Anke and Rike, who slept in the cottage. Rike, the younger of the sisters, was right at the end of a nine-month stay at Hohepa as a volunteer caregiver, and her sister Anke had just arrived from Germany, and was doing a few days' wwoofing before accompanying Rike on a South Island trip.

The following day, after weeding in the 'hort unit' (the vegetable gardens and glasshouses behind the main building), Vimbai asked me to go with her to check the steers' water. The farm manager was a warm, friendly woman from Zimbabwe, who had a ready laugh and an easy manner with residents, staff and wwoofers. As we walked, she pointed out various parts of the six-hectare farm.

'There are the compost heaps,' she said, indicating large piles over by the macrocarpa hedge. 'And that's the ram over there in that paddock.' He was eating grass in a rather awkward-looking position, kneeling down on his two front legs, with his rump sticking up in the air.

'Why is he kneeling like that?' I asked.

'I don't know. He often does that. Maybe it's just to get closer to the grass.'

We walked on, past a paddock with vegetables grown on a larger scale than in the hort unit. In this paddock there were large patches of corn and potatoes, and long rows of leeks, carrots, silverbeet and zucchini. Further on and we came to some small sheep yards and a hay barn, an orchard with mainly apples and pears, a pigsty with the proverbial three little pigs, and paddocks with sheep and cattle. There were three chook houses in separate paddocks, and as we went towards the steers' paddock, a delegation of clucking chooks toddled forward to meet us, and then chided us for not having brought any delicious scraps.

It was a hot day with a typical Canterbury nor'wester drying everything out. The steers were in a paddock without a pump-filled trough, so we had to get a hose and fill up some troughs and drums for the thirsty steers, who came running over as soon as they spotted us. Vestiges of my cattle-wariness sent a small shot of adrenaline through me at the sight of a dozen or more large horned beasts hoofing it straight towards me (the biodynamic practice is to leave the horns on), but I knew that they were just thirsty, and, besides, I was still on the other side of the gate. As soon as the water was flowing they started slurping it up with long, pink tongues.

'I'll leave you to fill these up,' said Vimbai, 'and would you mind checking on them and making sure they're topped up over the weekend? We'll move the steers to another paddock next week.'

During my six-week stay I got to know the steers a bit better and became used to them. I even began to give some of them names. My favourite was a shaggy, stocky Highland steer whom I called Boris, who had the most fantastic huge curved horns that came forward and towards the centre like hugging arms. Others I dubbed Gemini, and Number 21 (no prizes for guessing the number on his eartag).

The community as a whole was called Birchfield, and consisted of Hohepa Farm, where there were three residential houses (plus the wwoofer cottage), and the town property in Barrington Street, Christchurch, where there were several more houses, the main office and other buildings including a crafts workshop and an auditorium. Each house had three or four residents with learning disabilities, plus a live-in caregiver, and other caregivers who came to help with meals, showering and so on.

During the week many of the Barrington Street residents joined the Hohepa residents on the farm, where they worked in the gardens, fed the pigs, collected the eggs and so on. Some residents worked in the kitchen, cooking lunch, or baking bread, biscuits and pies for the residents' houses. Others worked in the workshop, making garden trellises, wooden toy animals, or children's block sets. Some of the Hohepa residents went to Barrington Street on certain days to do craftwork, and once a week for an assembly.

Work at Hohepa was carried out on a regular schedule. From Monday to Friday, the vans pulled up at 9.00 a.m., disgorging residents from town, who joined their Hohepa friends and all went to their respective workplaces – kitchen, workshop, farm or hort unit. Morning tea was from 10.15 to 10.45, lunch from 12.15 to 1.00, and afternoon tea at 3.00. The residents didn't go back to work after that, but enjoyed a social time while they waited for the vans to come and pick them up at around 4.00.

Having had little routine over the past couple of years' wwoofing, I enjoyed the stability of the time-bound pattern for a change, and the weekends off to go and socialise or explore the area, although, because staff members were not working over the weekend and we were on site, we wwoofers were sometimes asked to check on animals or do some watering in the glasshouse.

Most days I was working alongside two or three of the residents, sometimes keeping an eye on them, sometimes relying on their knowledge of the place to find things, and mostly enjoying my time with them, as many of them had great senses of humour. At that time of the year much of the work was harvesting vegetables and fruit.

'I'd like you to work with Jane today,' said Vimbai one morning, 'harvesting the tomatoes.'

'Great!' said Jane, a talkative and enthusiastic resident who had already introduced herself to me. 'I want to work with you.'

'Grab a wheelbarrow – if you can get one off the hort unit guys – and put a picking bin inside it,' Vimbai continued. 'That way you don't have to carry a heavy bin, and you can put the good tomatoes in the bin, and any seconds in the wheelbarrow – they can use them in the kitchen.'

Getting a wheelbarrow was the first hurdle. The residents who usually worked in the hort unit were very attached to the barrows, and sometimes could be seen wheeling one around even when they didn't need it for the job they were doing. They had to be reassured that we would return it as soon as we were finished. Picking tomatoes was easy and pleasant work in the warmth of the greenhouses, seeking out the abundant ripe red globes amongst the lush green profusion of leaves. Jane and I chatted while we worked. She proudly showed me her watch, which sported a picture of Mickey Mouse on the face, with his white-gloved hands rotating as the hands of the watch.

'What's the time, Philippa?' Jane asked after a while.

'You've got a watch,' I said. 'You tell me.'

'Morning tea time!' she announced. I smiled.

'Not yet. It's only half past nine,' I replied, having learnt very quickly to carry my mini alarm clock (my only timepiece) so I could tell when it was break time. I was impressed by the residents' inbuilt sense of when to knock off, until the mystery of this was solved and one of the staff members told me that you could hear, even from further away on the farm, the fan in the workshop being turned off at morning and afternoon tea and lunchtime.

There were at least three different varieties of tomatoes, and I never found out what they were. The most distinctive was a large, pink cooking variety, with a stripy effect near the calyx. We wheeled the laden barrow into the packing shed, lifted out the bin onto the large central table and put the seconds, which were softer, less perfect but still perfectly edible, into a separate bin and into the coolstore for later use in the kitchen, for soups, sauces or pizzas.

The orders were done twice a week in the packhouse. A paid worker (usually Gus, assistant to the farm manager, then Chris who succeeded him) supervised this operation, which involved making up boxes of vegetables, fruit, eggs, meat from the freezer and bread, pies and biscuits from the kitchen. Most of the boxes went to the various residential houses, whose house manager would have put in an order the day before. A few extra boxes went to private customers, and bulk orders also went out to the Christchurch organic shops – crates of corn, zucchinis, potatoes, tomatoes, apples and pears, and bundles of greens like silverbeet, rocket, mizuna and another Japanese green I hadn't heard of before: komatsuna, which had rounded leaves and could be used in salads when young, or cooked when older. The packhouse was a flurry of activity on orders days, with staff, residents and wwoofers harvesting vegetables and bringing them in to the packhouse where they were washed if necessary, put in bags, bunches, or simply straight in the boxes. We wwoofers and volunteers were also provided with farm produce, on an as-needed basis.

There was a block of corn out in the field, and picking corn had to be done at least a couple of times a week. Unfortunately the corn was being attacked by birds – pheasants I think were the main culprits – and they could sometimes be seen and heard flapping away as we approached. Some cobs were totally stripped of kernels, while others, even more frustratingly, were just picked into, making them unsaleable, but still perfectly useable for the residents or wwoofers.

Next to the corn were a couple of long rows of zucchinis, each plant grown inside a tyre, which helped keep the weeds away. They grew so fast that tiny finger-sized zucchinis swelled to the standard 15 centimetres or so in a couple of days, and if left for three or four days, or longer, ballooned into marrows, which there was far less call for. It was a matter of keeping on track and making sure they were harvested at least three times a week.

There were a couple of large potato patches, one in the paddock with the other vegetables grown on a large scale, and another right down the end of the farm, alongside a pumpkin patch. The potato harvest was carried out over several days, if not weeks, and required lots of us to dig them up. A couple of days I was working with some residents in the closer paddock, all of us armed with a fork, working in pairs, each pair with a wheelbarrow. Most of them worked away cheerfully, and beamed with a little encouragement.

'Well done! You've got heaps there,' I'd say.

Sometimes one of them would let out a cry of delight, holding up an extra-large tuber like a trophy.

'Look at this big one!'

One of our harvesting crew (whom I'll call Eric) was unearthing potatoes at an astounding rate, but leaving them where they were on the ground. I wasn't quite sure how to deal with this, but first I tried asking.

'Eric, you're doing a great job of digging up all those potatoes. Could you put them in the wheelbarrow please?' Silence. Eric just kept on digging. Then I tried reason.

'If we leave them in the light they'll go green and poisonous,' I said, confident that Eric would understand this. He had some kind of autism, apparently, and was intelligent. Silence. I guess he was in his own world. Then I tried a trick, removing his fork at one point when he wasn't looking, but he continued on without comment, scrabbling at the rich, soft earth with his bare hands, his speed barely reduced by the lack of a tool. Eventually I gave up, and a couple of us went around after him collecting them all, but even so we couldn't keep up with his rapid rate.

Other days I went down to the further away potato paddock with a couple of the residents. Digging potatoes was Blair's favourite job, and he was an especially good worker, digging away tirelessly at a constant rate, and only letting up at break time. He was careful with the potatoes and hardly ever speared them with his fork. The other worker with us was not quite so enthusiastic, dawdling in his task and eventually stopping. Time for a change, I thought.

'How about we do a bit of weeding in the pumpkin patch?' I asked him. The pumpkins were in the same paddock.

'OK,' he replied, and we walked over.

'Here, these are the weeds we need to pull up,' I said, pointing out the fathen, which was the main weed, and indicated a rich soil. My companion seemed hesitant, or unmotivated. At morning tea he mentioned something about gloves, so I made sure he had gloves when we returned. Still he was reluctant.

'I might get prickled,' he said. There were thistles here and there, it was true, but the gloves would have protected him. He seemed more interested in the steers, who had come over to the fence line to see what was going on. Finally I thought of a job he might like.

'I think the steers want to eat the fathen,' I said. 'How about feeding some to them and seeing if they like it?' He carefully picked up some of the piles of weeds and gingerly tossed them over the fence, where the cattle promptly set upon them with gusto, jostling each other to get at the weeds. At last, I'd found a suitable job for him, and he happily continued to dispense my weed piles over the fence, talking quietly to the animals as he did so. Fathen (*Chenopodium album*) is rich in iron, and is quite palatable to humans too. I've tried it chopped up in a salad, and added to soups or stews.

Once harvested, the potatoes were cleaned in a machine that consisted of a wide, gently sloping tube made of slatted wood, into which the potatoes were loaded, and were then hosed down with water while the tube rotated. The potatoes bumped their way down, shedding most of their dirt on the way through the joint action of water and friction, and emerged onto a wide trellis-like tray. Several of us stood around the tray and removed any rotten or damaged potatoes, while the really small ones fell through the holes. When the good ones were dry we packed them in the storeroom in boxes covered in newspaper.

A few times I went with some of the residents to feed the pigs with kitchen scraps and weeds from the vege gardens and orchard, and on the same run we collected eggs from the hens, and checked their water and feed. The residents put the eggs carefully into buckets, and when we returned, they wiped them with a damp cloth and put them into cartons. I never saw a broken egg.

Picking apples and pears was another activity as summer turned into a golden autumn. My gang was generally enthusiastic about this task, and enjoyed filling up the large wooden bin, which Charles later picked up with the tractor's forklift prongs and transported to the chiller. Charles was a retired farmer who lived nearby, and who came over to Hohepa several times a week to help out, doing mainly stock and tractor work. He was small and wiry, pretty well-preserved for 80, and had a lifetime of farming experience. The chooks free-ranged in the orchard, trying valiantly to peck into any windfall fruit. We split some open for them so they could eat, and tried out the different varieties ourselves.

If we had a bit of time to spare and it wasn't quite time for a break, we would collect the walnuts that had fallen on the ground near the main building. The residents found this easy and satisfying, and several of us could collect a few bags in a short space of time. We then emptied out the bags onto an old wire-wove bed, which served as an excellent drying rack. There the nuts would stay for a few weeks, and would shed their outer green husk if they hadn't already, before being stored. My walnut cravings were still strong and I couldn't resist trying some, even though I knew few of them would be ready. On the whole, they were still slightly soft, a pale cream colour or even tinged with pink, and many were too astringent to be palatable, but occasionally there'd be a decent crisp one that had matured enough for my taste buds.

One day I helped Gus, the paid farm worker, to check a mob of ewes and a few wethers for flystrike. Gus was a tall, quiet man in his early 20s, who was keen on organics and doing some environmental study at nearby Lincoln University.

'It's not going to be a pleasant job,' he warned. Grimacing, I remembered back to my first experience with flystrike at my brother's place, and poor little Kowhai, who had eventually died.

'Here are some overalls,' said Gus, 'and I'll bring some gloves.' We walked down to the paddock by the sheep yards, and began rounding up the sheep. Charles happened to be passing and gave us a hand to get them all into the yards. Once the sheep were penned, Gus and I donned our overalls and gloves and got in amongst them, picking off one animal at a time. At first Gus did all the catching, and held the animals while I checked their rear ends. Once checked, they went into the next pen. I was glad to have the gloves, as some of their rear ends were a bit daggy.

'I want to have a go at catching,' I said after a while. It wasn't as easy as it looked, even in a small space. Gus gave me a few tips, such as pulling their heads around so they were looking back, which more or less stopped them in their tracks, as they naturally moved in the direction their head was facing.

Catching sheep was a skill that would obviously take a while to perfect, and much more practice than a dozen or so sheep, but I was certainly more successful than I had been back at Waihi Bush, even if my technique must have looked like an unco-ordinated flying tackle. In the end, we found evidence of flystrike on only one sheep, and it was just a small clump of pale yellow eggs, which were easily removed.

Perhaps because Hohepa was run biodynamically, it attracted a lot of German wwoofers and volunteers, as biodynamics originated in Europe and is popular in Germany. During my six-week stay there were no fewer than seven German wwoofers and volunteers. The only exception was an Australian wwoofer called Ros who had arranged to stay for a month. At 53, she had oodles of life experience (and gardening experience), and a direct and friendly manner. When she immediately set about doing a bit of a clean-up in the cottage, which had suffered somewhat from the lack of continuity of habitation, I knew at once that we were going to get along well. Together we reorganised the pantry and kitchen cupboards, and threw out bits of junk that had accumulated.

Ros and I often worked alongside each other and the residents in the hort unit, hoeing and weeding amongst the vegetables, or on rainy days, mixing up seed mix and sowing seed, or pricking out vegetable seedlings from seed trays and putting them into trays with separate little compartments for each seedling. Then we put them into a glasshouse to grow on a bit before they were transplanted into the hort unit. As we worked we talked, and Ros outlined her plans to have an organic macadamia farm when she returned to Queensland. It was something of a relief to me to have a mature, reliable wwoofer alongside me for a whole month, someone I could have decent in-depth conversations with, and it was a reminder that I missed seeing my friends and having a normal social life.

Close to the cottage there was a small shed in which 60 chicks were being reared, and when Achim left, it became my job to check on them in the evenings and on the weekends and make sure they had mash and water. During the day a worker checked and fed them. They were kept in an enclosure made of cartons immediately below a low-hanging heat lamp, which was on all the time to keep them warm, simulating a mother hen. In the daytime the lamp was raised up a little bit, and then lowered again for the night. As the chicks grew we made the enclosure bigger until eventually they had the run of the shed, and we added green stuff to their diet, things like silverbeet, clover, chickweed and fathen. They devoured the silverbeet with particular relish.

Unfortunately many of the chicks became affected by some unknown disease that began as a black encrustation on their feet, which caused their feet to curl up so they couldn't walk, couldn't get to their food or water, and gradually became weaker. Several died around the time of this discovery, and it was a situation we had to get on top of immediately as it looked as though more of them were afflicted. Vimbai phoned the vet, but he said he couldn't diagnose the problem with the information given and said even an autopsy might not diagnose the cause of the problem.

In the meantime Vimbai felt we had to do something, so we brought the chicks into the office, removed the encrustations with olive oil, which loosened them, and then used tea tree oil on their feet in case it was a fungal infection of some kind. Unfortunately a number of them died, possibly from the unknown disease, or maybe from the tea tree fumes, which were quite strong in the small office space where we had them overnight with the heater on for warmth, or even from the stress of being handled.

Someone suggested it might be coccidiosis, a disease that is passed on through droppings – but Charles said the symptoms weren't the same. Just to be on the safe side, Ros and I cleaned out the shed thoroughly and put in fresh hay, and we put the remaining chicks back in the shed, keeping an eagle eye – so to speak – on them.

Sadly, more of the chicks died. When I left there were only 13 chicks left, and I heard later that the number had dropped down to six – a tenth of the original number. They had reared chicks plenty of times before at Hohepa and never had such a problem, but it just showed how vulnerable chicks can be, and how quickly disease can spread.

After six weeks at Hohepa I had got to know the staff and many of the residents, and felt sad to be moving on. They put on a special morning tea for me just before I left, with scones and jam and cream. Vimbai had regretfully left the job and moved away because of her husband's work, so the new farm manager, Godwell, who was also from Zimbabwe, thanked me for my work. I was also treated to items from a couple of the residents: a rendition of the national anthem on the recorder from Andrew, and a haka from Hayden, and was presented with a woven scarf that had been made in the Barrington Street workshops. It was very moving and I felt humbled that they had organised this, but the residents loved an event! Some months later I put together a photo montage of Hohepa farm and residents, and dropped by for an unannounced afternoon tea visit to deliver it. They were delighted, and immediately put it up on the wall in the dining room. It was a good feeling to be part of this community in some small way.

'When are you coming back?' they asked me, and I had to tell them I wasn't. My wwoofing journey by then was over, having come to a natural end.

23
HOW ORGANIC
IS ORGANIC?

I was fairly choosy about the farms that I visited, and before moving on to the next one would spend some time poring through the WWOOF book debating my next move, weighing up the various factors of location, type of farm and recommendations from others. A number of farmers were already known to me, if not personally through organic networks, then by reputation, and many hosts made helpful suggestions of places to go – or in some cases to avoid. Farms that were certified organic, or stated a strong commitment to organic philosophy were my preference.

But as I discovered, people have different ideas of what organic is, and there are quite divergent lifestyles among organic farmers, or at least among WWOOF hosts, not all of whom are in fact organic. The scheme has become increasingly popular in recent years, with the number of hosts jumping from about 650 in 2002 to over 1000 in 2007. The numbers of wwoofers have increased year by year and reached a peak of 4756 in 2002 and then flattened off to 4588 in 2005.

There is no practical way to police hosts on how organic they are – and indeed this would be against the philosophy of trust that the scheme is built on. Someone once asked me why not limit the scheme to certified organic hosts? But that would reduce the number of hosts greatly, as the majority are not certified organic, either because they cannot afford it, or it isn't necessary because they aren't selling produce but are mainly growing for themselves. As the scheme is now, all hosts simply declare what their organic status is. Some are certified, some simply declare themselves as organic, or spray-free, or using permaculture or biodynamic principles, some say they are 'in transition' (which is ambiguous: it could mean in transition to being certified, or it could mean in transition from conventional farming to organic).

One place I stayed at sounded great from its description; there were a number of different projects going on at this farm, including several different crops, a few livestock and some processing. It was certified organic, and conveniently located in the direction I was heading.

Little detective work was required on arrival to realise that my hosts, Sharon and Steve (not their real names) were smokers, and I was glad to have my own smoke-free sleepout. At that time of year, both of them were doing some off-farm work and, after giving me instructions in the morning, they left me to work on my own. Sharon showed me around the kitchen, pointing out the bread, tinned spaghetti, baked beans and so on that I was to help myself to for lunch.

The only organic food on the menu seemed to be meat, but of course I was a vegetarian. The cupboards were full of tins and packets of processed and convenience foods, probably much like many Kiwi homes, but in sharp contrast to the jars of organic lentils, rolled oats and brown rice that had been the standard fare in my journey so far. I found it hard to reconcile their lifestyle with their certified organic farm. It was as though the house was an island that was exempt from organic standards in the middle of the farm.

One evening I set about making dinner. Sharon was out, and Steve was working away on the computer in the little office off the living room.

'I'm going to make some fried rice,' I called. 'I'll make enough for you and the kids too if you like.'

'Oh, don't worry about me,' he said, 'I'll grab something later.' Rummaging through the cupboards to find some ingredients, I came across a line of ants marching in and out of an opened packet of chocolate biscuits. Just as I was about to clean it up, Steve suddenly swooped down brandishing a can of Black Flag fly spray and gave the cupboard a generous squirt.

'Hey! What are you doing?' I exclaimed, racing to put lids on the food already cooking on the stove.

'Aw, they won't take my Bio-Gro licence away for a bit of Black Flag,' he said. I was gobsmacked. This was the first time I had encountered such an attitude. All of the organic farmers I'd stayed with so far were organic in their whole philosophy and lifestyle, into recycling, renewable energy and other such ideas – like me. Were Steve and Sharon simply into organics to make some money? Were they believers in organic principles but hadn't put all of those principles into practice in their home life? Or were they simply human beings with inconsistencies like us all? The farm certainly seemed to be well-run and no doubt they complied with the certification regulations. Their lifestyle was really their own business, but it certainly shook my purist tendencies and challenged my notions of organic farmers, making me realise that people have different reasons for going organic. Well, I might not entirely agree with their lifestyle – or it might not agree with me – but I'd pay good money for their products.

During my wwoofing journey I had numerous conversations with hosts and fellow wwoofers about the culture of wwoofing, which seems to be changing. On the one hand, there has been exponential growth in the scheme, due possibly in part to the fact that organics is becoming more mainstream, due to the growing number of people living on lifestyle blocks, and to the increasing numbers of young backpackers travelling around New Zealand. On the other hand, the scheme seems to have become somewhat diluted and less about organics.

Being organic is intrinsic to the organisation – indeed WWOOF NZ has for many years clearly stated it is only for organic farms. At the very least, I think, hosts ought to be committed to learning about organic principles and gradually putting them into practice. Some hosts specify in their directory listing that they are organic except for some gorse control in one or two paddocks, for example, and I appreciate this honesty.

But some hosts are openly non-organic, like a couple of hosts (who are no longer in the directory) whose directory listing stated that they weren't organic, but that their products were 'natural without additives'. What could this have meant? Did they think that Round-Up or other synthetic chemical sprays and fertilisers are 'natural'? Another host I met said she had 'tried to go organic but it was just too hard with young kids'. And there seems to be an increasing number of hosts who have conventional farms, but have an organic home vege garden. Or maybe not even that. As one (definitely organic) host joked to me: '400-hectare conventional sheep and beef farm, one transitional pot of parsley.'

One non-organic farmer said money was a serious barrier to his converting his farm to organics. He was worried his income might dip during the three-year conversion period and then he wouldn't be able to meet his financial commitments, but his home garden, orchard and vegetable patch were all organic. I guess it's a step in the right direction.

But on the whole, most hosts seem to be dedicated to organics, and lots of them loved talking about organics till the cows come home, and were happy to share their knowledge and experience. For me, this was just as valuable as the hands-on learning. Some hosts lamented the fact that the learning aspect of the scheme has diminished, especially when they got wwoofers who were patently not interested in organics at all. They say that the type of wwoofer has changed over the years, with more environmentally conscious, organic types previously, but now there are more backpackers who are just using the scheme to travel around New Zealand cheaply. Many are not interested in organics or even farming necessarily.

Several wwoofers I met unwittingly ended up in non-organic situations, and/or at places where their duties consisted mainly or entirely of housework, childcare, house painting etc. They were disappointed not to be doing gardening or farmwork. Of course some housework is often expected, and that's fine, but for it to be your whole WWOOF experience is not what the scheme is about. Generally they don't complain to their hosts or to the WWOOF organisers – they just move on and chalk it up to experience. The organisers are now placing more emphasis on getting feedback from wwoofers.

Another recent change is the increase in hosts whose primary business is not land-based, but some sort of accommodation and/or café, which would otherwise normally employ paid staff. Are these hosts taking advantage of the scheme? Or is it OK as long as they are committed to organic principles (for example, use organic ingredients and eco-friendly cleaning products, do recycling, etc.)? Also puzzling to me is the inclusion of two meditation centres openly charging money to stay there, on top of the wwoofing work required.

In 2004 I wrote an article for the *WWOOF NZ Newsletter* titled 'Hosts: How Organic Are You?', in which I outlined many of these concerns, and what the WWOOF organisers, Andrew and Jane Strange, were doing to address them.

There is another similar but non-organic scheme called Farm Helpers in New Zealand, and Andrew and Jane direct potential hosts to this other scheme if they are not organic. Farmers applying to join WWOOF must now have a referee who is an existing host, which gives the organisers a second opinion as to a potential host's suitability. While not a 100 per cent guarantee of a farmer's organicness, it does emphasise the requirements of the scheme. The organisers do not hesitate to remove hosts who prove unsuitable. For the most part, though, hosts are welcoming, caring and into organics.

It is pertinent to remember that none of us is perfect – we can all make improvements in our organic practices and in the way we live on this fragile planet. WWOOF is a powerful organisation within the organics movement, and as such plays a positive part in the growth of organics, by giving opportunities for learning, and providing workers to what is often a labour-intensive sector of farming. For me, wwoofing meant connecting with this land and its people in a direct, practical way, and making a meaningful contribution towards improving the environment and producing healthy food.

EPILOGUE

After two-and-a-half years' wwoofing it became obvious that I needed to slow down and chill out after all that gadding about the countryside. Eventually, after a stint of motel-minding and house-sitting, three years after my journey began I moved back to my house in Dunedin to take up residence once again with my cats. My neglected garden was all long grass, convolvulus, ivy, tumble-down sheds and cherry laurels crowding around the orchard trees and blocking out the light. I considered becoming a wwoof host, just to get people in to help me restore the garden to its former beauty and productivity, but the thought of having strangers coming and going was just too much. I needed to reclaim my own space.

The post-wwoofing year was a hard one for me: a return to earth, to my own earth, with a jolt. A chronic health problem had developed, with the result that I had little energy to whip the garden into shape. Bang went the notion that, after so long wwoofing, I ought to be some kind of paragon of garden virtue! Although my garden has remained rather overgrown since I got back, each season it continues to surprise and delight me.

In the winter the two rampant kiwifruit vines that had entwined themselves amongst the boards and roof of the top shed rewarded me with a bowlful of fruit – despite no pruning or composting. Two broccoli plants self-sowed themselves in the vege garden, producing surprisingly good heads considering they most likely cross-pollinated with other brassicas in the neighbourhood (such a promiscuous plant family), but they still bore the distinct colouring of the Purple Sprouting variety I had sowed there four years before.

In spring the flax flowers bloomed right outside my windowsill, attracting tui and korimako, who dipped their beaks systematically into each and every flower. Potatoes came up in several places, including some heirloom Maori varieties sown in a bed that had reverted to lawn. A few Jerusalem artichokes began to peep up, and the blackcurrant and redcurrant bushes were studded with ripening fruit.

Midsummer and the plum trees were laden as I'd never seen them before, and, although they were pelted with wind and rain, there was plenty there for me and the birds. Pairs of plump kereru flapped gracefully around the garden, to settle clumsily in the tops of the big cherry plum tree, and tuck into the fruit I couldn't reach. This kitchen witch was kept busy making batches of jam, jelly and sauce from the currants and plums, and my favourite: plum, date and ginger chutney.

In the autumn my energy began returning, and I was out in the garden, weeding out grass and ivy, convolvulus and cleavers, spreading eelgrass (a kind of seaweed) on the garden as mulch, and planting lettuces, broccoli, mizuna, coriander, kale and silverbeet. One apple tree in particular bore well, and tomatoes, capsicums and basil flourished on a sunny windowsill, as my glasshouse was still too much of a jungle.

I think back now to the beginning of my wwoofing journey, and the sad death of Kowhai, the sheep, from flystrike. With the distance of time and the wisdom of experience, it seems to me that coming to know Nature is to accept her rhythms, to accept the cycle of birth, life, death and decay, and know that the death of a plant or animal simply makes compost for future life. By the same token, my experiences, both good and bad, are being transformed into a metaphorical compost that will nourish my future growth. Coming to know Nature also means doing what you can to improve things, but accepting that you can't change everything. Likewise, I have come to accept my own rhythms and limitations, and acknowledge that my ill-health was a sign that I needed to give myself a break from the busyness of 'doing', and enjoy a more contemplative period of 'being'.

The dreams I had at the start of the journey have not all been fulfilled, but have changed along the way. The desire for my own farmlet and a more self-sufficient life has been put to one side as I live within my current health limits and as I pursue other things, including writing, and the delightfully satisfying role of marriage and civil union celebrant. At the same time I have a new appreciation for the city garden I have got to know and love over the past 14 years, and realise what incredible potential there is in such a small plot of land for food production and for simply delighting in nature. I've learnt to live more in the moment, to enjoy the little things, like dew-laden spider webs, spectacular sunsets, scrumptious organic food and good company.

There's no sign of a partner on the horizon, either, but I've made lots of friends, mostly my hosts, some wwoofers, and others I've met along the way. The people I've met and the experiences I've had have made the world less black and white for me, but rather a multi-hued rainbow of colour, of diversity. I am, I hope, less judgemental about some of the choices people make about the way they live, and more willing to enter into a dialogue with others who hold different views. The journey challenged some of my beliefs, and led to changes in my life. After having been a vegetarian for 27 years, I ate organic meat for a while because of my health, and my notion of identity changed from lesbian to bisexual.

More than anything, my wwoofing journey has strengthened my commitment to organics. I continue to write about organics and am now a member of the Soil and Health National Council. Over the past few years organics has moved from being on the fringe to becoming much more accepted and mainstream. If New Zealand is to truly live up to its 'clean green' reputation, we need a lot more people farming and living in a truly sustainable manner, and substantial government funding to support organic initiatives. Becoming an increasingly organic nation will result in improved health and a cleaner environment, not to mention good export earnings. Not only that, but, compared with conventional agriculture, organic farming sequesters more carbon, has lower greenhouse gas emissions, and is less dependent on fossil fuels.

The positive contribution being made by organic farmers and growers all over the country is inestimable, and I salute all those farmers and growers living with respect and love for the earth and all its creatures, actively seeking knowledge to live in harmony with the land.

Philippa Jamieson
Autumn Equinox 2007

APPENDIX
ORGANIC ORGANISATIONS
IN NEW ZEALAND

Agriquality, Private Bag 14946, Panmure, Auckland
  tel: 09 573 8000, fax: 09 573 8001
  email: info@agriquality.com, website: www.agriquality.co.nz

Bio Dynamic Farming and Gardening Association in New Zealand
  PO Box 39045, Wellington Mail Centre
  tel: 04 589 5366, fax: 04 589 5365
  email: biodynamics@clear.net.nz

Bio-Gro (New Zealand Biological Producers and Consumers Council
  Inc), PO Box 9693, Marion Square, Wellington
  tel: 04 801 9741, fax: 04 801 9742
  email: info@biogro.co.nz, website: www.biogro.co.nz

Organic Aotearoa New Zealand, PO Box 1926, Wellington
  tel: 04 890 3769, fax: 04 890 3766
  email: ken.shirley@oanz.org.nz, website: www.oanz.org.nz

Organic Farm New Zealand, PO Box 36-170, Northcote,
  Auckland 9
  tel: 09 419 4536, fax: 09 419 4556
  email: info@organicnz.org, website: www.organicfarm.org.nz

Permaculture Institute of New Zealand, c/- Simon Thomson
  61 Matawha Rd, RD2 Raglan
  website: www.permaculture.org.nz

Soil and Health Association of New Zealand, PO Box 36-170
Northcote, Auckland 9
tel: 09 419 4536, fax: 09 419 4556,
email: info@organicnz.org, website: www.organicnz.org

Te Waka Kai Ora, c/- Percy Tipene, RD3 Kaikohe
tel: 09 401 4837
email: tipenep@xtra.co.nz

WWOOF New Zealand, Andrew and Jane Strange, PO Box 1172,
Nelson
tel/fax: 03 544 9890
email: a&j@wwoof.co.nz, website: www.wwoof.co.nz

Other organic organisations in New Zealand include sector groups
(e.g. dairy, wine), seed saving groups and environment centres. A
useful website for all things organic is www.organicpathways.com

SELECT BIBLIOGRAPHY

Ashworth, Suzanne, *Seed to Seed: Seed Saving and Growing Techniques for Vegetable Gardeners*, Seed Savers Exchange, Decorah, 2003

Bio Dynamic Farming and Gardening Association in New Zealand (ed. Gita Henderson), *Biodynamic Perspectives: Farming and Gardening*, Random House, Auckland, 2001

Bio Dynamic Farming and Gardening Association in New Zealand, *Biodynamics: New Directions for Farming and Gardening in New Zealand*, Random House, Auckland, 1989

Fisk, Trisha, *Practical Organics for New Zealand Farmers*, Reed Publishing, Auckland, 2003

Fukuoka, Masanobu, *The One-Straw Revolution*, Rodale Press, Emmaus, 1978

Reader's Digest Encyclopaedia of Gardening (Australian and New Zealand Edition), Reader's Digest, Sydney, 1995

Williams, Morgan, *Growing for Good: Intensive Farming, Sustainability and New Zealand's Environment*, Parliamentary Commissioner for the Environment, Wellington, 2004

WWOOF NZ, *World Wide Opportunities on Organic Farms New Zealand* (directory), 2004 edition

INDEX